Other Books by Jeff Smith

Published by Cartoon Books

BONE One Volume Edition Paperback (in the original Black & White)
BONE One Volume Edition Hardcover Slipcase (in Full Color)
BONE: CODA
RASL Book One: The Drift
RASL Book Two: Romance at the Speed of Light
RASL Book Three: The Fire of St. George
RASL One Volume Edition Hardcover

Published by Graphix (an imprint of Scholastic)

BONE Color Series
Bone Volume 1: Out from Boneville
Bone Volume 2: The Great Cow Race
Bone Volume 3: Eyes of the Storm
Bone Volume 4: The Dragonslayer
Bone Volume 5: Rock Jaw, Master of the Eastern Border
Bone Volume 6: Old Man's Cave
Bone Volume 7: Ghost Circles
Bone Volume 8: Treasure Hunters
Bone Volume 9: Crown of Horns
Bone Handbook
Bone: Rose (Written by Jeff Smith, Painted by Charles Vess)
Bone: Tall Tales (Written by Jeff Smith and Tom Sniegoski, Illustrated by Jeff Smith)
Bone: Out from Boneville Tribute Edition
BONE Adventures (Featuring Finders Keepers & Smiley's Dream)

Published by Toon Books

Little Mouse Gets Ready!

Published by DC Comics

Shazam! The Monster Society of Evil

Available in fine bookstores and comic shops everywhere
For more information visit us at boneville.com
Facebook: The OFFICIAL Jeff Smith Page
Twitter: @jeffsmithsbone
Instagram: the_official_jeffsmith_insta
Tumblr: theofficialjeffsmithcartoonist
YouTube: The Official Jeff Smith YouTube Channel

For more information about the BONE color series visit: scholastic.com/bone
For more information about Little Mouse visit: toon-books.com

TUKI
Fight for Fire

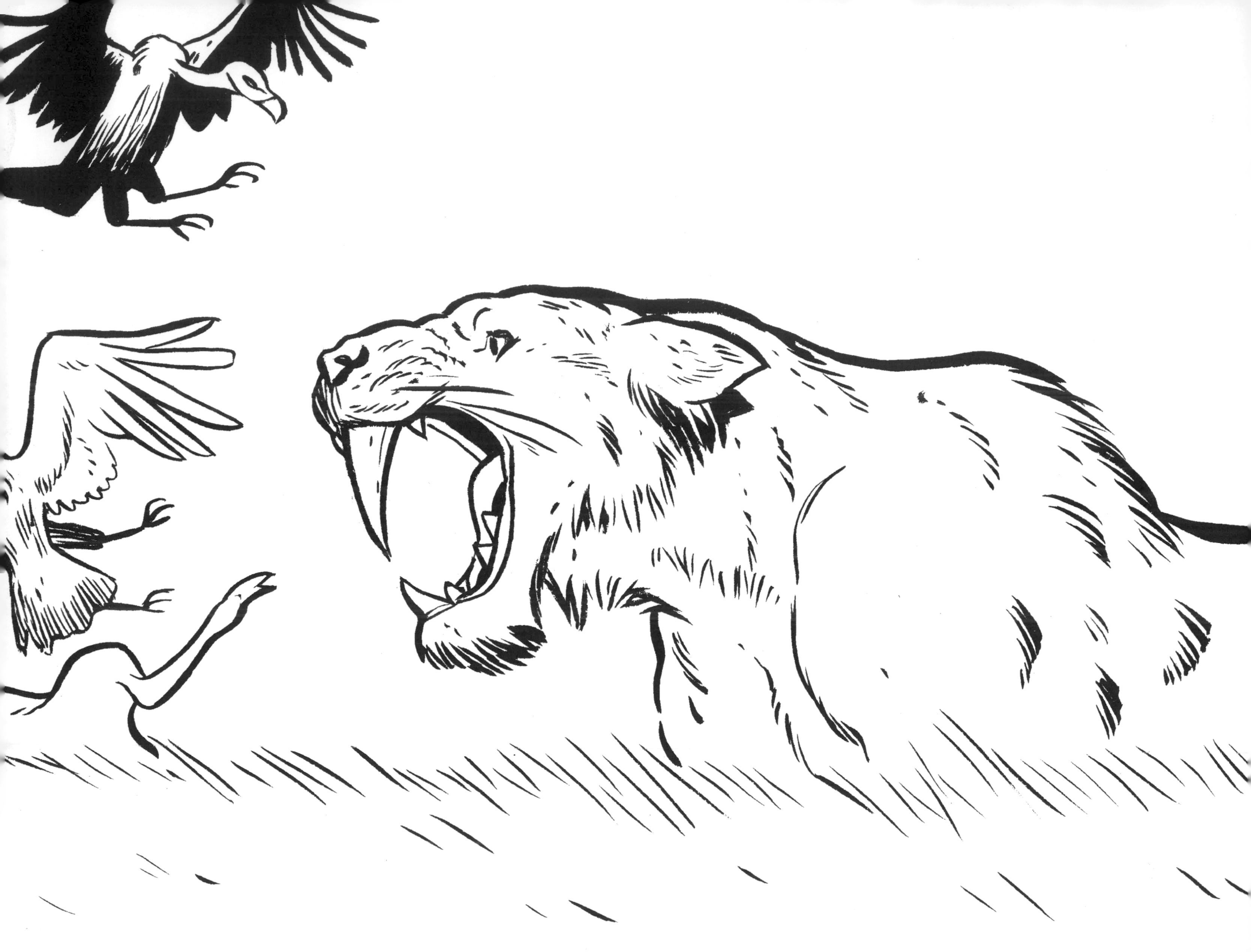

Tuki

Fight for Fire by Jeff Smith

Cartoon Books
Columbus, Ohio

Cover Art by Jeff Smith
Cover Color by Tom Gaadt

For information write:
Cartoon Books
P.O. Box 16973
Columbus, OH 43216

Softcover Regular Edition ISBN: 978-1-888963-75-5
Softcover Special Edition ISBN: 978-1-888963-79-3
Hardcover Regular Edition ISBN: 978-1-888963-80-9
Hardcover Special Edition ISBN: 978-1-888963-81-6

eISBN: 978-1-888963-76-2

10 9 8 7 6 5 4 3 2 1

Printed in Canada

Table of Contents

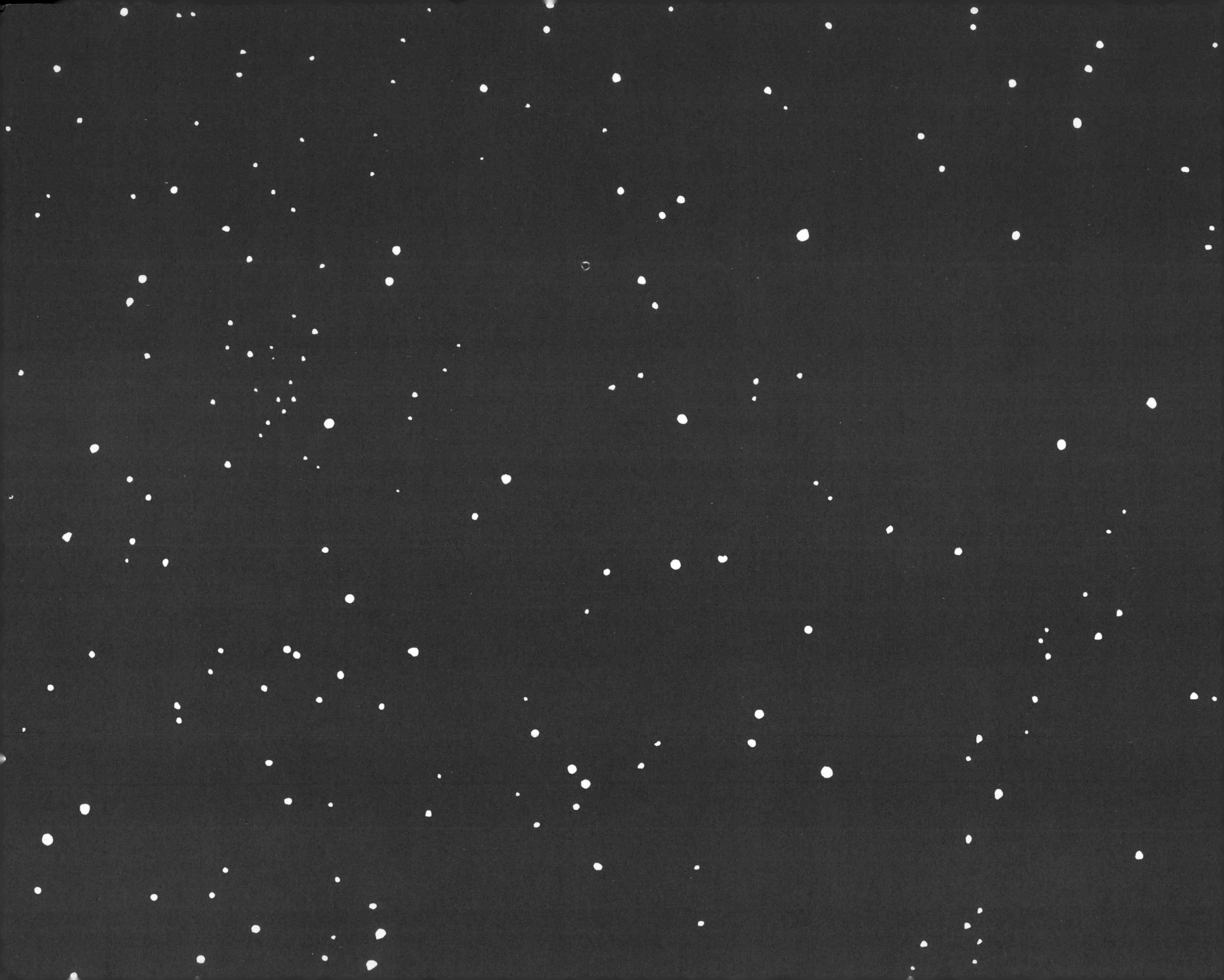

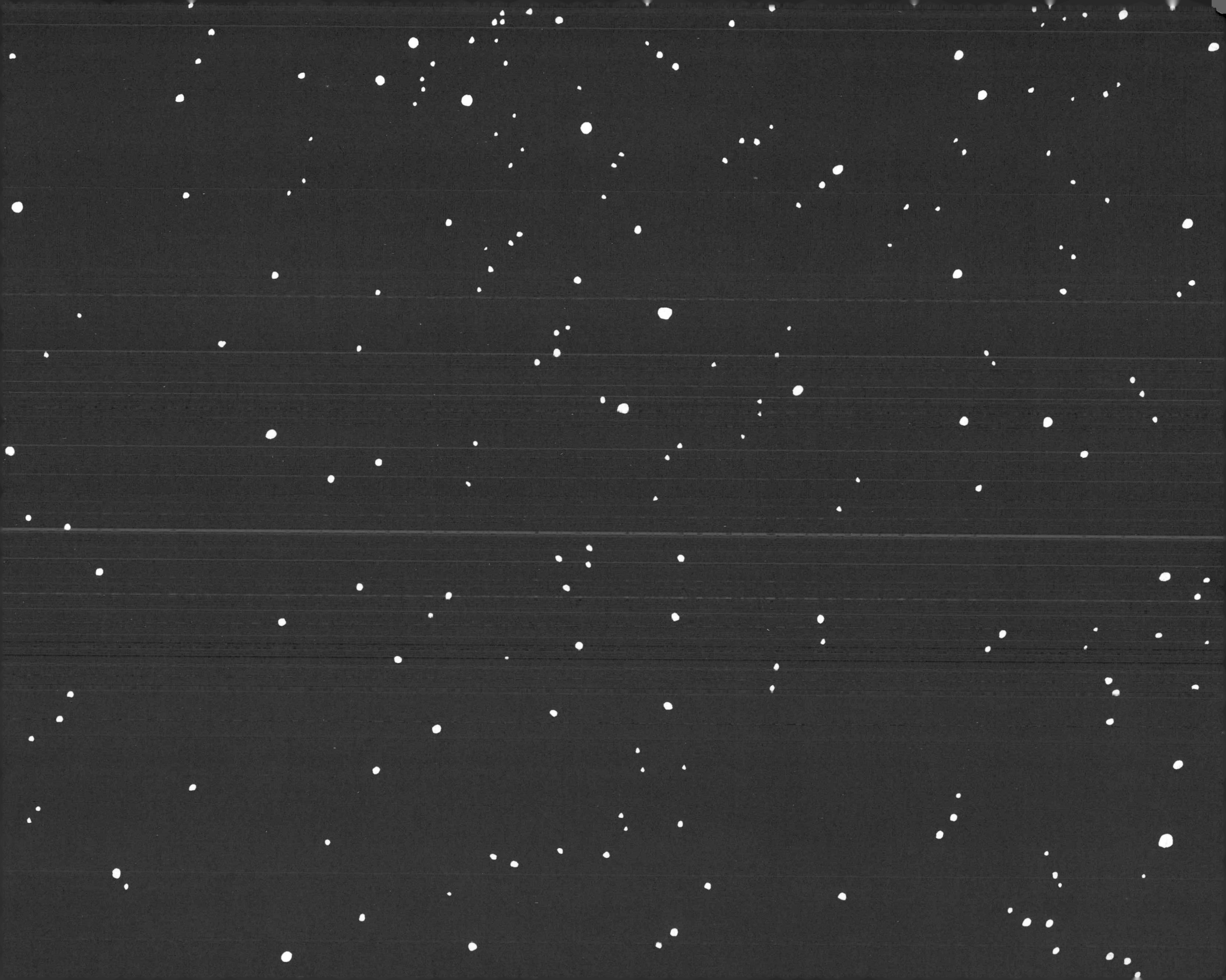

Part One

A Note on Paleoanthropology

Evolution, unlike the neat bumper sticker that shows a single line of primates slowly standing upright, was very messy and scattershot. Isolated groups evolved separately over hundreds of thousands or even millions of years. 1. 8 million years ago, multiple human species existed together during a period of catastrophic climate change, including the great traveler & fire starter Homo erectus, our forebearer. Each of the characters in TUKI is based on a human species known to have existed at that time.

HUMAN SPECIES ALIVE AROUND
2 MILLION BCE

Australopithecus africanus
Paranthropus boisei
Australopithecus sediba
Homo habilis
Homo rudolfensis
Homo erectus

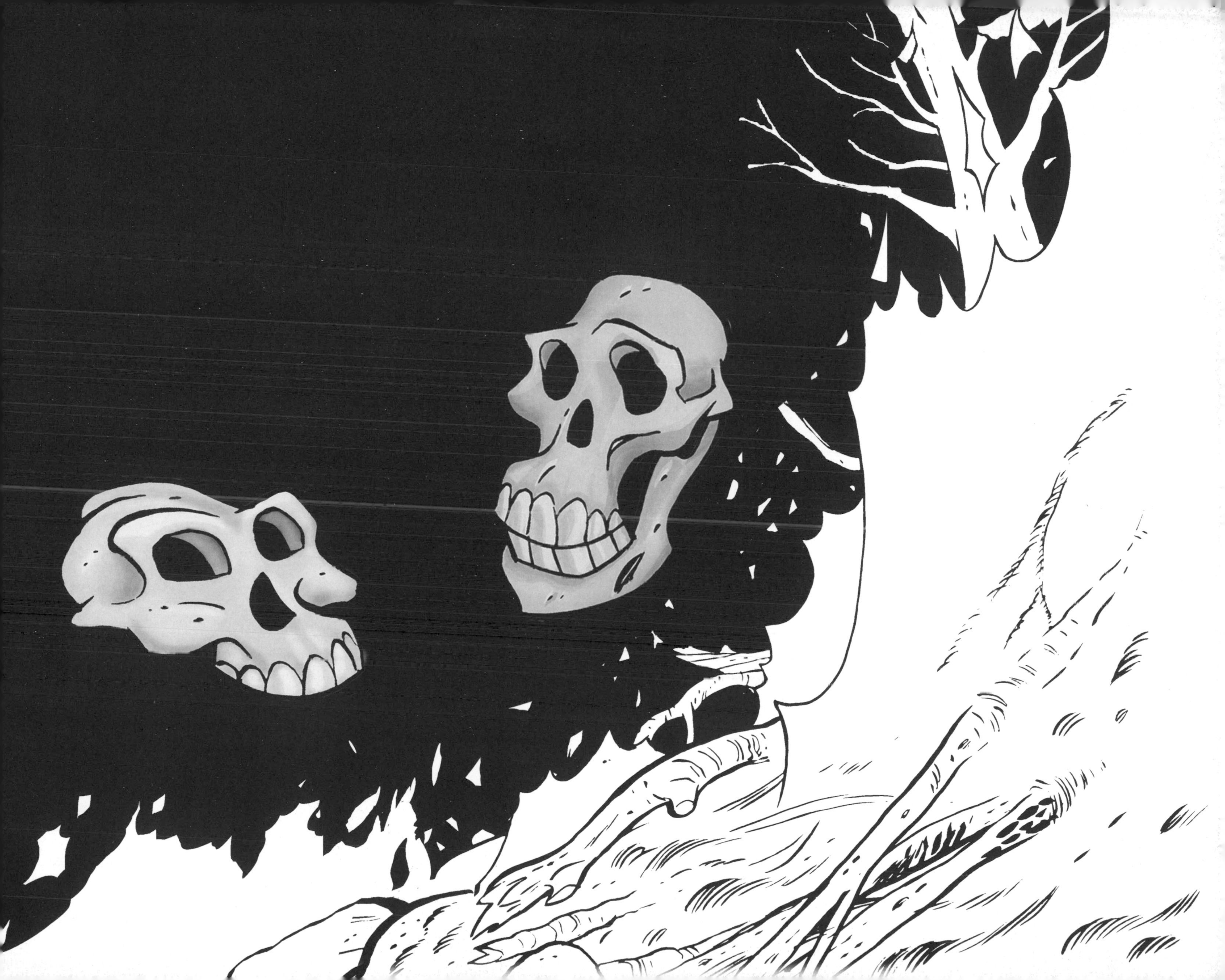

"This is the book of thy descent . . .

Here begin the terrors,
Here begin the marvels."

- the Holy Grail

PROLOGUE

2 Million BCE

ARE YOU SURE?

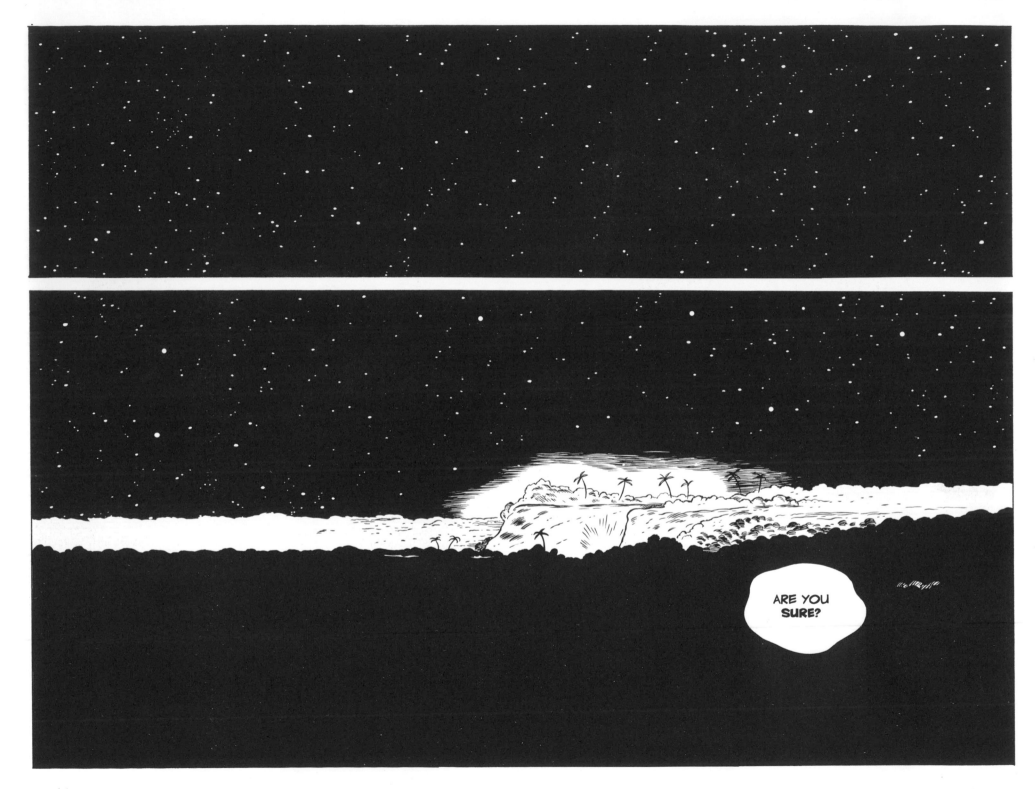

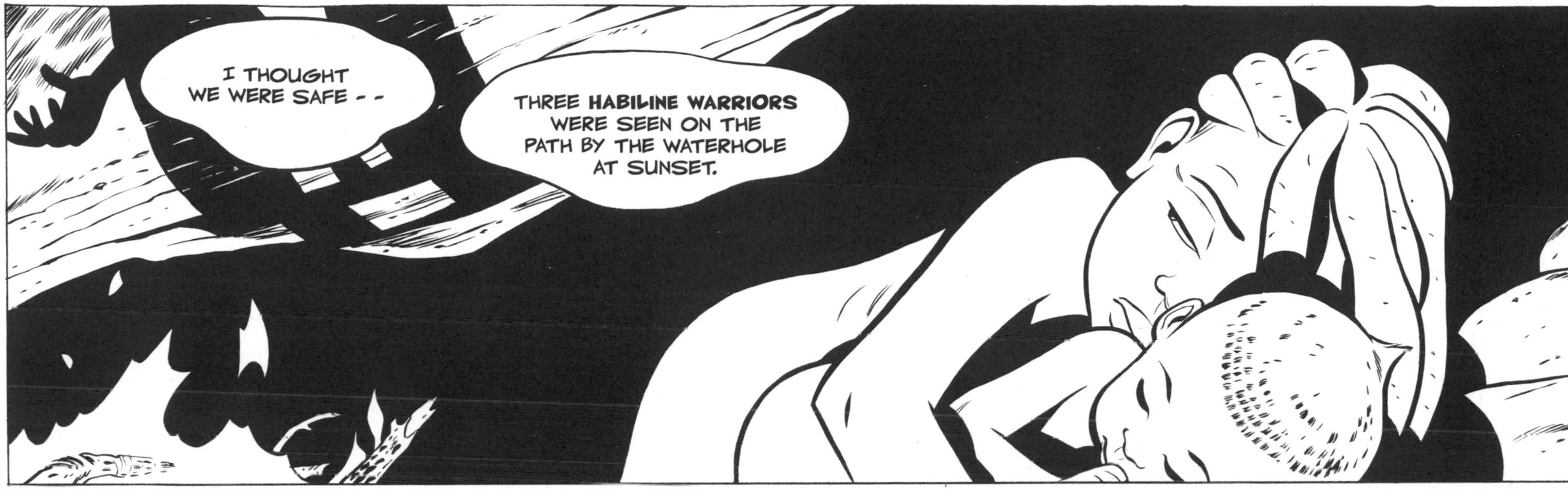
I THOUGHT WE WERE SAFE - -
THREE **HABILINE WARRIORS** WERE SEEN ON THE PATH BY THE WATERHOLE AT SUNSET.

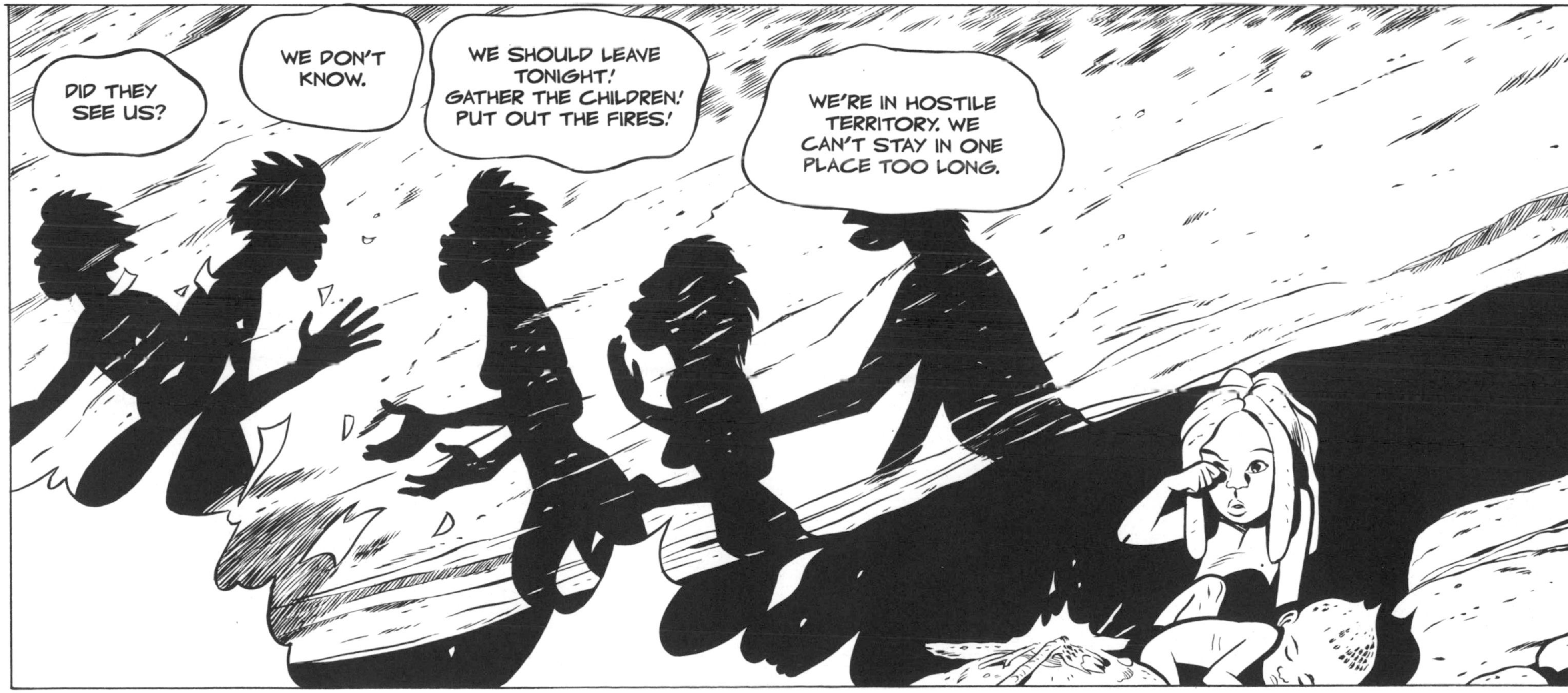
DID THEY SEE US?
WE DON'T KNOW.
WE SHOULD LEAVE TONIGHT! GATHER THE CHILDREN! PUT OUT THE FIRES!
WE'RE IN HOSTILE TERRITORY. WE CAN'T STAY IN ONE PLACE TOO LONG.

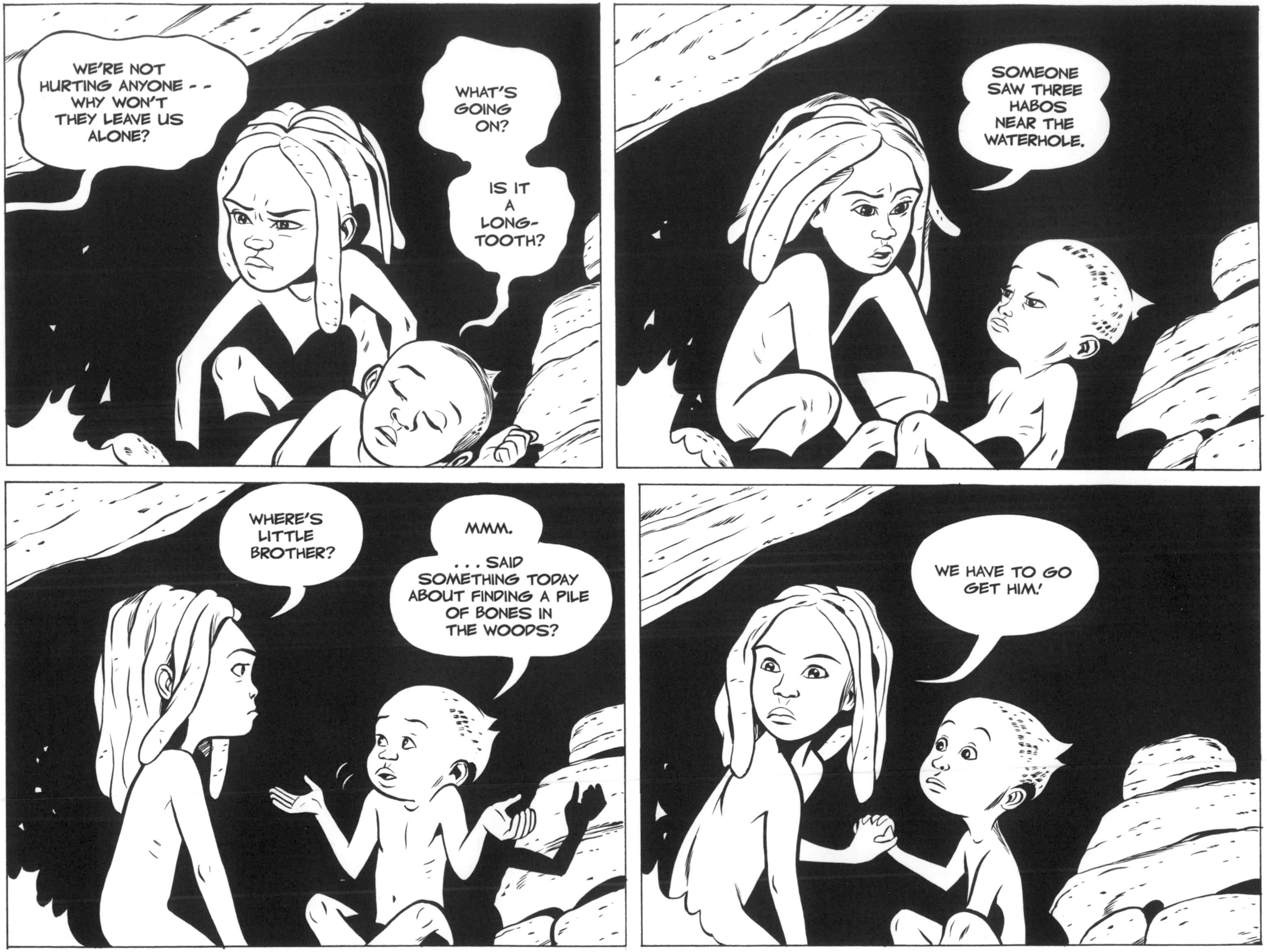
WE'RE NOT HURTING ANYONE - - WHY WON'T THEY LEAVE US ALONE?
WHAT'S GOING ON?
IS IT A LONG-TOOTH?
SOMEONE SAW THREE HABOS NEAR THE WATERHOLE.
WHERE'S LITTLE BROTHER?
MMM.
. . . SAID SOMETHING TODAY ABOUT FINDING A PILE OF BONES IN THE WOODS?
WE HAVE TO GO GET HIM!

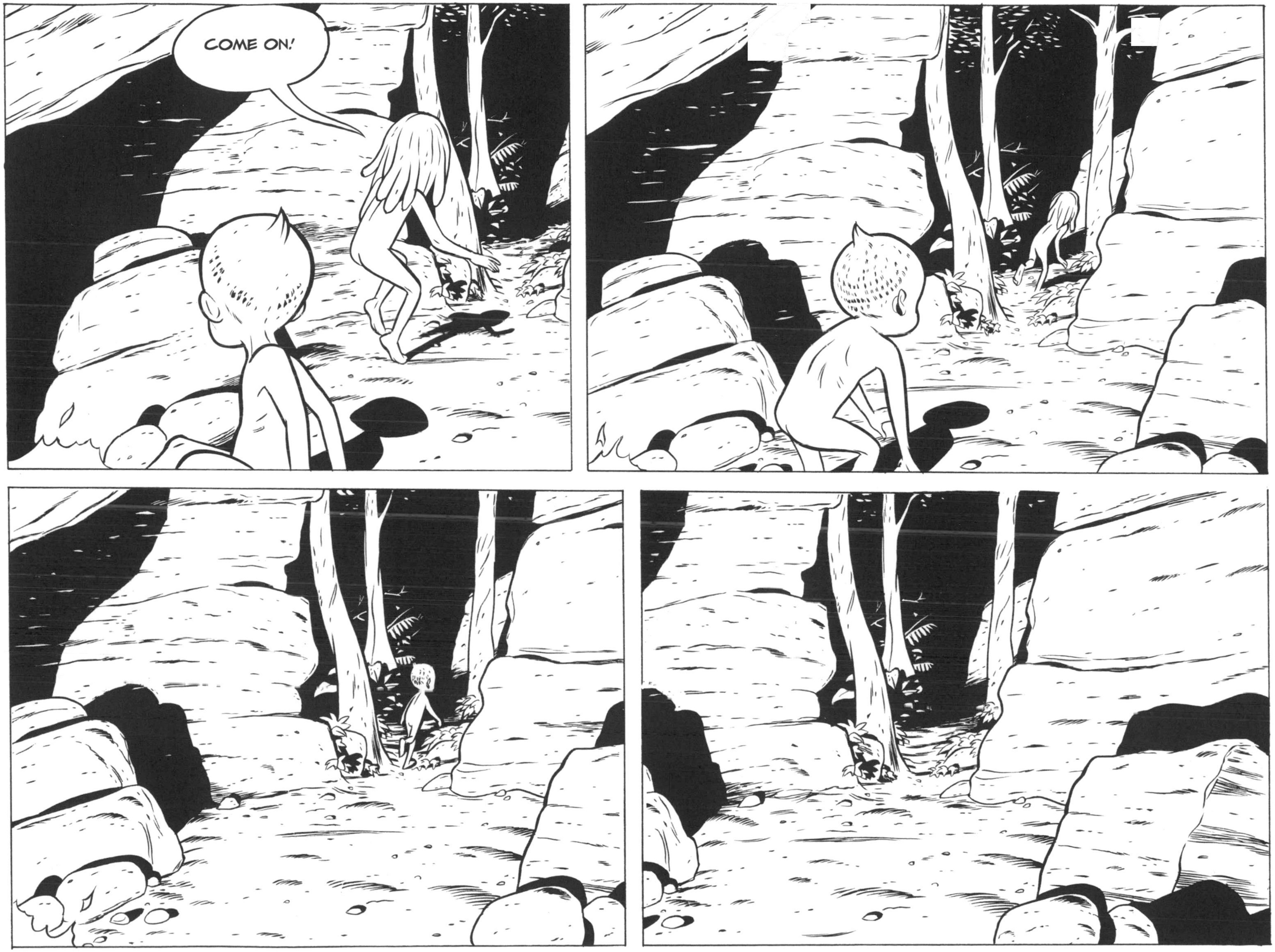
COME ON!

One

Tuki

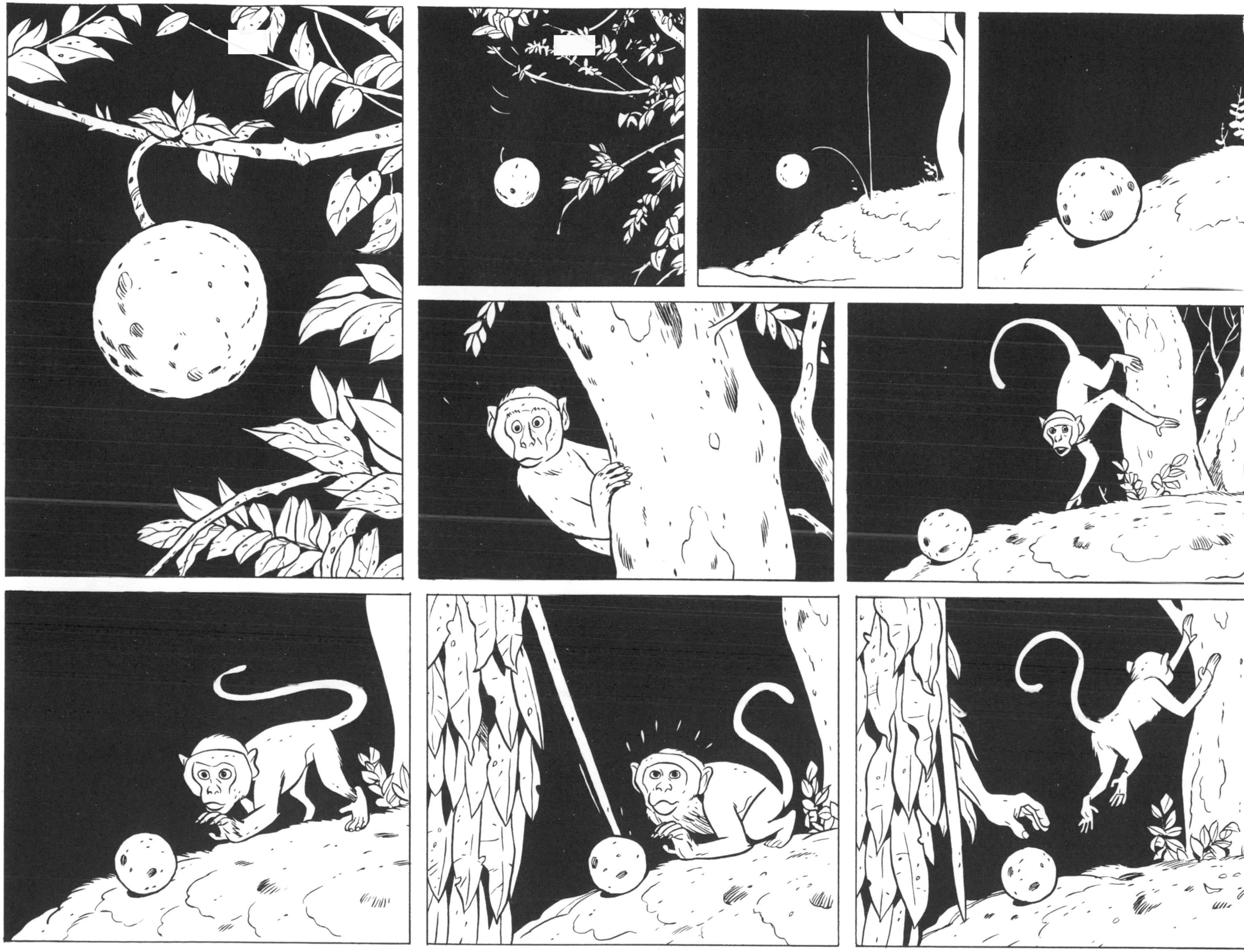

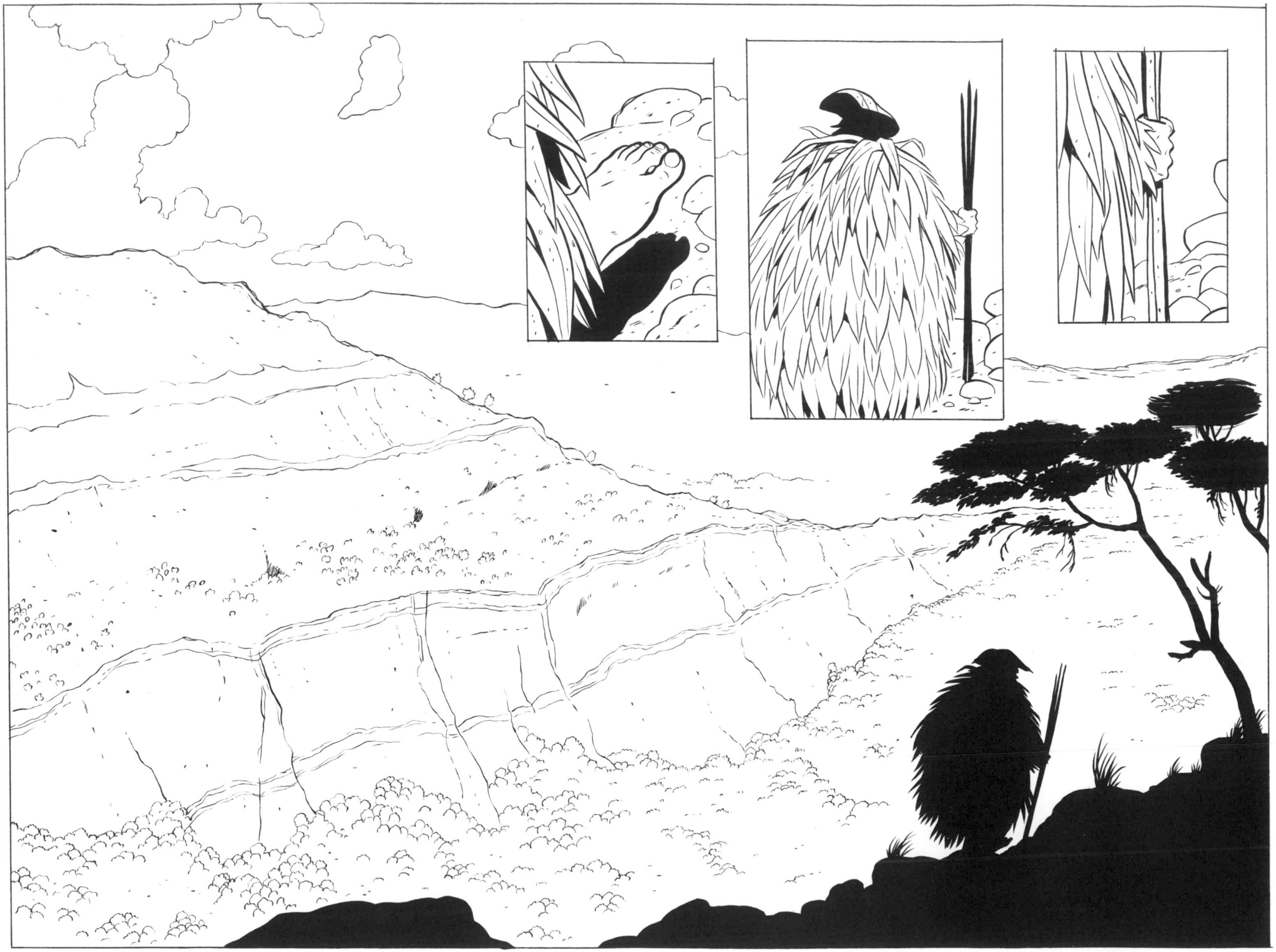

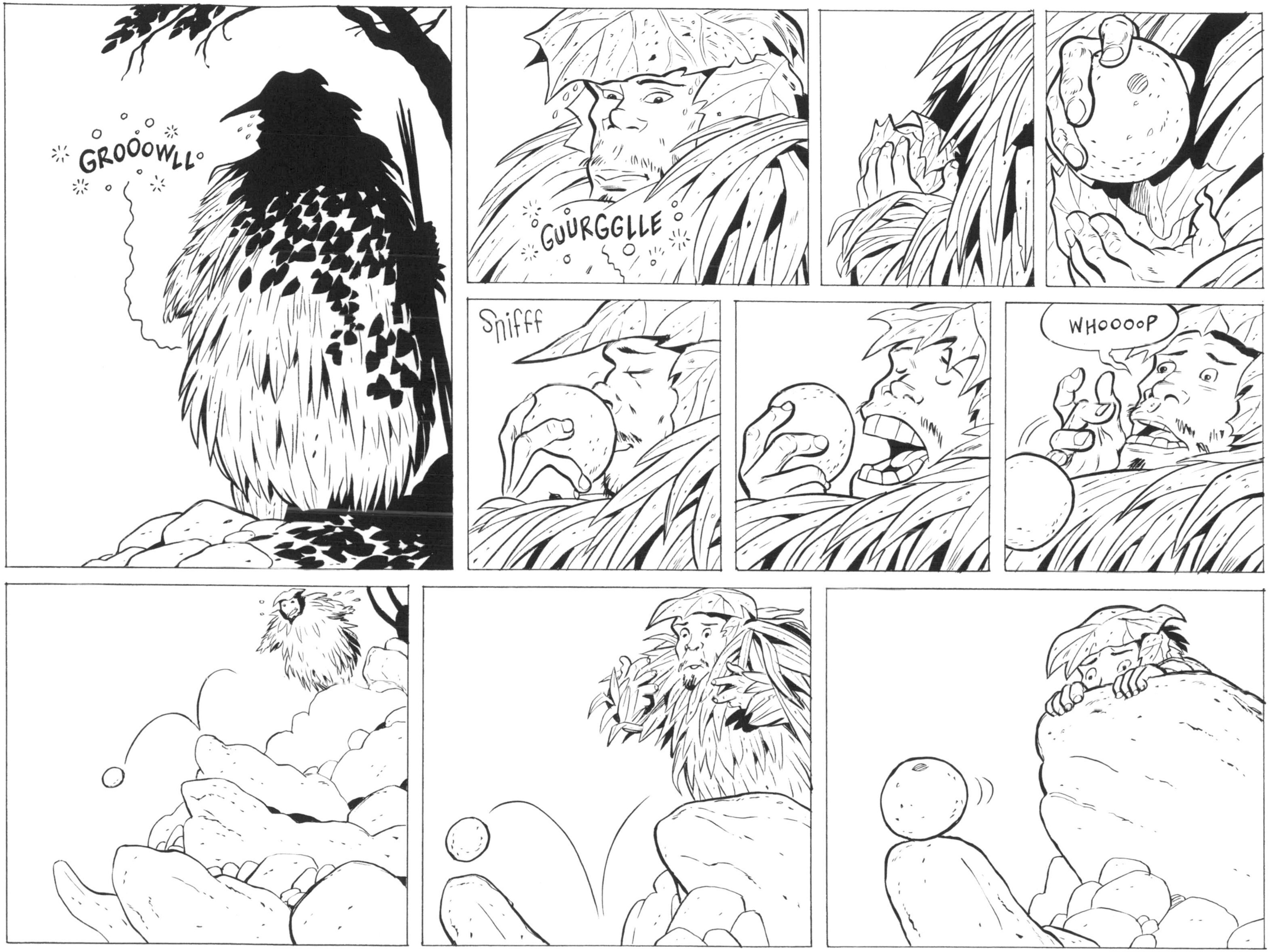
GROOOWLL
GUURGGLLE
Sniff
WHOOOOP

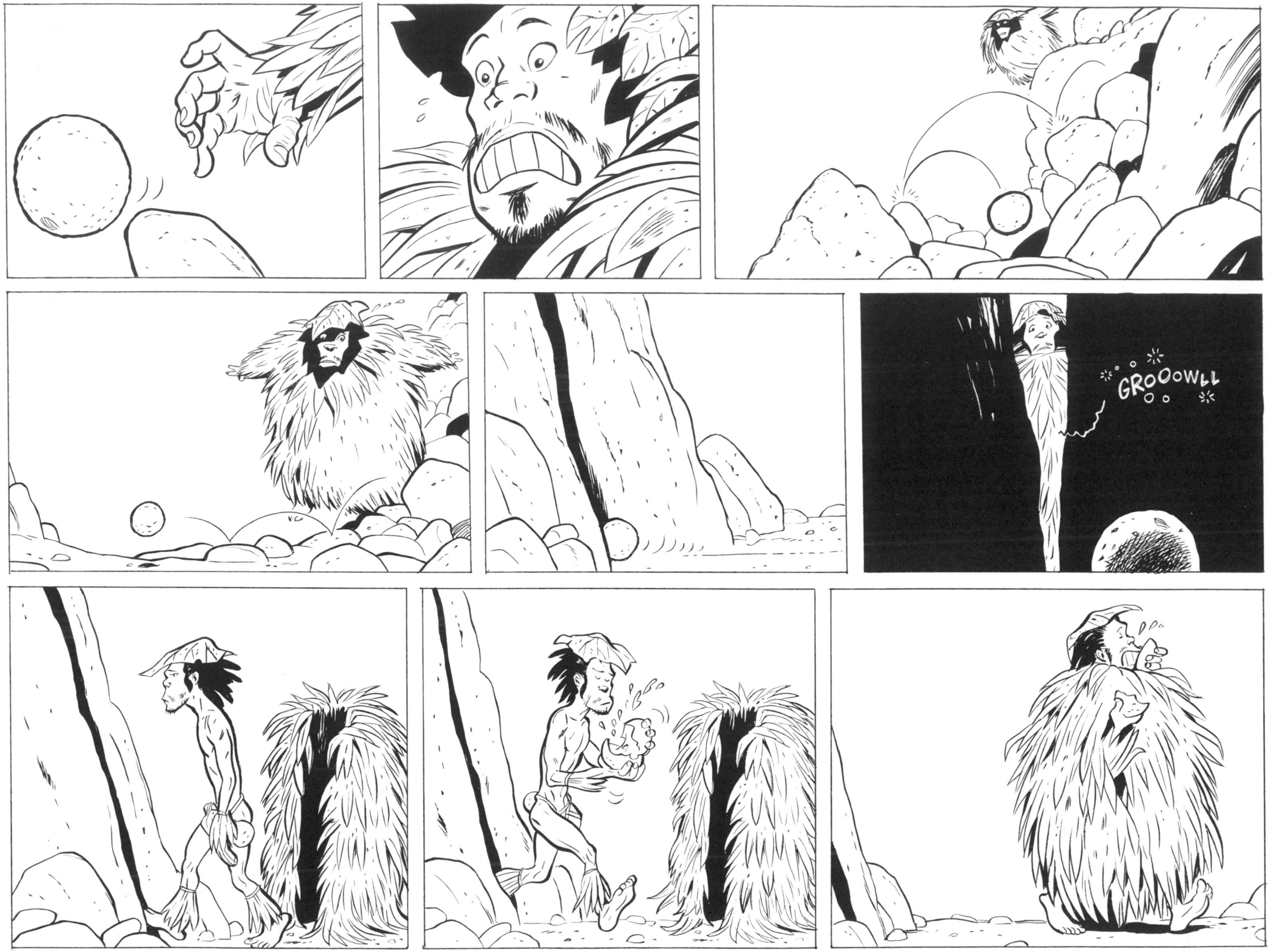
GROOOWLL

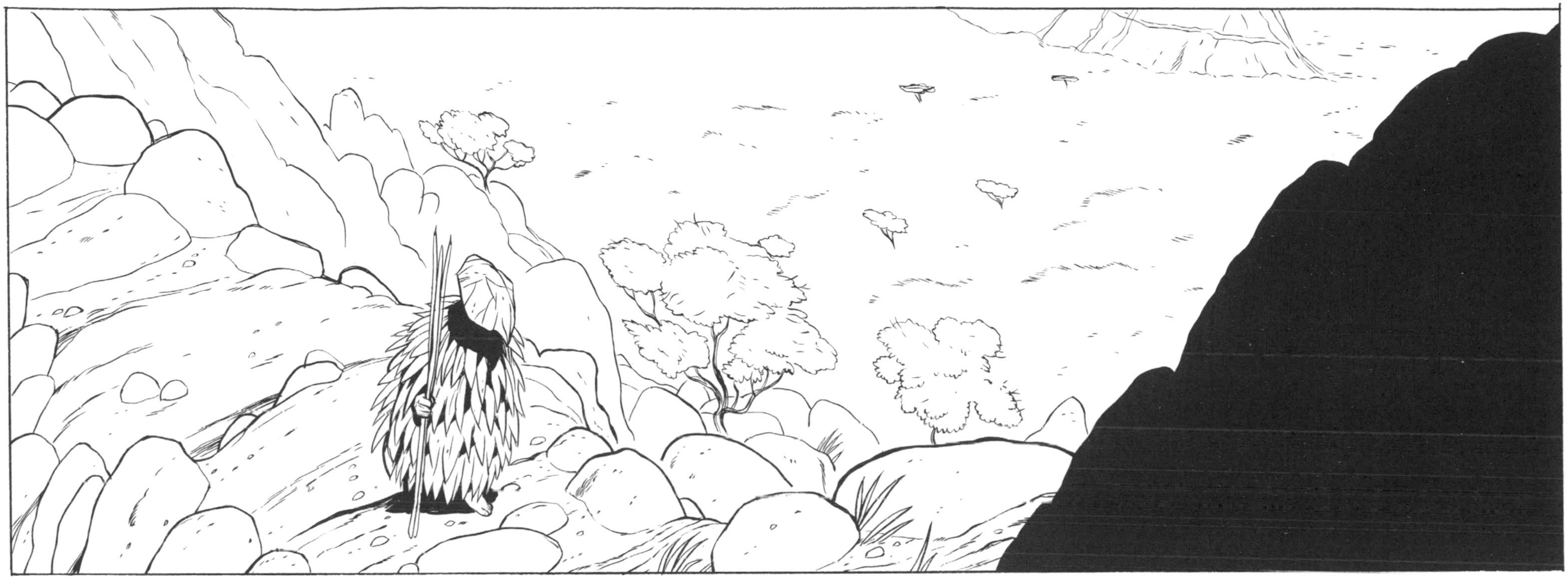

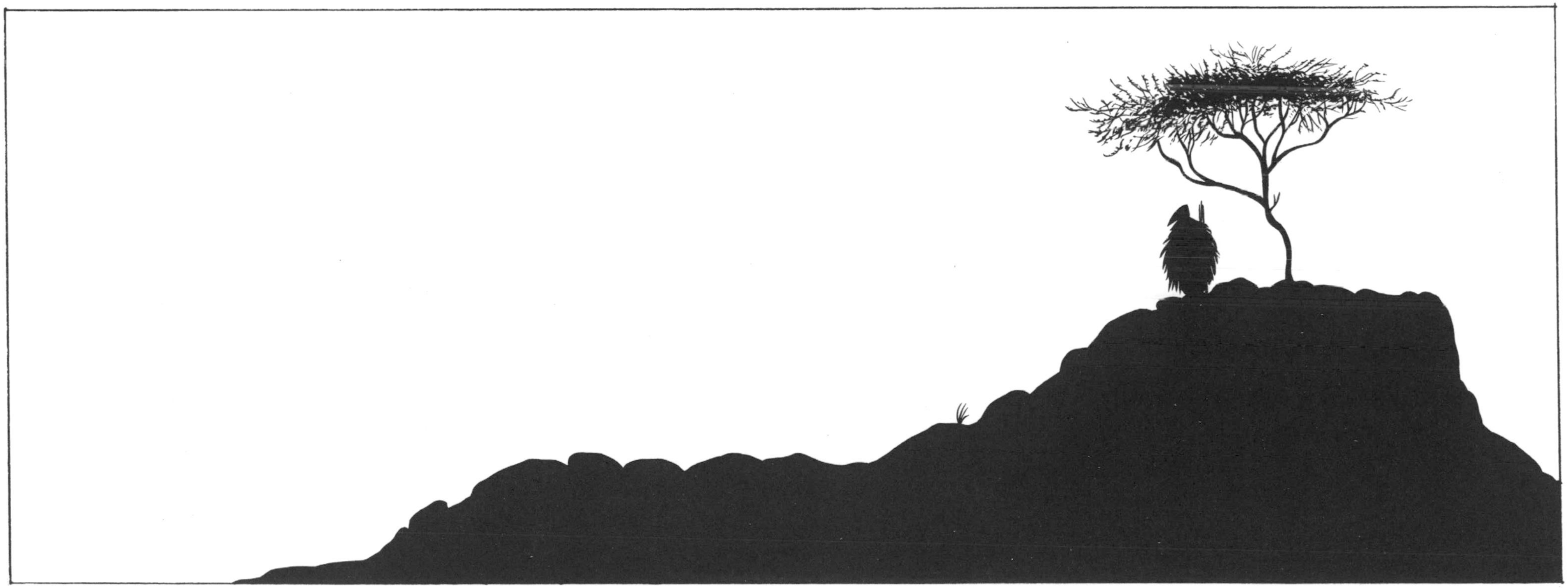

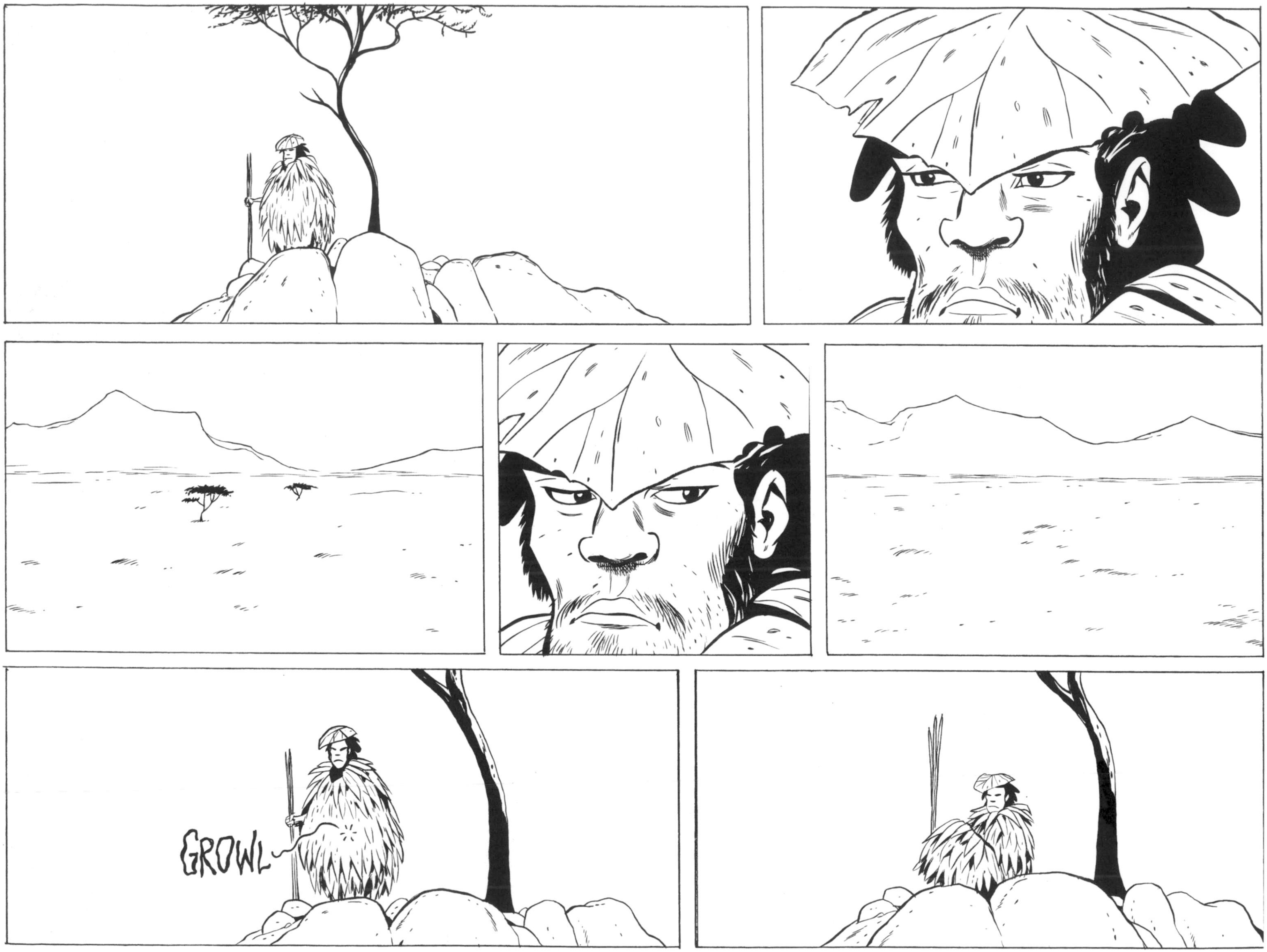
GROWL

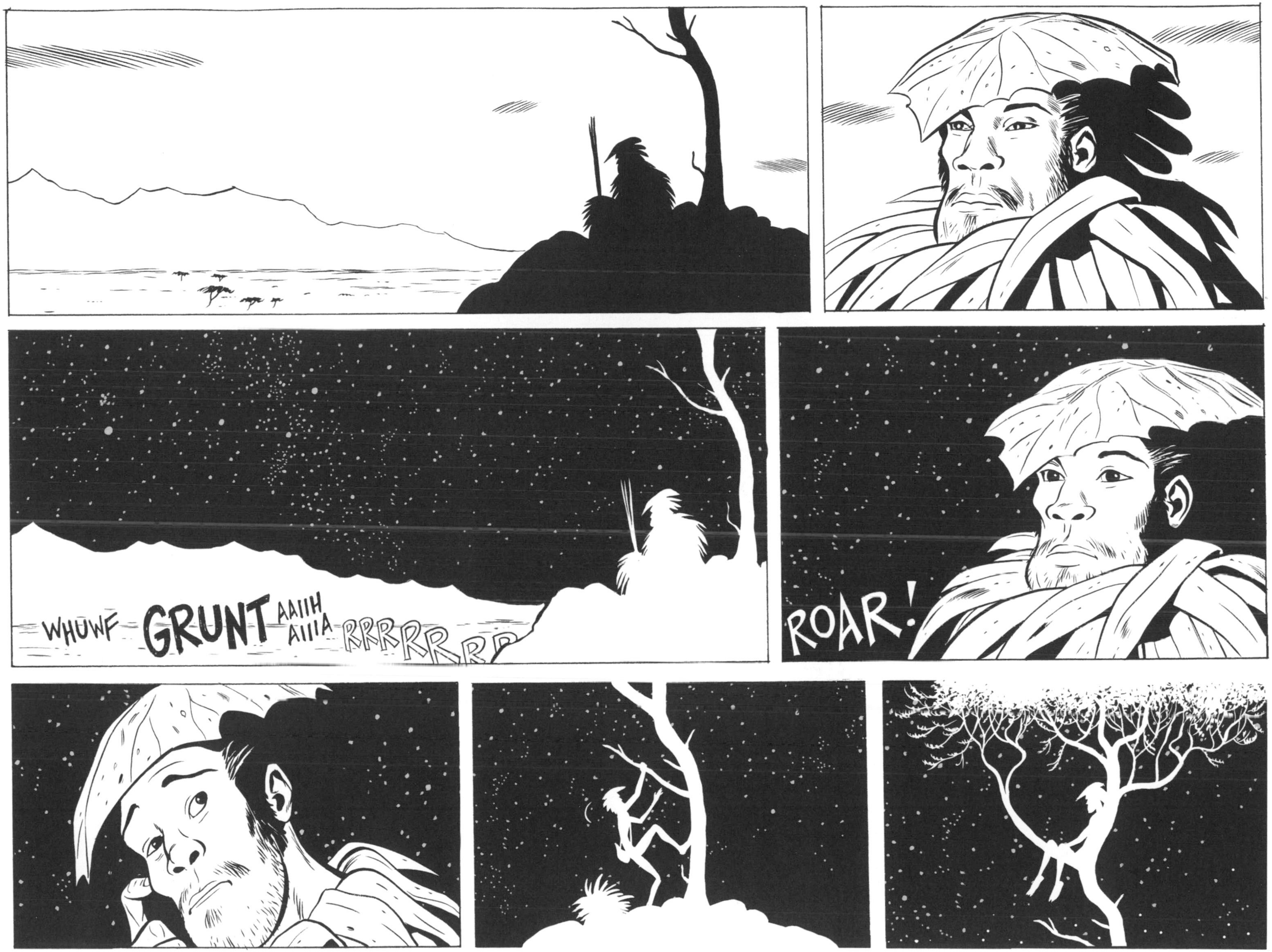
WHUWF
GRUNT
AAIIH AIIIA
RRRRRRRR
ROAR!

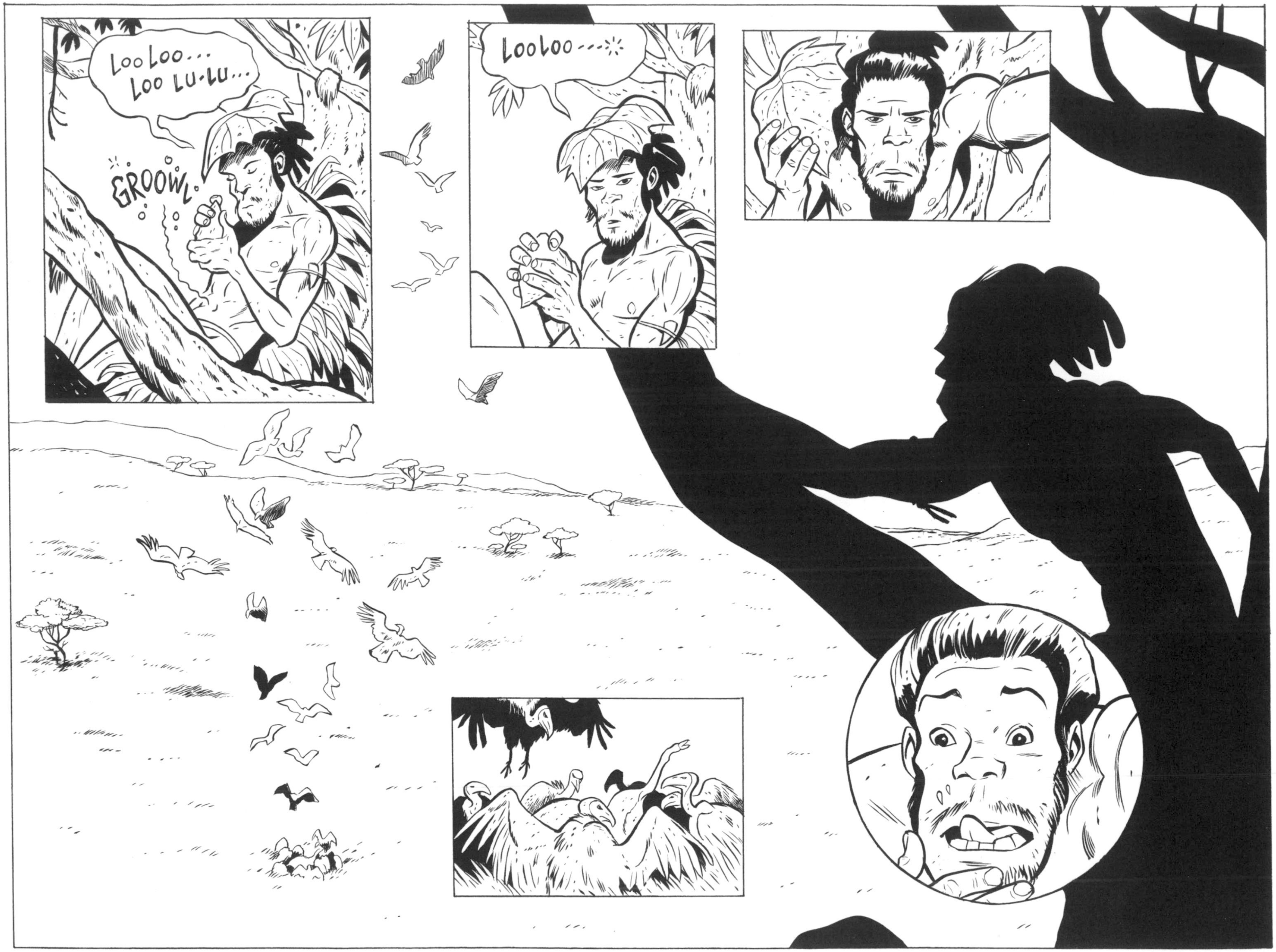
LooLoo...
LooLu-Lu...
GROOWL
LooLoo...

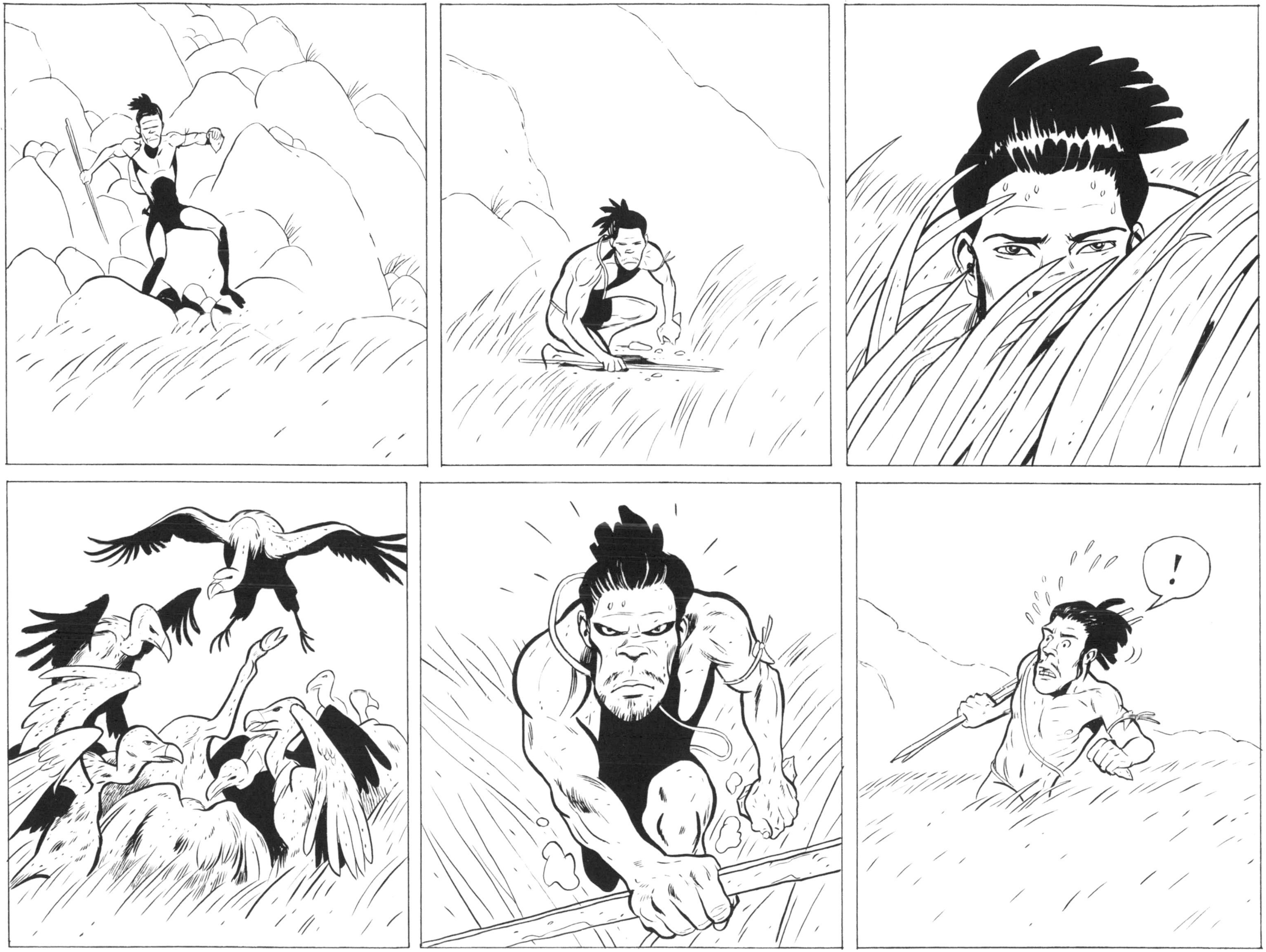
!

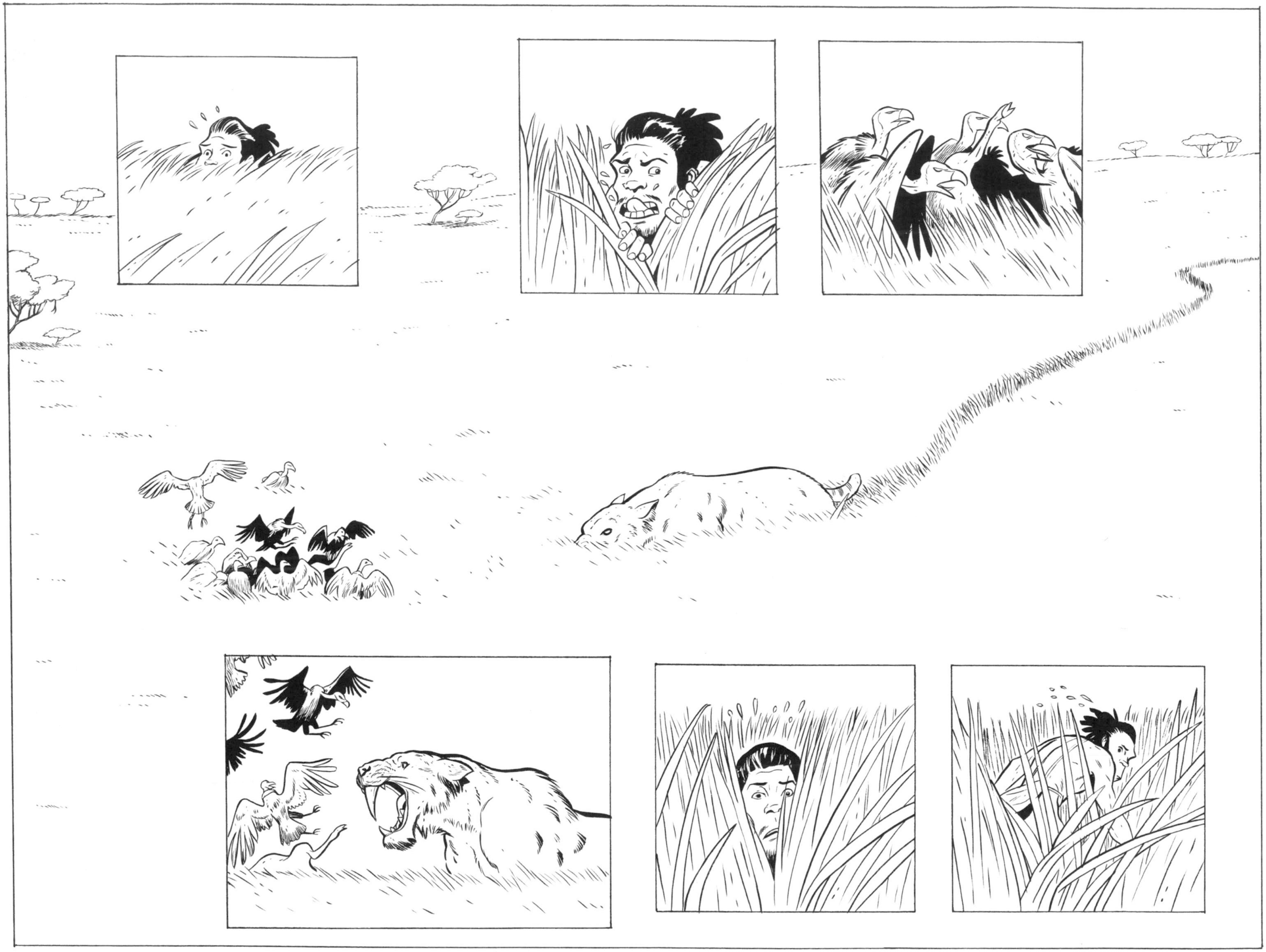

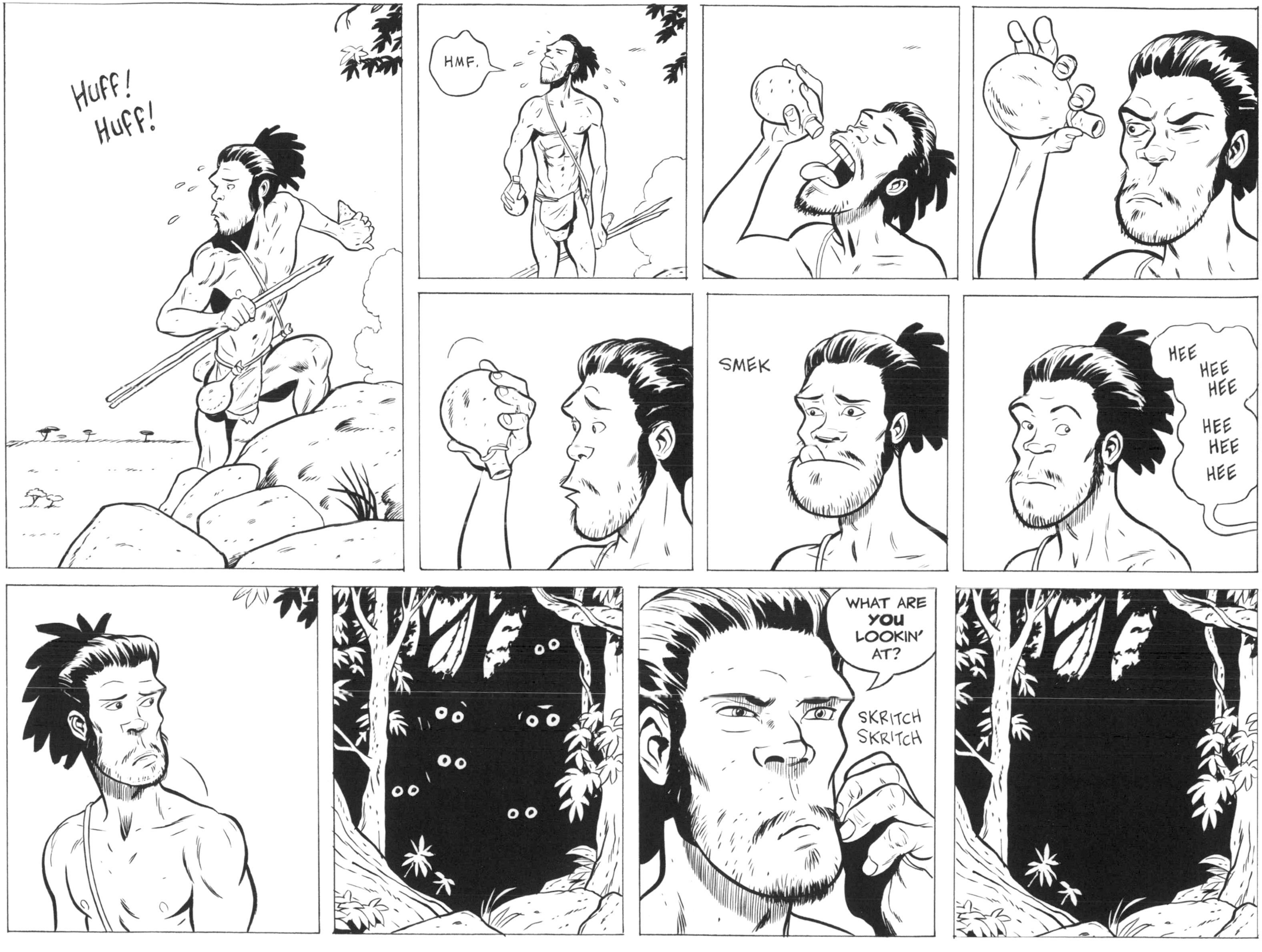
HUFF! HUFF!
HMF.
SMEK
HEE HEE HEE HEE HEE HEE
WHAT ARE YOU LOOKIN' AT?
SKRITCH SKRITCH

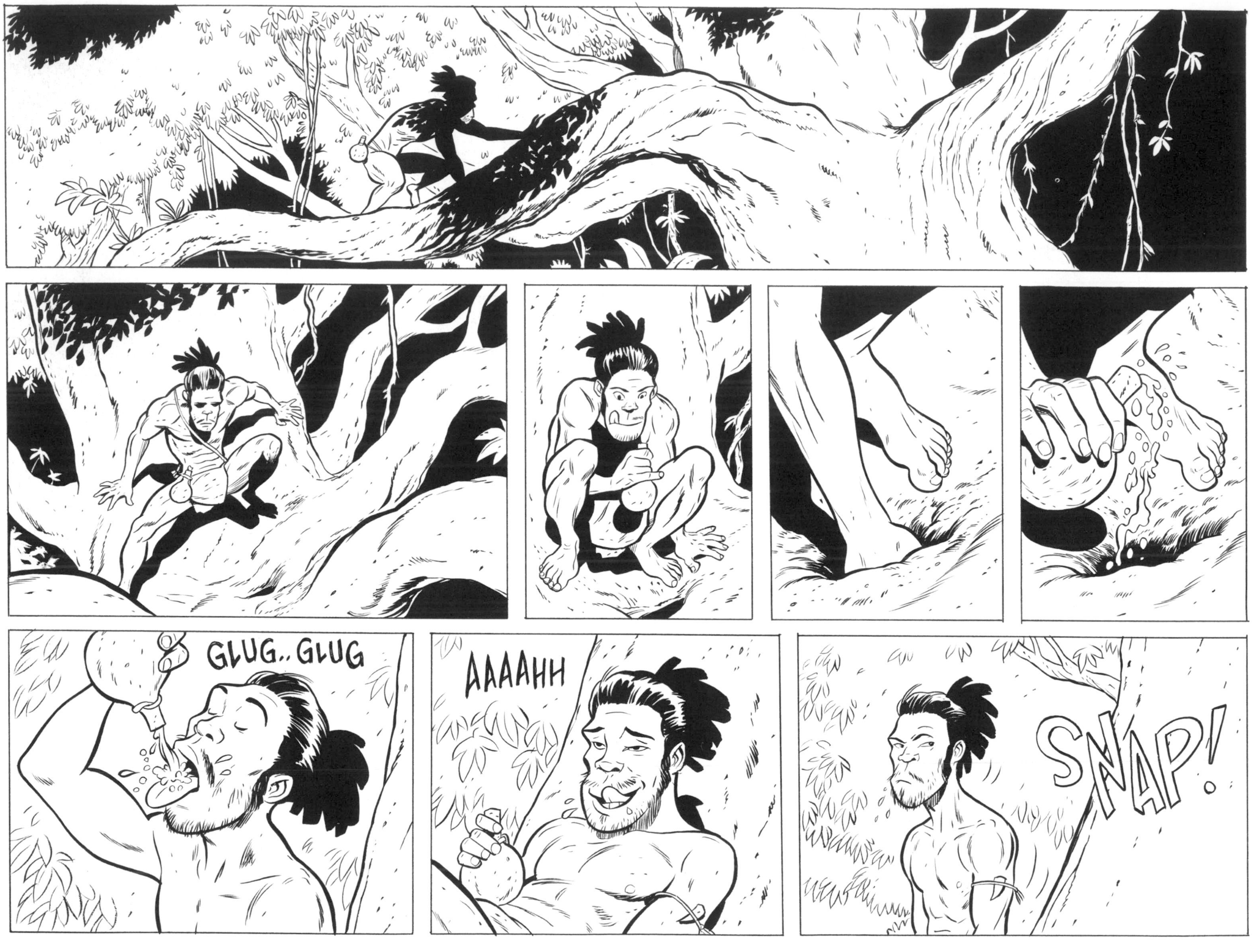
GLUG.. GLUG
AAAAHH
SNAP!

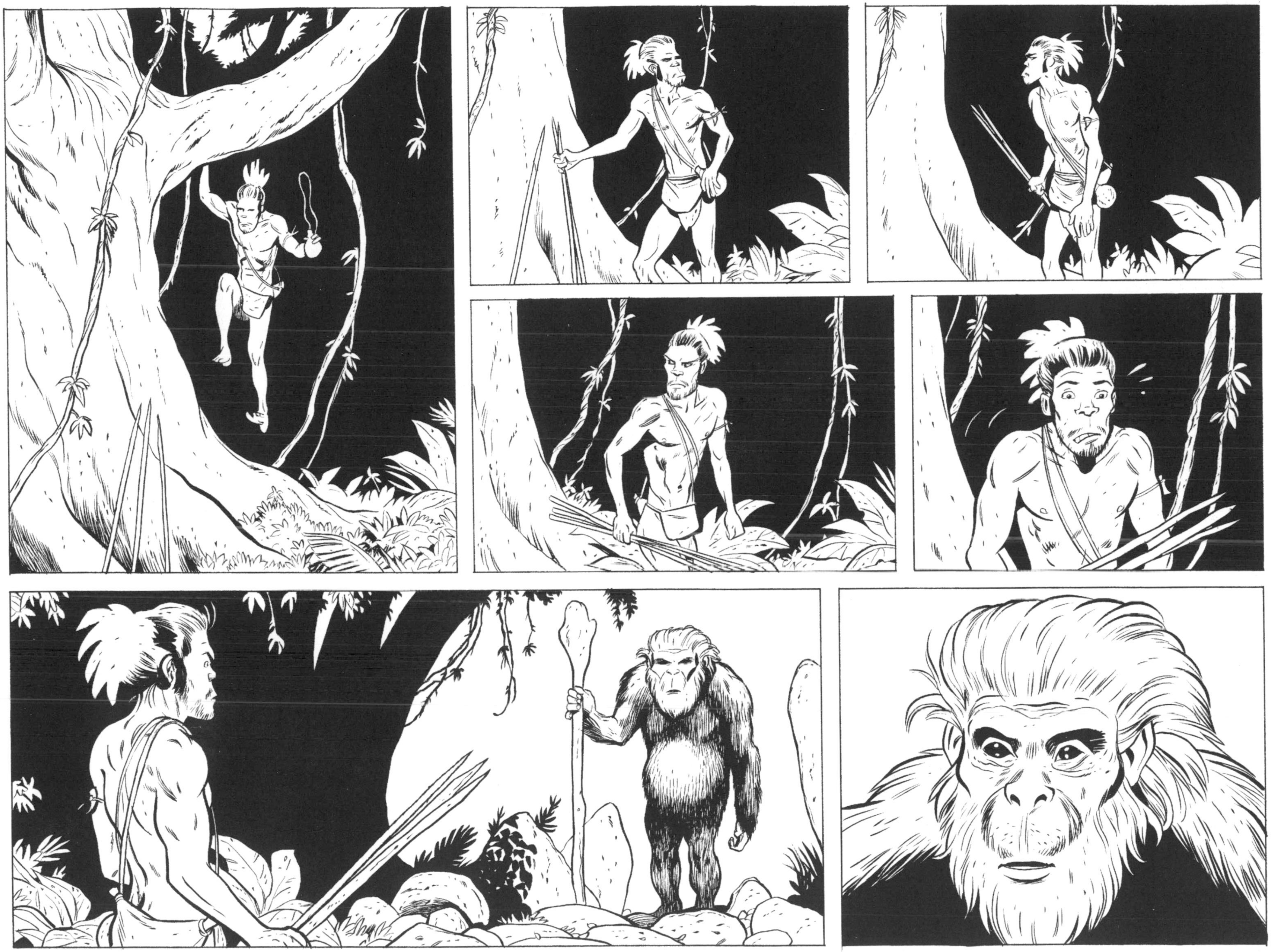

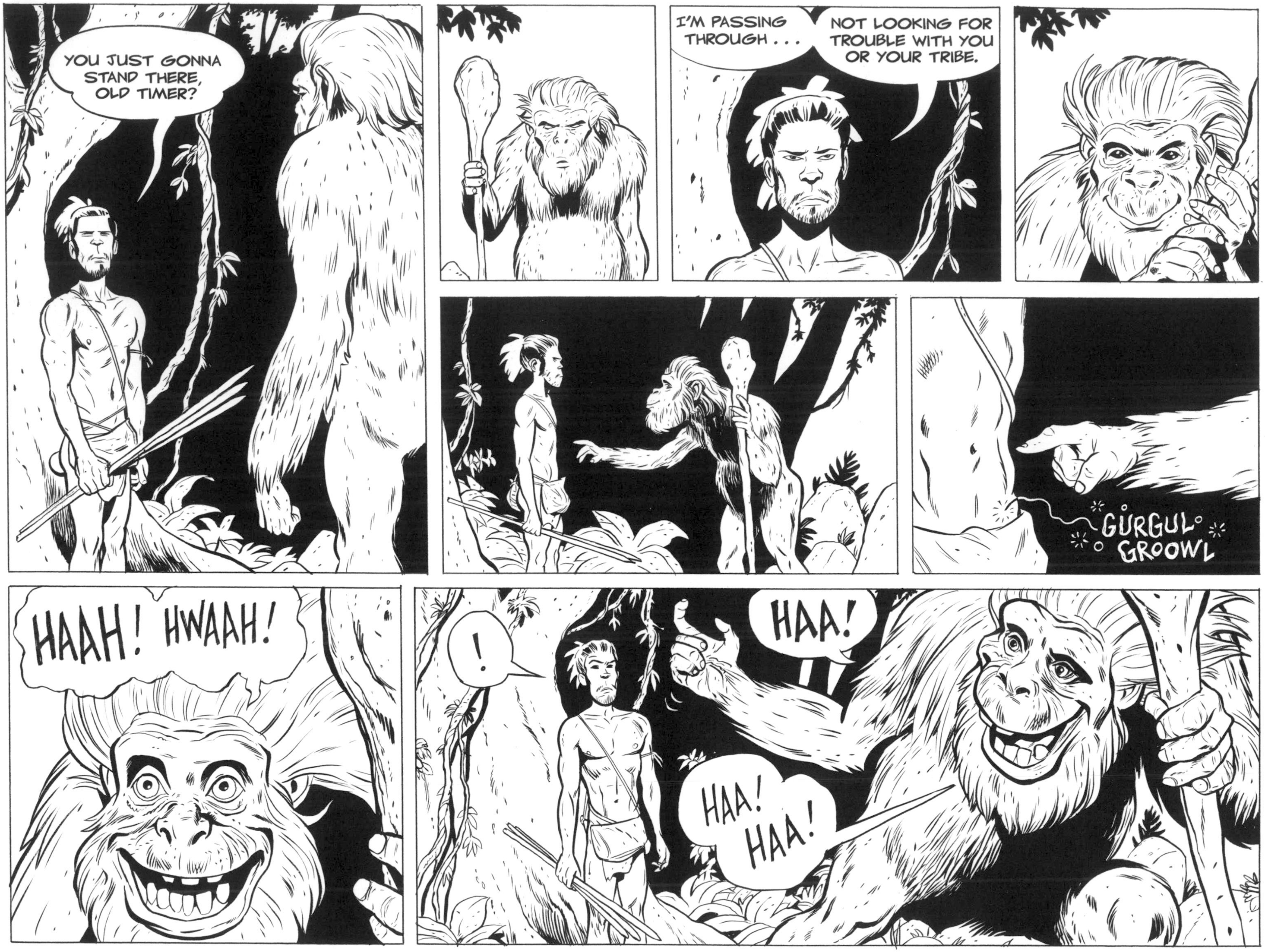

YOU JUST GONNA STAND THERE, OLD TIMER?
I'M PASSING THROUGH . . .
NOT LOOKING FOR TROUBLE WITH YOU OR YOUR TRIBE.
GURGUL GROOWL
HAAH! HWAAH!
!
HAA!
HAA! HAA!

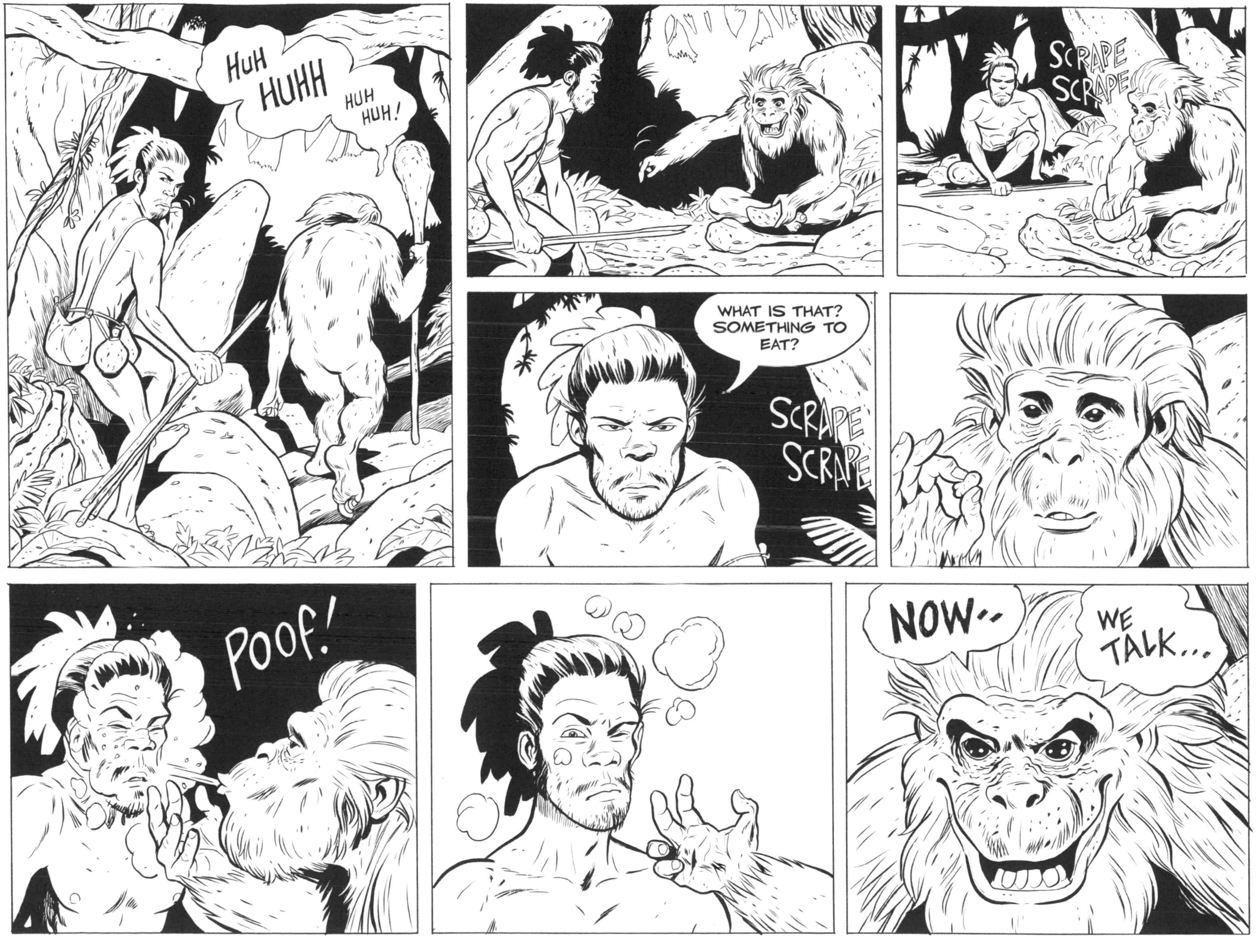
HUH HUHH
HUH HUH!
SCRAPE SCRAPE
WHAT IS THAT? SOMETHING TO EAT?
SCRAPE SCRAPE
POOF!
NOW..
WE TALK...

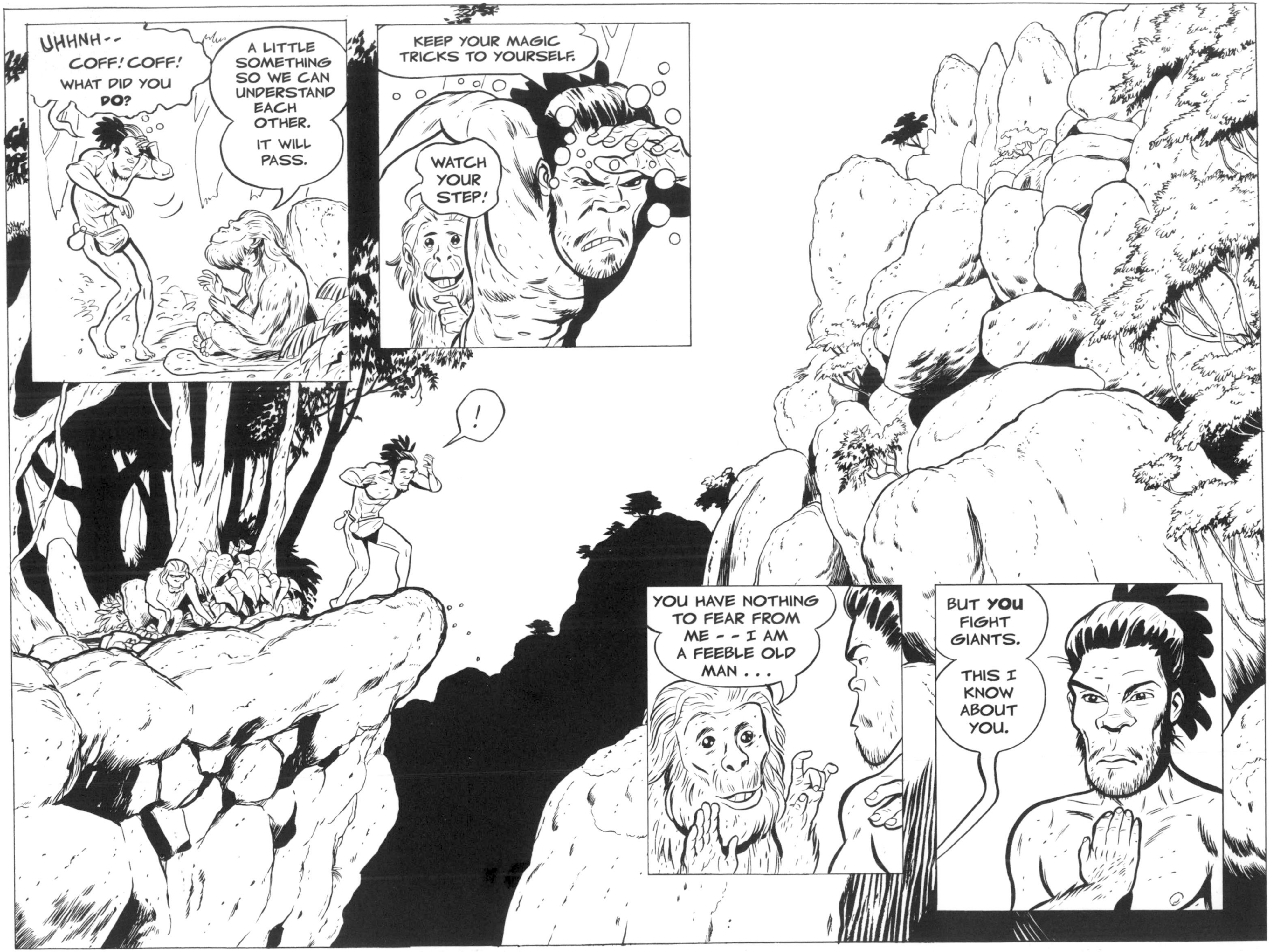
UHHNH--
COFF! COFF!
WHAT DID YOU DO?
A LITTLE SOMETHING SO WE CAN UNDERSTAND EACH OTHER.
IT WILL PASS.
KEEP YOUR MAGIC TRICKS TO YOURSELF.
WATCH YOUR STEP!
!
YOU HAVE NOTHING TO FEAR FROM ME - - I AM A FEEBLE OLD MAN . . .
BUT YOU FIGHT GIANTS.
THIS I KNOW ABOUT YOU.

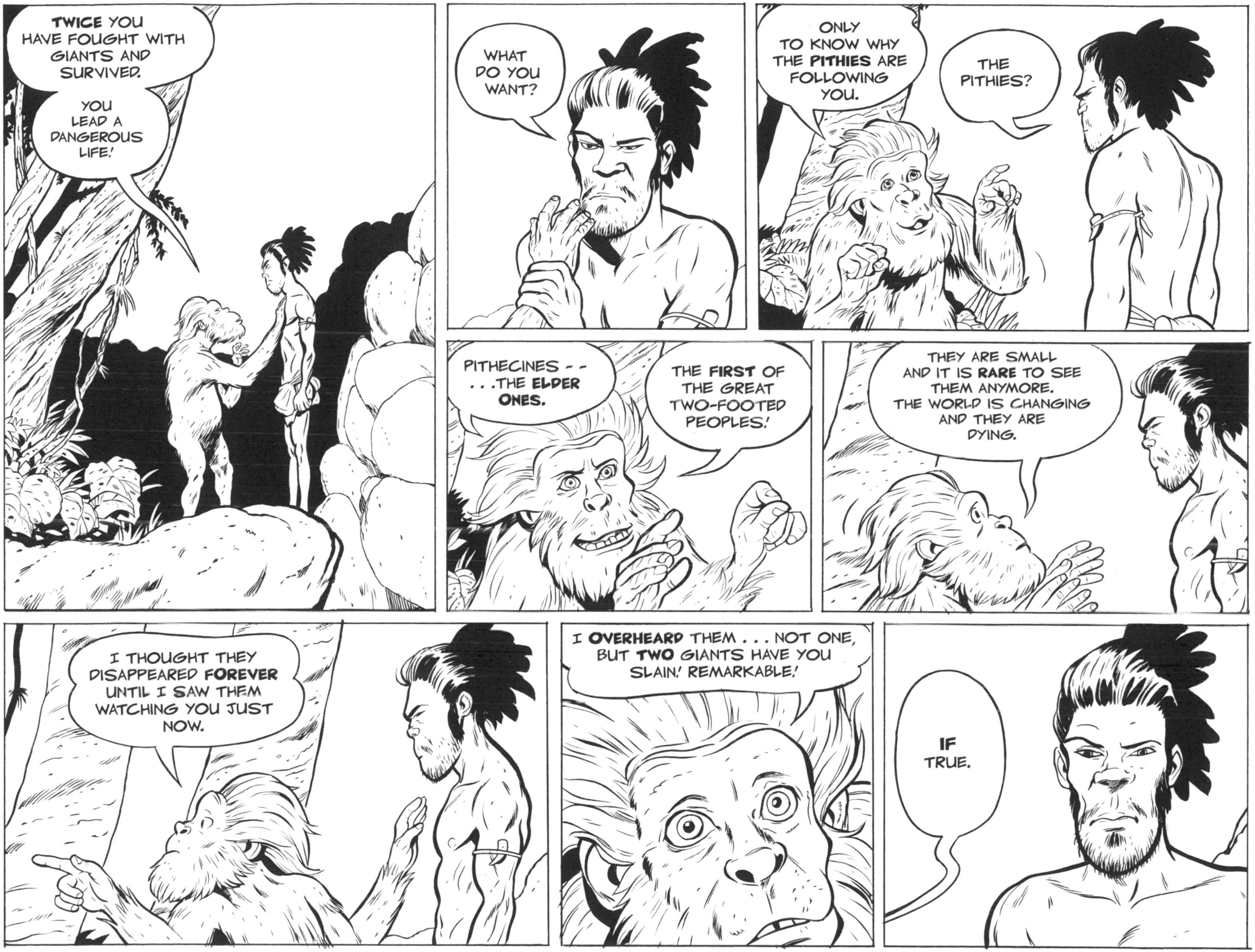
TWICE YOU HAVE FOUGHT WITH GIANTS AND SURVIVED.
YOU LEAD A DANGEROUS LIFE!
WHAT DO YOU WANT?
ONLY TO KNOW WHY THE PITHIES ARE FOLLOWING YOU.
THE PITHIES?
PITHECINES - - . . .THE ELDER ONES.
THE FIRST OF THE GREAT TWO-FOOTED PEOPLES!
THEY ARE SMALL AND IT IS RARE TO SEE THEM ANYMORE. THE WORLD IS CHANGING AND THEY ARE DYING.
I THOUGHT THEY DISAPPEARED FOREVER UNTIL I SAW THEM WATCHING YOU JUST NOW.
I OVERHEARD THEM . . . NOT ONE, BUT TWO GIANTS HAVE YOU SLAIN! REMARKABLE!
IF TRUE.

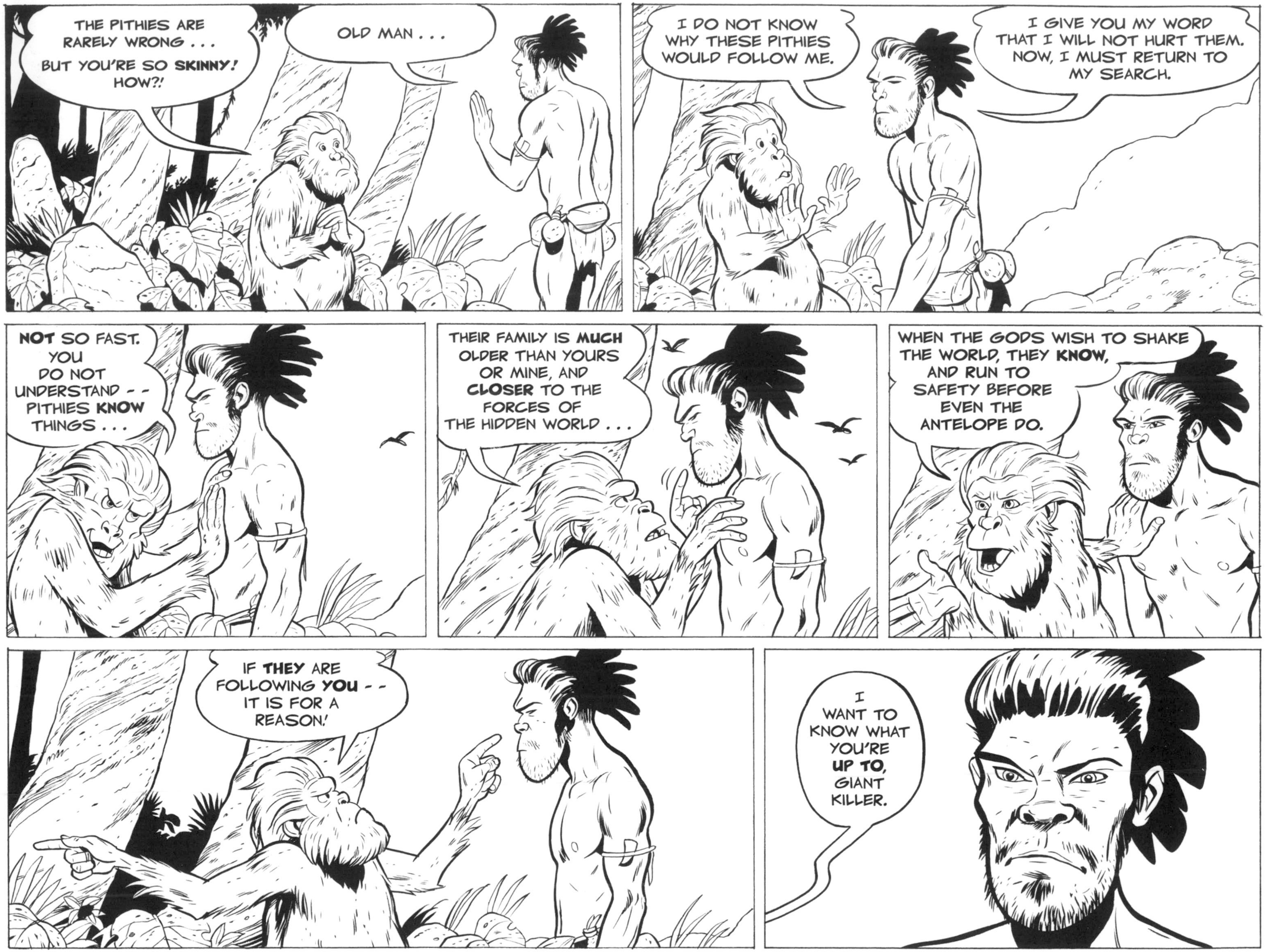
THE PITHIES ARE RARELY WRONG . . . BUT YOU'RE SO SKINNY! HOW?!
OLD MAN . . .
I DO NOT KNOW WHY THESE PITHIES WOULD FOLLOW ME.
I GIVE YOU MY WORD THAT I WILL NOT HURT THEM. NOW, I MUST RETURN TO MY SEARCH.
NOT SO FAST. YOU DO NOT UNDERSTAND -- PITHIES KNOW THINGS . . .
THEIR FAMILY IS MUCH OLDER THAN YOURS OR MINE, AND CLOSER TO THE FORCES OF THE HIDDEN WORLD . . .
WHEN THE GODS WISH TO SHAKE THE WORLD, THEY KNOW, AND RUN TO SAFETY BEFORE EVEN THE ANTELOPE DO.
IF THEY ARE FOLLOWING YOU -- IT IS FOR A REASON!
I WANT TO KNOW WHAT YOU'RE UP TO, GIANT KILLER.

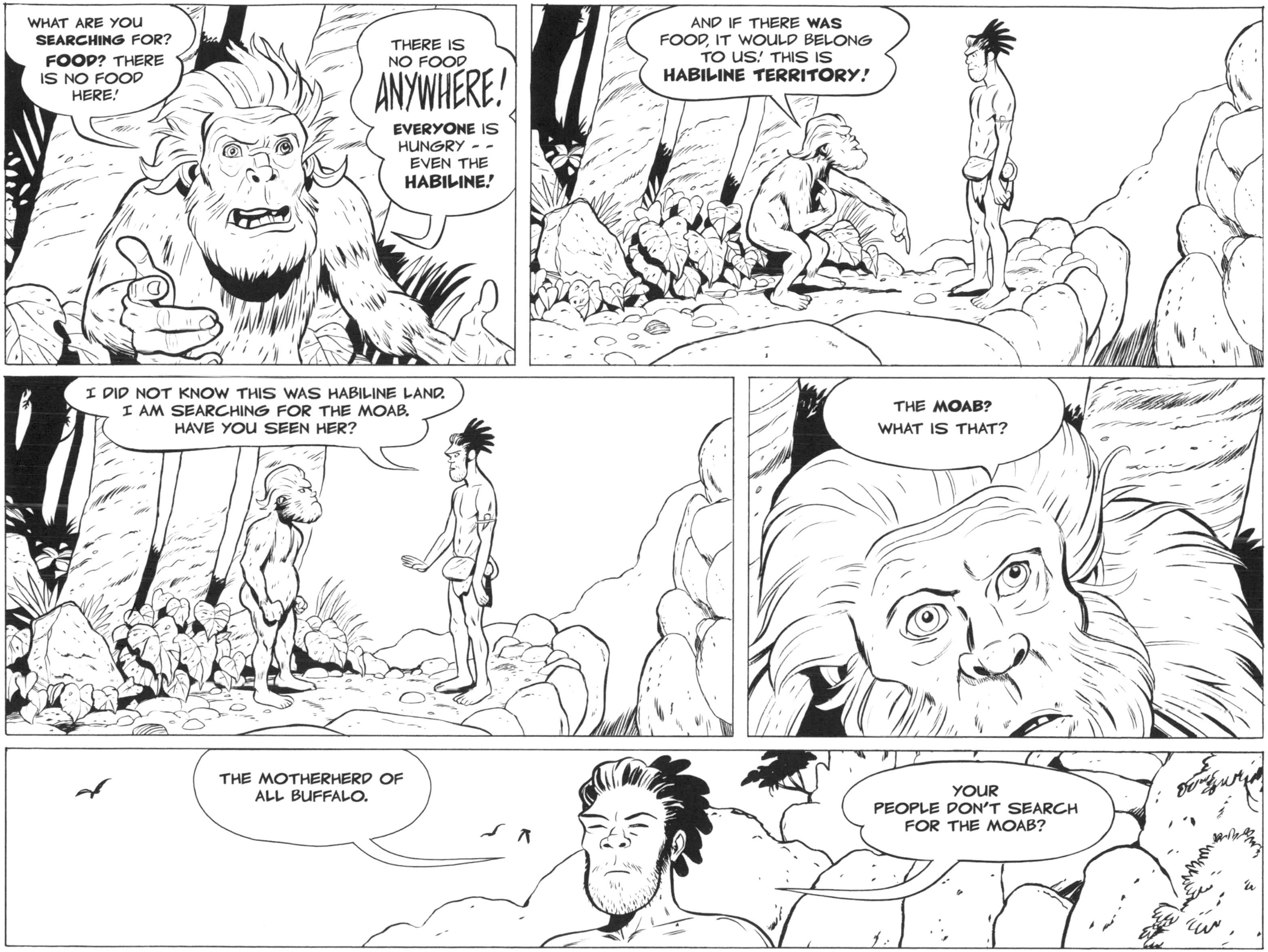
WHAT ARE YOU SEARCHING FOR? FOOD? THERE IS NO FOOD HERE!
THERE IS NO FOOD ANYWHERE! EVERYONE IS HUNGRY -- EVEN THE HABILINE!
AND IF THERE WAS FOOD, IT WOULD BELONG TO US! THIS IS HABILINE TERRITORY!
I DID NOT KNOW THIS WAS HABILINE LAND. I AM SEARCHING FOR THE MOAB. HAVE YOU SEEN HER?
THE MOAB? WHAT IS THAT?
THE MOTHERHERD OF ALL BUFFALO.
YOUR PEOPLE DON'T SEARCH FOR THE MOAB?

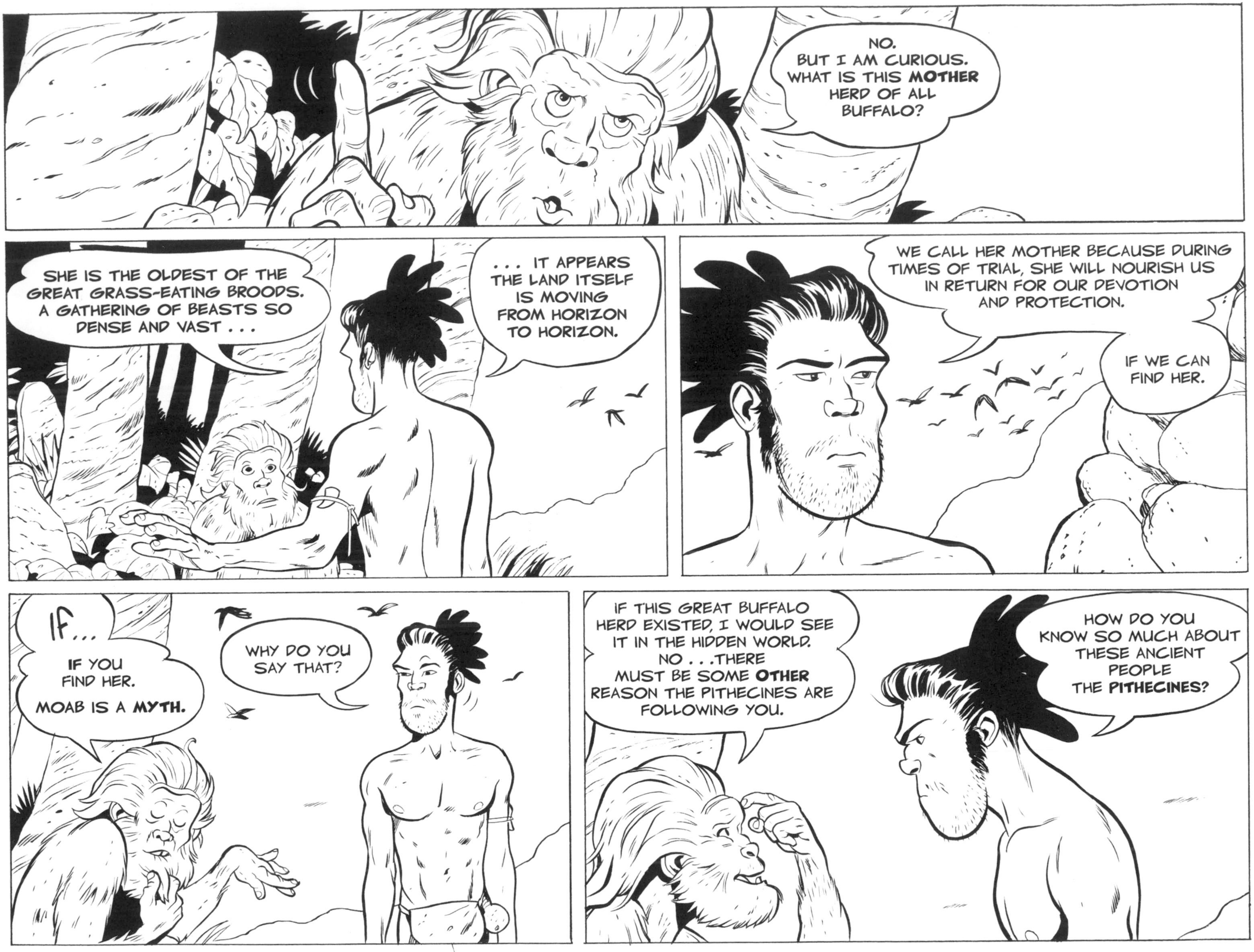

NO. BUT I AM CURIOUS. WHAT IS THIS **MOTHER** HERD OF ALL BUFFALO?
SHE IS THE OLDEST OF THE GREAT GRASS-EATING BROODS. A GATHERING OF BEASTS SO DENSE AND VAST . . .
. . . IT APPEARS THE LAND ITSELF IS MOVING FROM HORIZON TO HORIZON.
WE CALL HER MOTHER BECAUSE DURING TIMES OF TRIAL, SHE WILL NOURISH US IN RETURN FOR OUR DEVOTION AND PROTECTION.
IF WE CAN FIND HER.
IF...
IF YOU FIND HER.
MOAB IS A **MYTH.**
WHY DO YOU SAY THAT?
IF THIS GREAT BUFFALO HERD EXISTED, I WOULD SEE IT IN THE HIDDEN WORLD. NO . . .THERE MUST BE SOME **OTHER** REASON THE PITHECINES ARE FOLLOWING YOU.
HOW DO YOU KNOW SO MUCH ABOUT THESE ANCIENT PEOPLE THE **PITHECINES**?

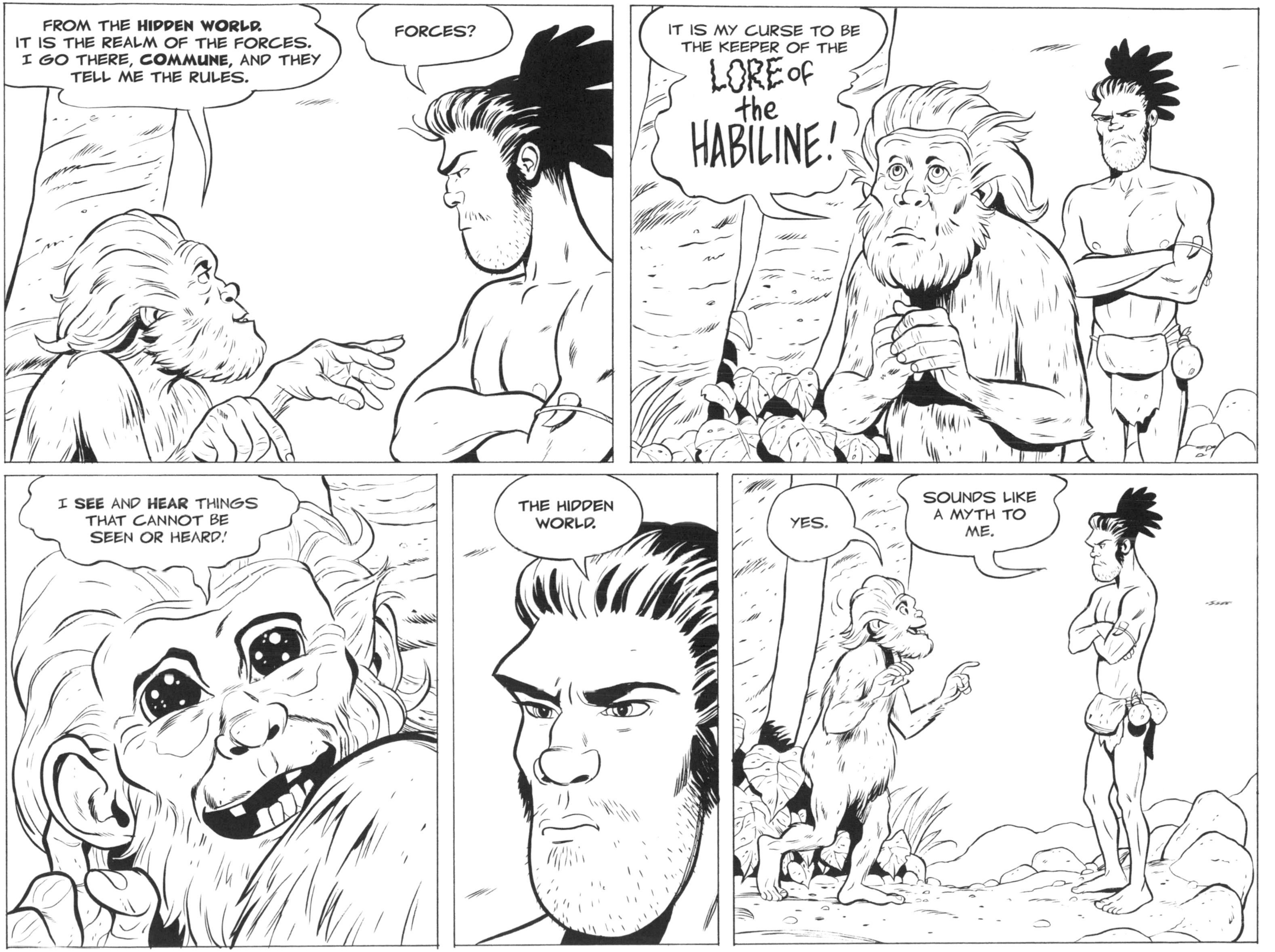
FROM THE HIDDEN WORLD. IT IS THE REALM OF THE FORCES. I GO THERE, COMMUNE, AND THEY TELL ME THE RULES.
FORCES?
IT IS MY CURSE TO BE THE KEEPER OF THE LORE of the HABILINE!
I SEE AND HEAR THINGS THAT CANNOT BE SEEN OR HEARD!
THE HIDDEN WORLD.
YES.
SOUNDS LIKE A MYTH TO ME.

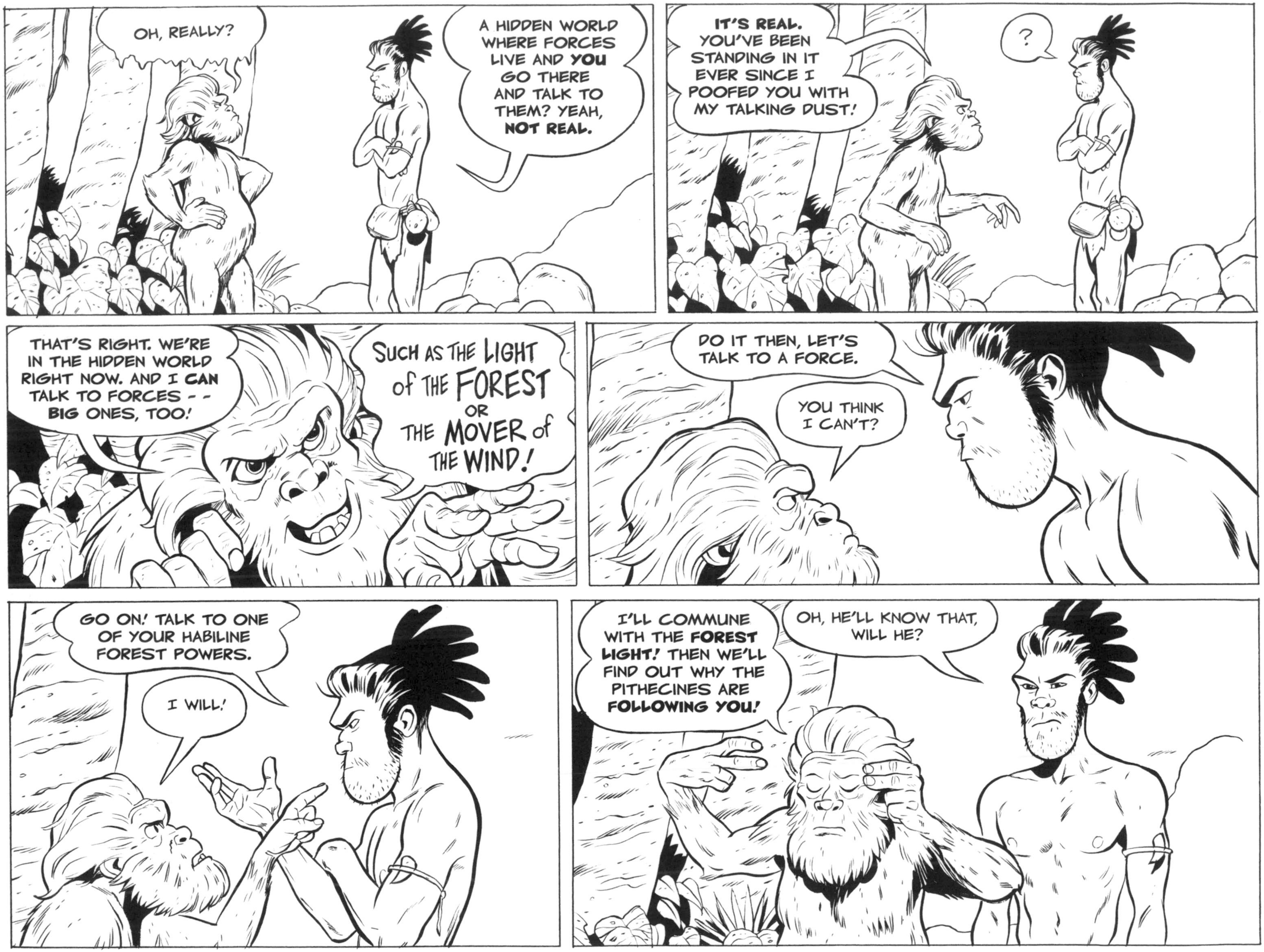
OH, REALLY?
A HIDDEN WORLD WHERE FORCES LIVE AND YOU GO THERE AND TALK TO THEM? YEAH, NOT REAL.
IT'S REAL. YOU'VE BEEN STANDING IN IT EVER SINCE I POOFED YOU WITH MY TALKING DUST!
?
THAT'S RIGHT. WE'RE IN THE HIDDEN WORLD RIGHT NOW. AND I CAN TALK TO FORCES - - BIG ONES, TOO!
SUCH AS THE LIGHT OF THE FOREST OR THE MOVER OF THE WIND!
DO IT THEN, LET'S TALK TO A FORCE.
YOU THINK I CAN'T?
GO ON! TALK TO ONE OF YOUR HABILINE FOREST POWERS.
I WILL!
I'LL COMMUNE WITH THE FOREST LIGHT! THEN WE'LL FIND OUT WHY THE PITHECINES ARE FOLLOWING YOU!
OH, HE'LL KNOW THAT, WILL HE?

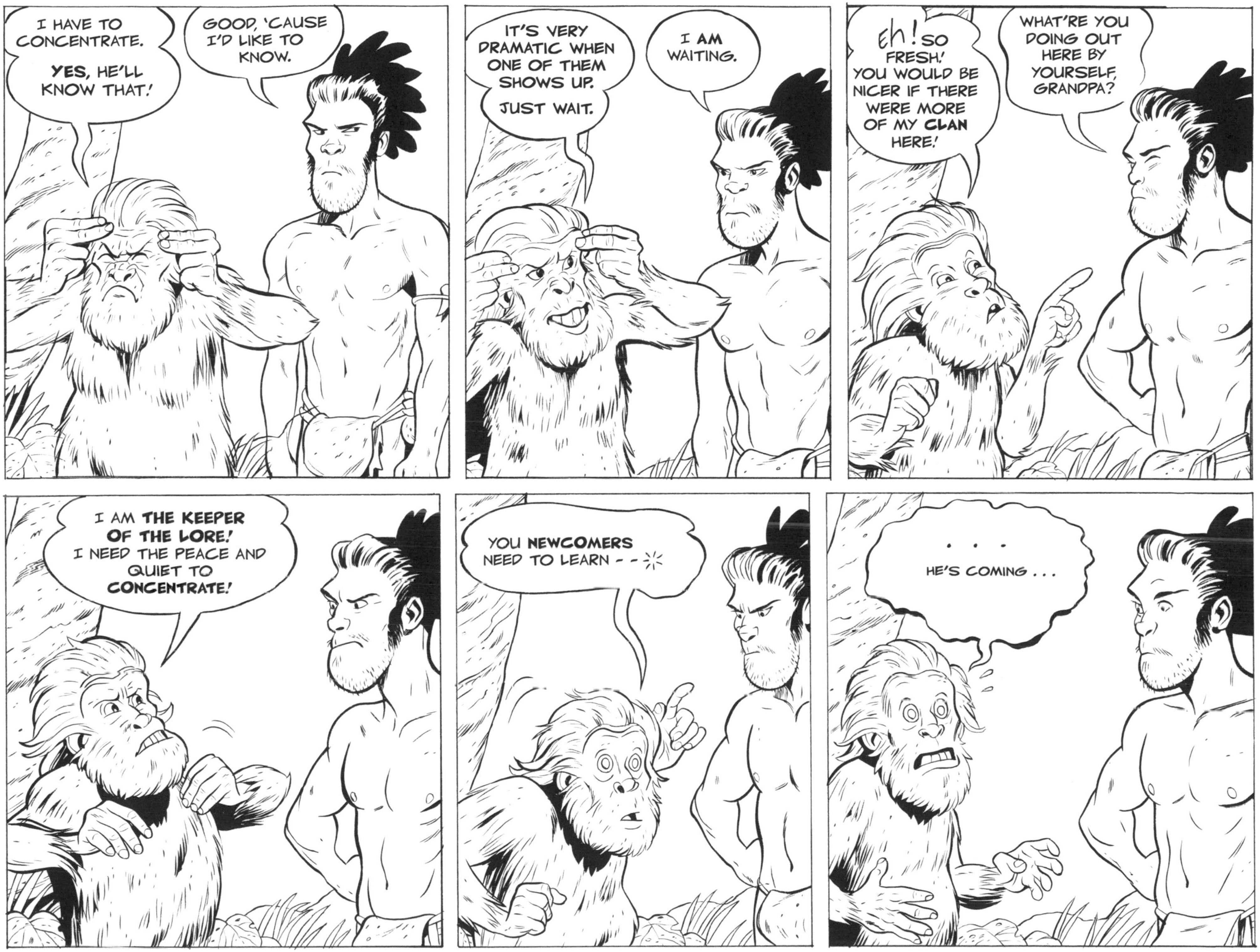
I HAVE TO CONCENTRATE.
YES, HE'LL KNOW THAT!
GOOD, 'CAUSE I'D LIKE TO KNOW.
IT'S VERY DRAMATIC WHEN ONE OF THEM SHOWS UP.
JUST WAIT.
I AM WAITING.
Eh! SO FRESH! YOU WOULD BE NICER IF THERE WERE MORE OF MY CLAN HERE!
WHAT'RE YOU DOING OUT HERE BY YOURSELF, GRANDPA?
I AM THE KEEPER OF THE LORE! I NEED THE PEACE AND QUIET TO CONCENTRATE!
YOU NEWCOMERS NEED TO LEARN - -
. . .
HE'S COMING . . .

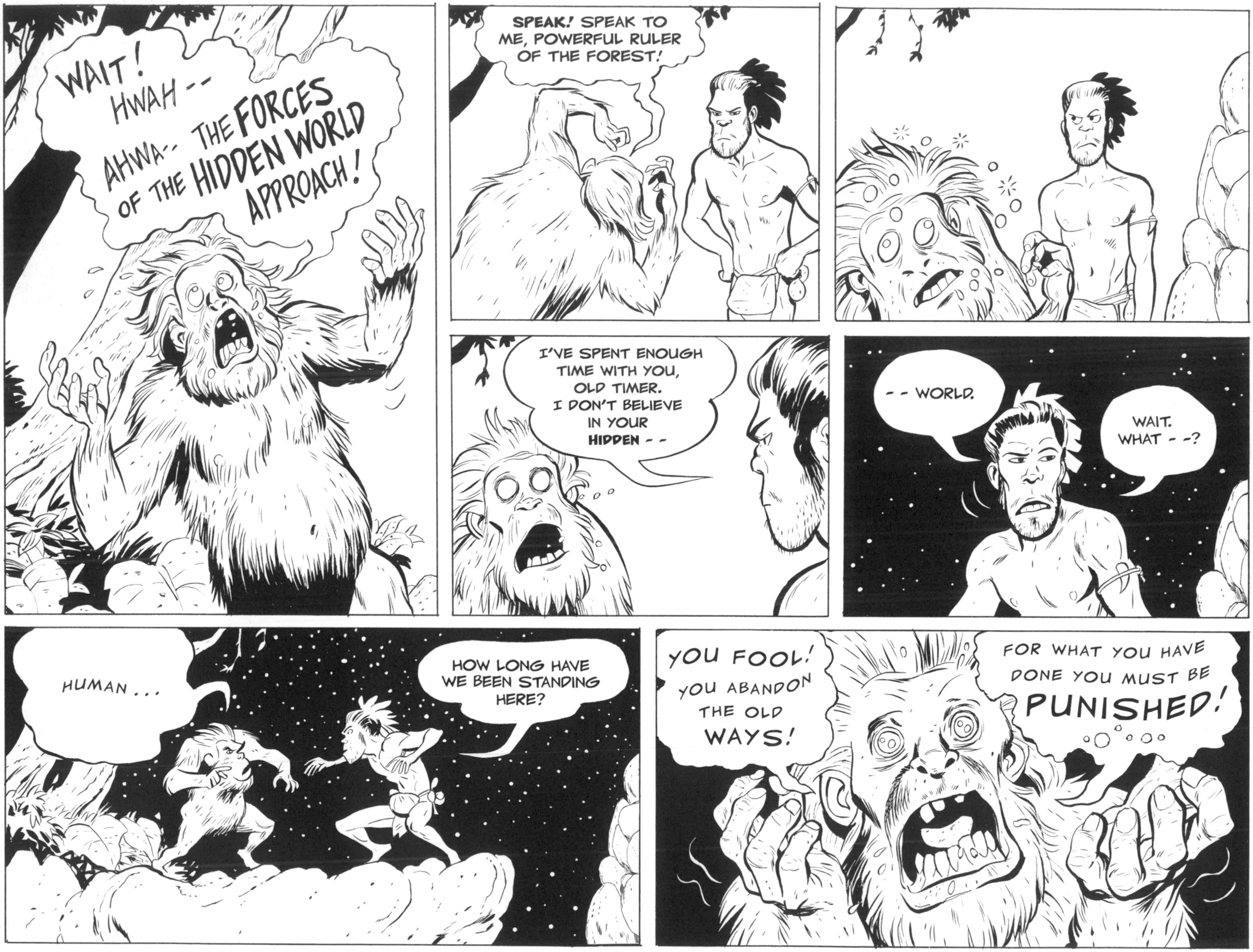
WAIT! HWAH -- AHWA-- THE FORCES OF THE HIDDEN WORLD APPROACH!
SPEAK! SPEAK TO ME, POWERFUL RULER OF THE FOREST!
I'VE SPENT ENOUGH TIME WITH YOU, OLD TIMER. I DON'T BELIEVE IN YOUR HIDDEN --
-- WORLD.
WAIT. WHAT --?
HUMAN...
HOW LONG HAVE WE BEEN STANDING HERE?
YOU FOOL! YOU ABANDON THE OLD WAYS!
FOR WHAT YOU HAVE DONE YOU MUST BE PUNISHED!

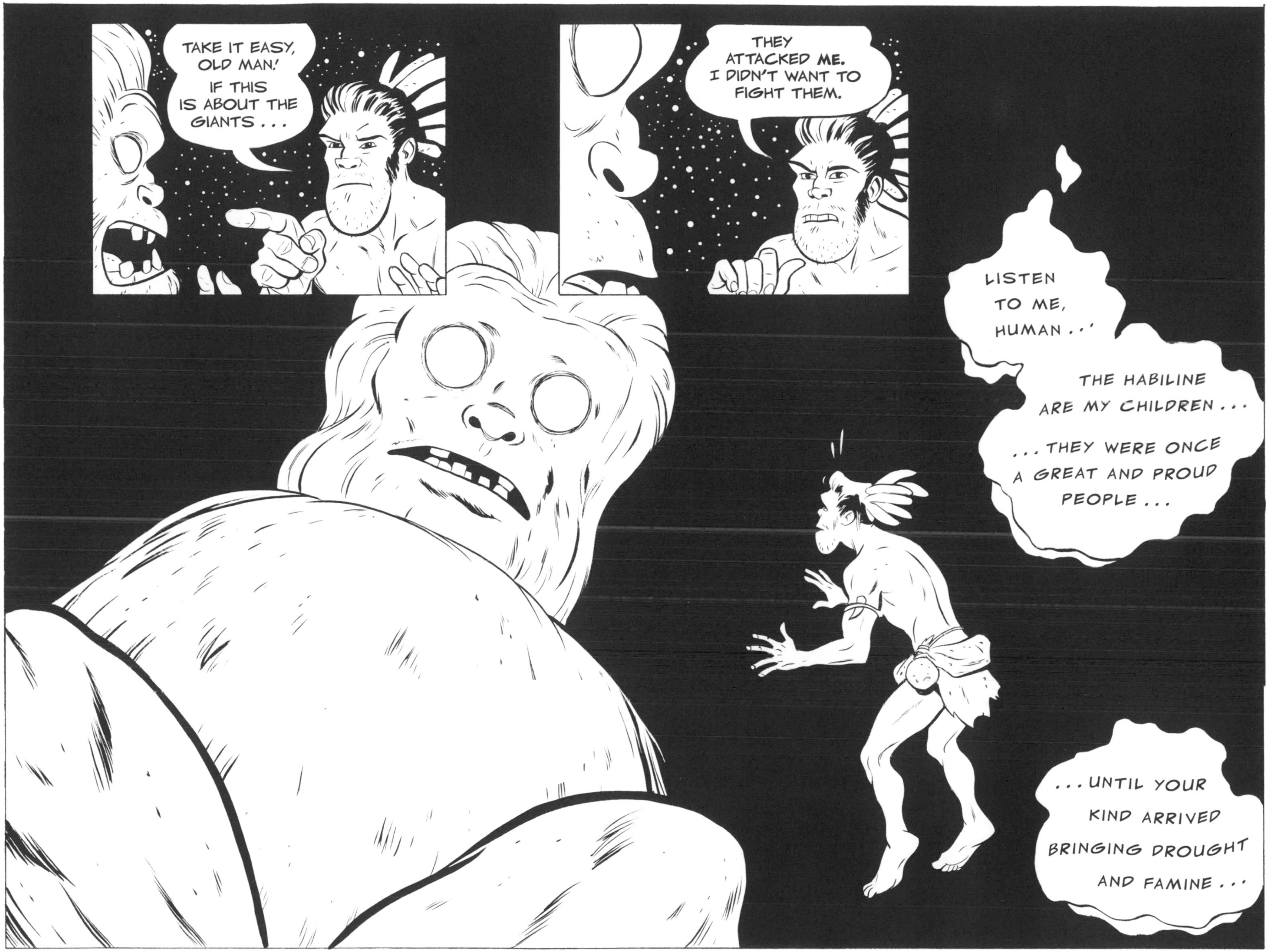
TAKE IT EASY, OLD MAN! IF THIS IS ABOUT THE GIANTS . . .
THEY ATTACKED **ME.** I DIDN'T WANT TO FIGHT THEM.
LISTEN TO ME, HUMAN . . .
THE HABILINE ARE MY CHILDREN . . .
. . . THEY WERE ONCE A GREAT AND PROUD PEOPLE . . .
. . . UNTIL YOUR KIND ARRIVED BRINGING DROUGHT AND FAMINE . . .

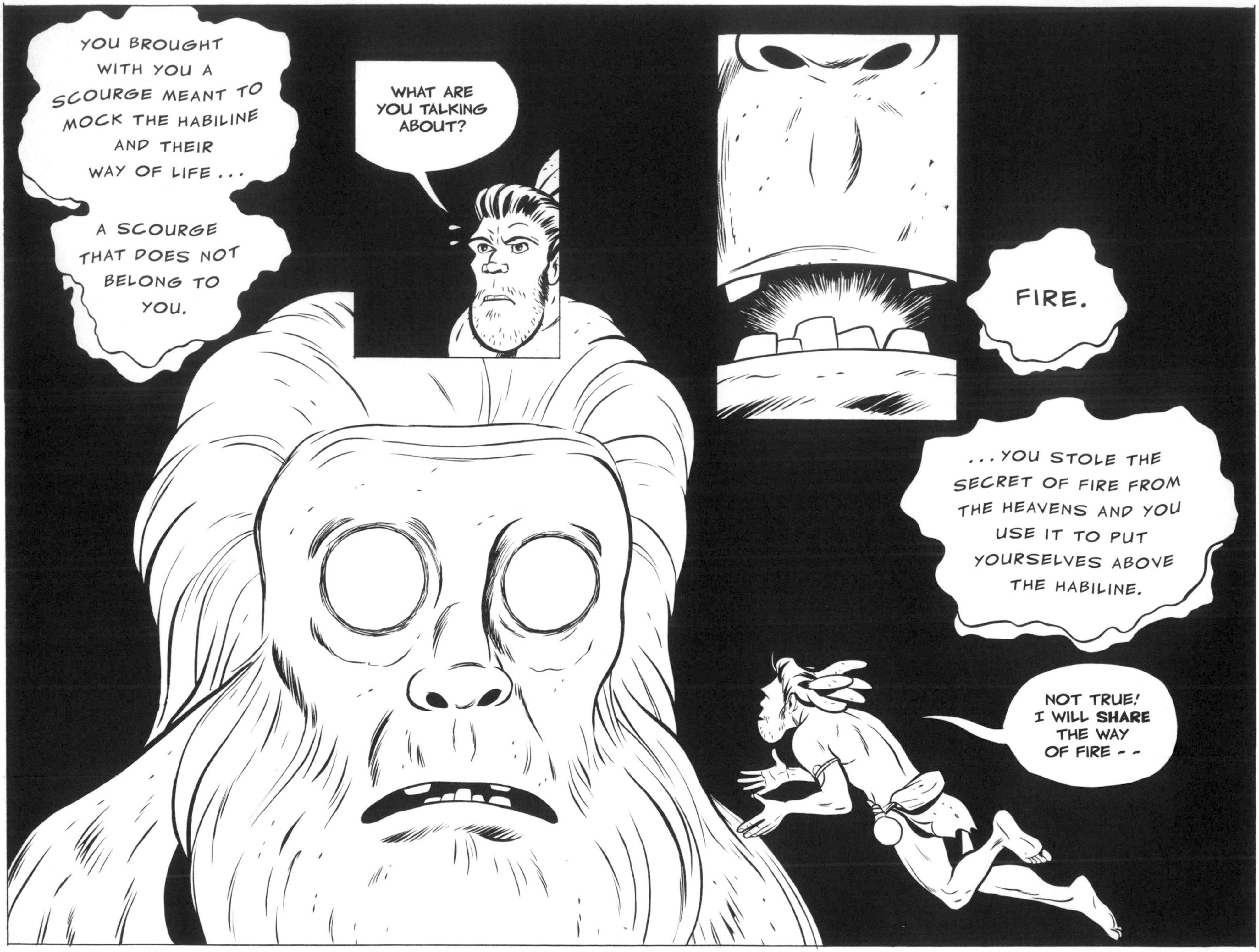
YOU BROUGHT WITH YOU A SCOURGE MEANT TO MOCK THE HABILINE AND THEIR WAY OF LIFE...
A SCOURGE THAT DOES NOT BELONG TO YOU.
WHAT ARE YOU TALKING ABOUT?
FIRE.
...YOU STOLE THE SECRET OF FIRE FROM THE HEAVENS AND YOU USE IT TO PUT YOURSELVES ABOVE THE HABILINE.
NOT TRUE! I WILL **SHARE** THE WAY OF FIRE --

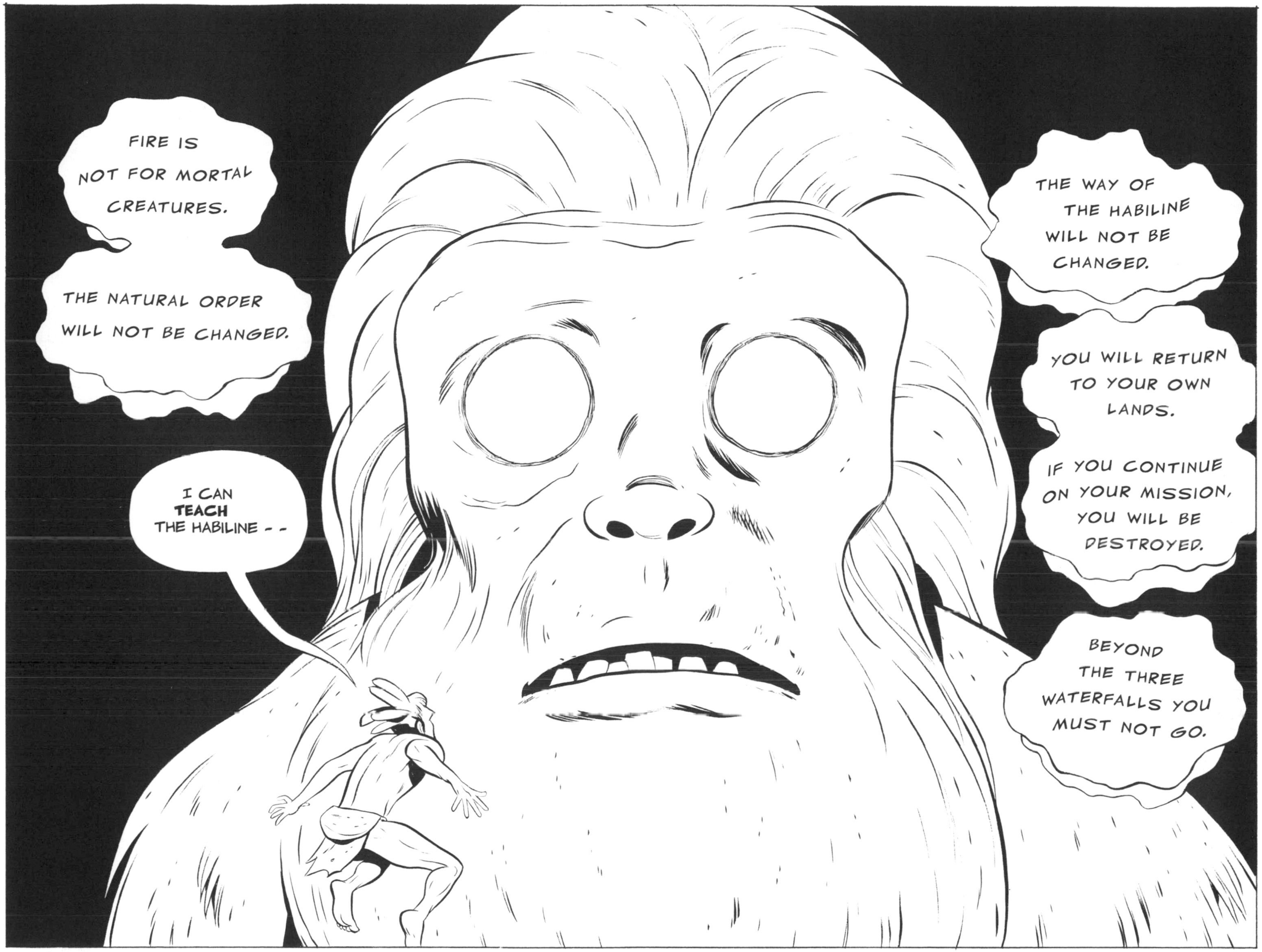
FIRE IS NOT FOR MORTAL CREATURES.
THE NATURAL ORDER WILL NOT BE CHANGED.
I CAN **TEACH** THE HABILINE - -
THE WAY OF THE HABILINE WILL NOT BE CHANGED.
YOU WILL RETURN TO YOUR OWN LANDS.
IF YOU CONTINUE ON YOUR MISSION, YOU WILL BE DESTROYED.
BEYOND THE THREE WATERFALLS YOU MUST NOT GO.

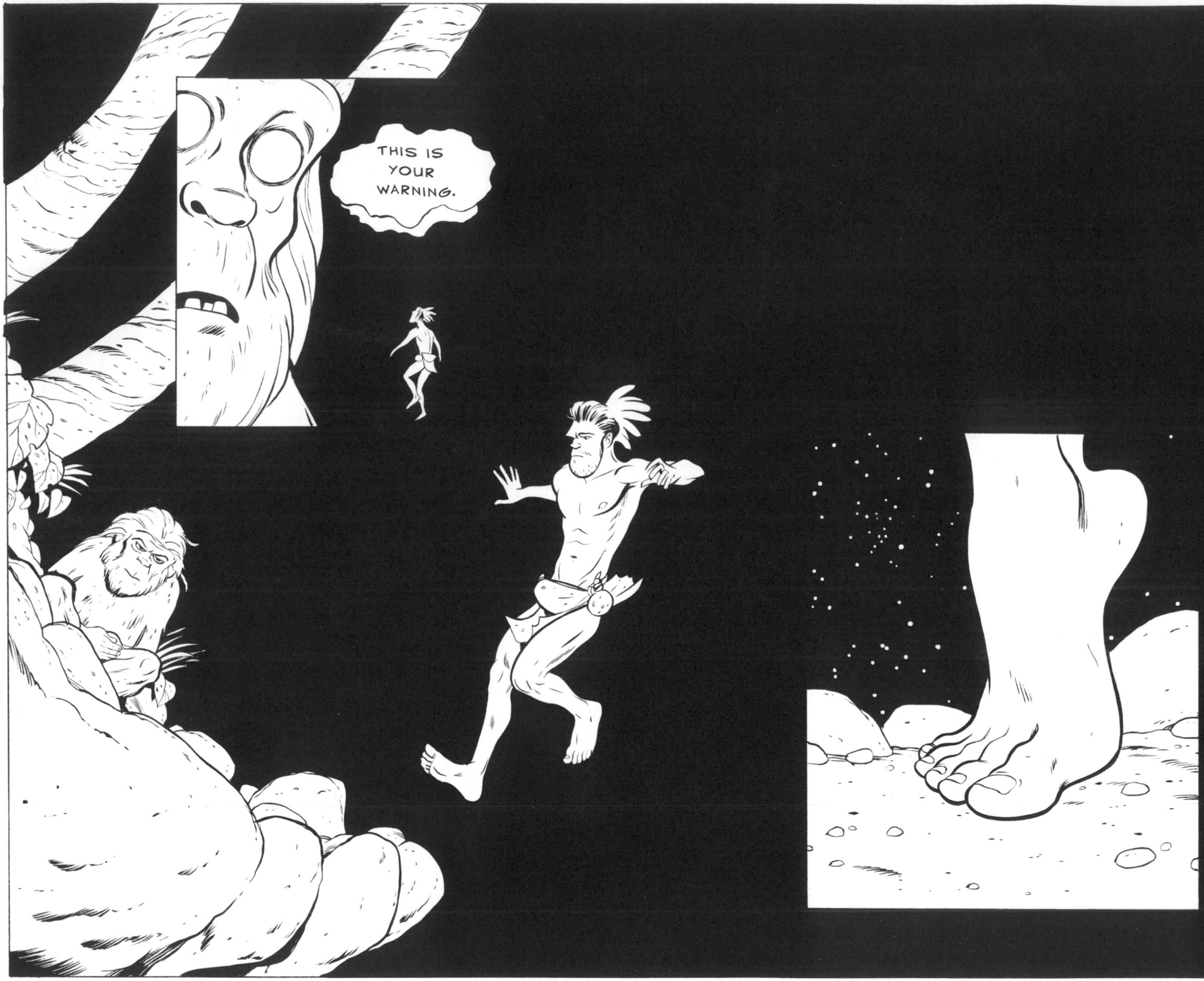
THIS IS YOUR WARNING.

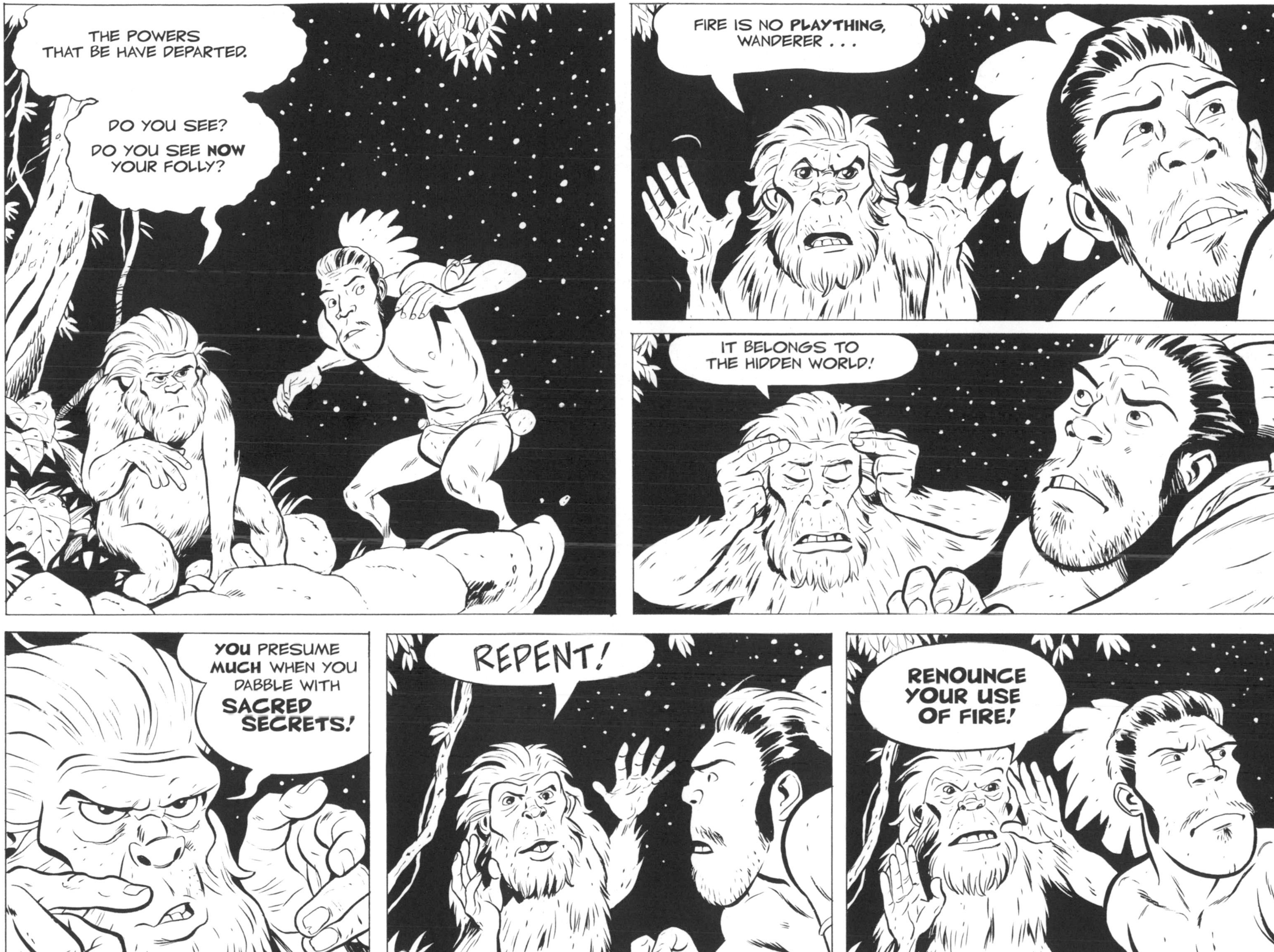
THE POWERS THAT BE HAVE DEPARTED.
DO YOU SEE? DO YOU SEE NOW YOUR FOLLY?
FIRE IS NO PLAYTHING, WANDERER . . .
IT BELONGS TO THE HIDDEN WORLD!
YOU PRESUME MUCH WHEN YOU DABBLE WITH SACRED SECRETS!
REPENT!
RENOUNCE YOUR USE OF FIRE!

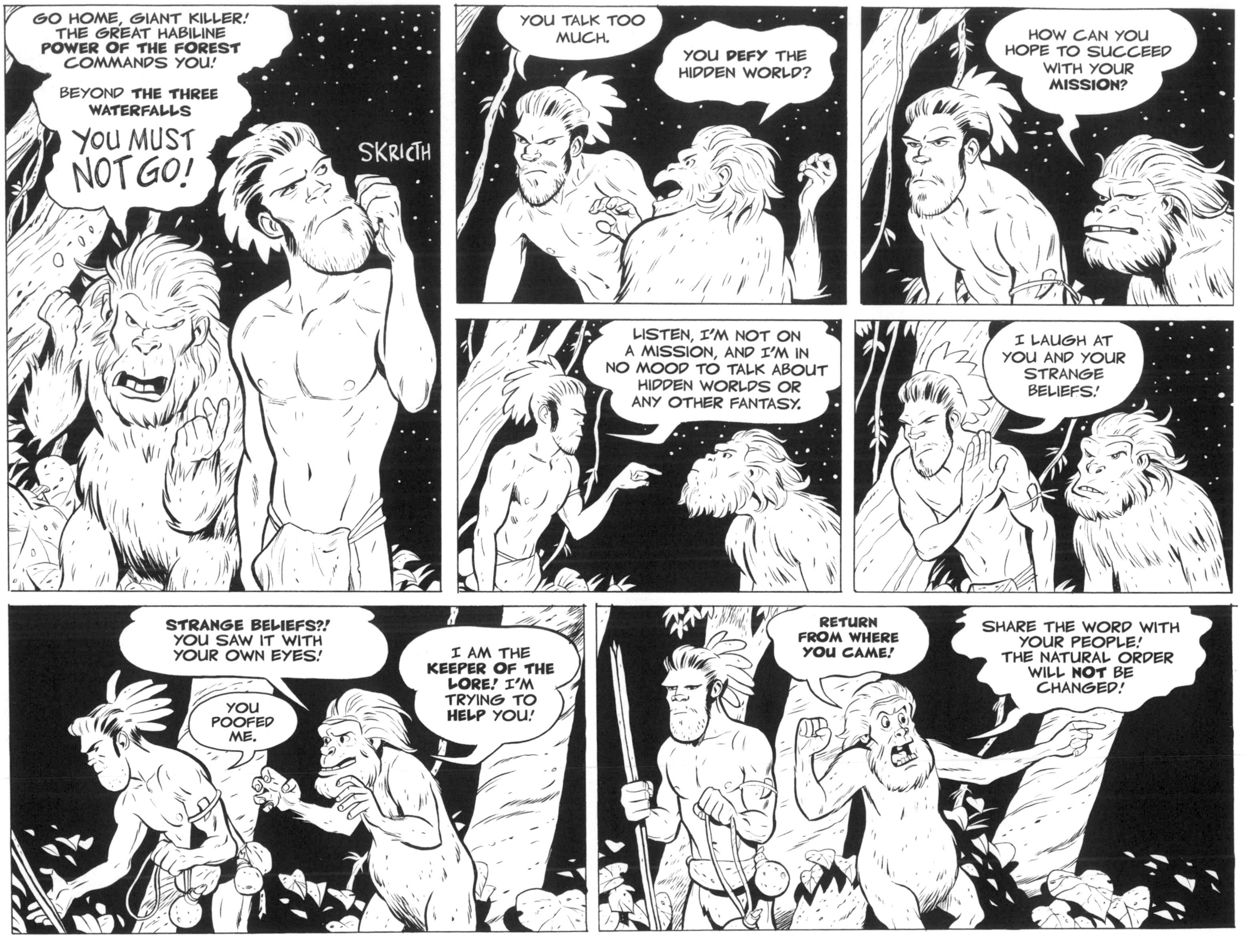

GO HOME, GIANT KILLER! THE GREAT HABILINE **POWER OF THE FOREST** COMMANDS YOU!
BEYOND **THE THREE WATERFALLS**
YOU MUST NOT GO!
SKRICTH
YOU TALK TOO MUCH.
YOU **DEFY** THE HIDDEN WORLD?
HOW CAN YOU HOPE TO SUCCEED WITH YOUR **MISSION?**
LISTEN, I'M NOT ON A MISSION, AND I'M IN NO MOOD TO TALK ABOUT HIDDEN WORLDS OR ANY OTHER FANTASY.
I LAUGH AT YOU AND YOUR STRANGE BELIEFS!
STRANGE BELIEFS?! YOU SAW IT WITH YOUR OWN EYES!
YOU POOFED ME.
I AM THE **KEEPER OF THE LORE!** I'M TRYING TO **HELP** YOU!
RETURN FROM WHERE YOU CAME!
SHARE THE WORD WITH YOUR PEOPLE! THE NATURAL ORDER WILL **NOT** BE CHANGED!

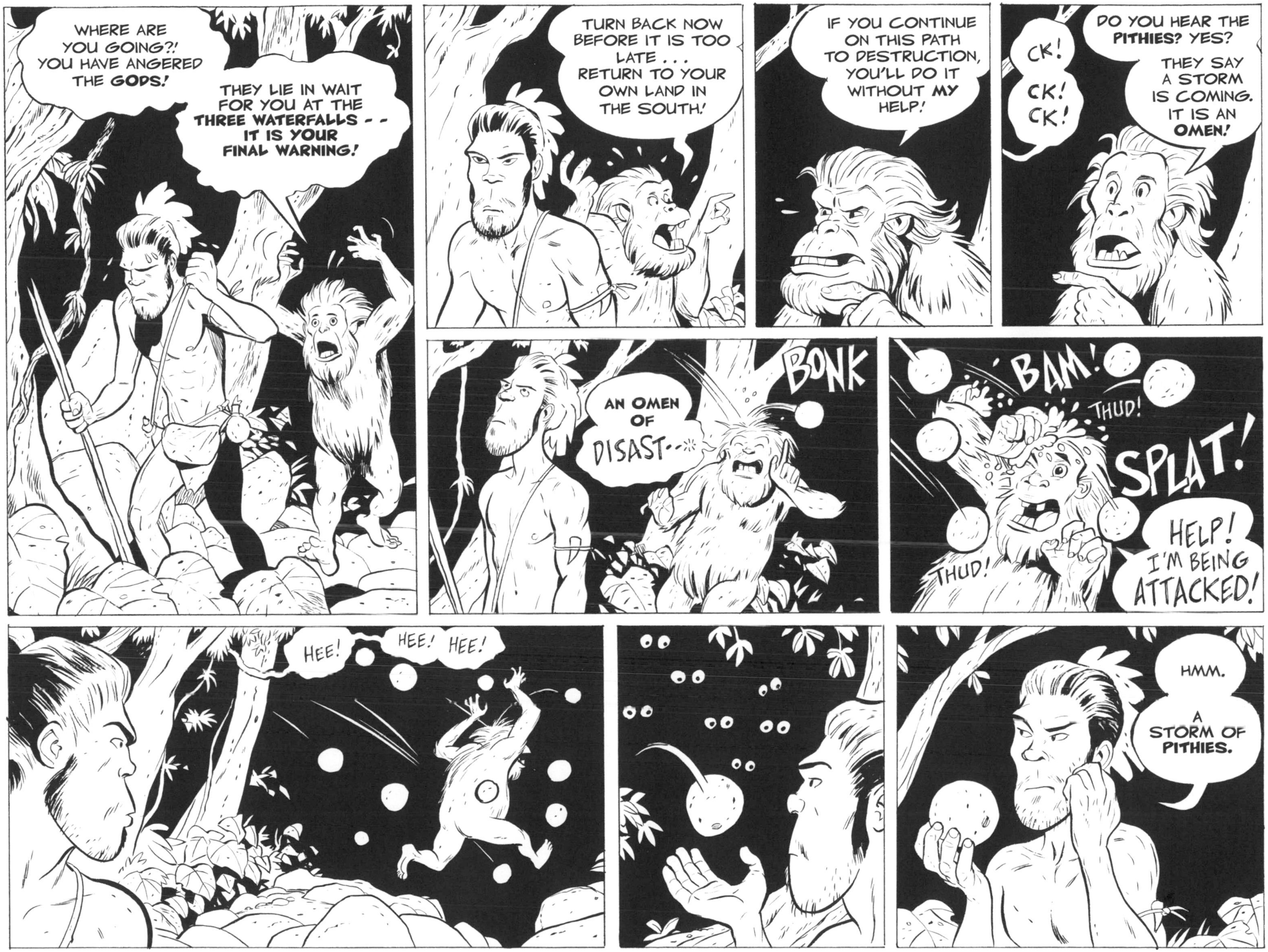
WHERE ARE YOU GOING?! YOU HAVE ANGERED THE **GODS!**
THEY LIE IN WAIT FOR YOU AT THE **THREE WATERFALLS - - IT IS YOUR FINAL WARNING!**
TURN BACK NOW BEFORE IT IS TOO LATE . . . RETURN TO YOUR OWN LAND IN THE SOUTH!
IF YOU CONTINUE ON THIS PATH TO DESTRUCTION, YOU'LL DO IT WITHOUT **MY** HELP!
CK!
CK! CK!
DO YOU HEAR THE **PITHIES?** YES?
THEY SAY A STORM IS COMING. IT IS AN **OMEN!**
AN OMEN OF DISAST- -
BONK
BAM!
THUD!
SPLAT!
THUD!
HELP! I'M BEING ATTACKED!
HEE! HEE! HEE!
HMM.
A STORM OF **PITHIES.**

Two

The Miracle

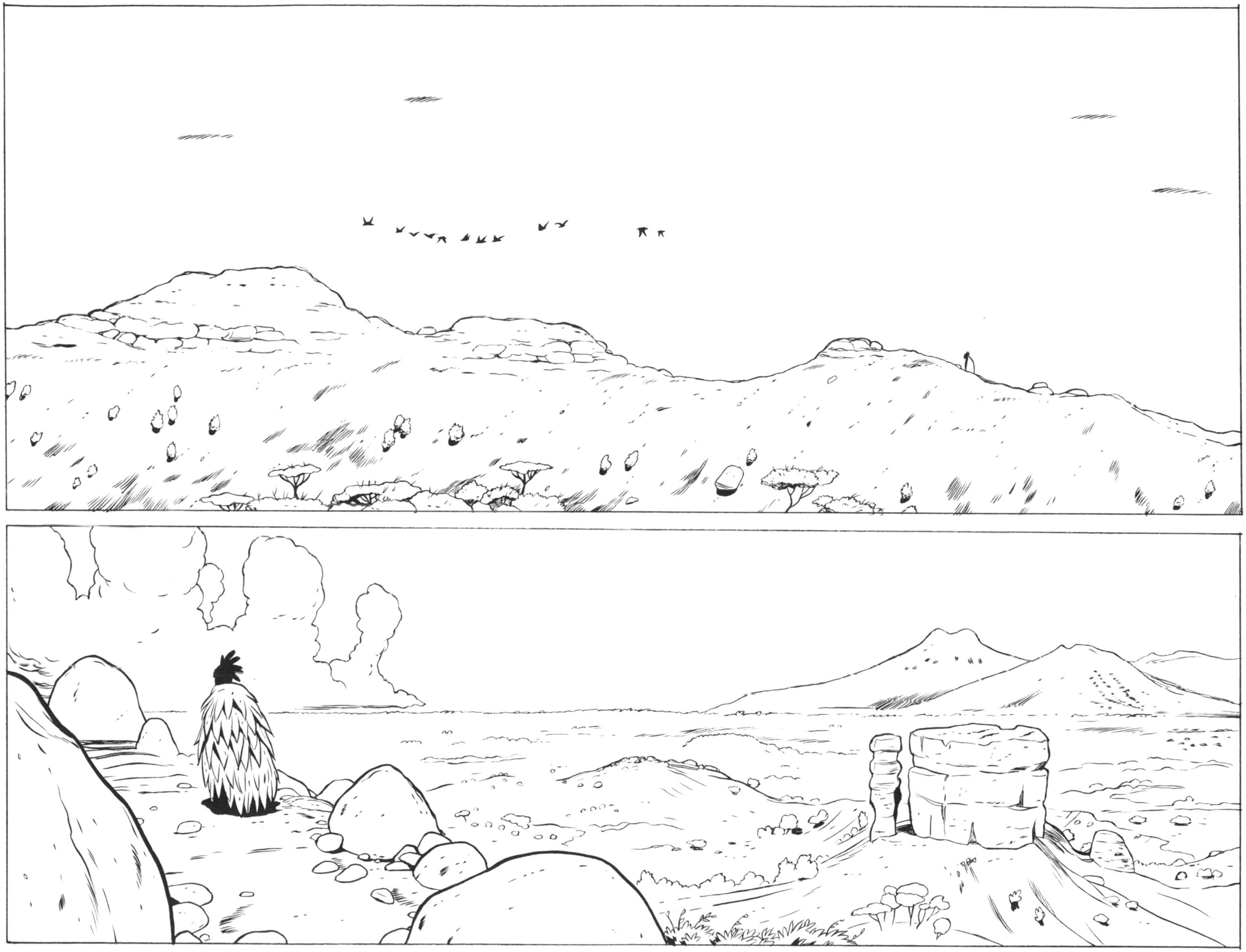

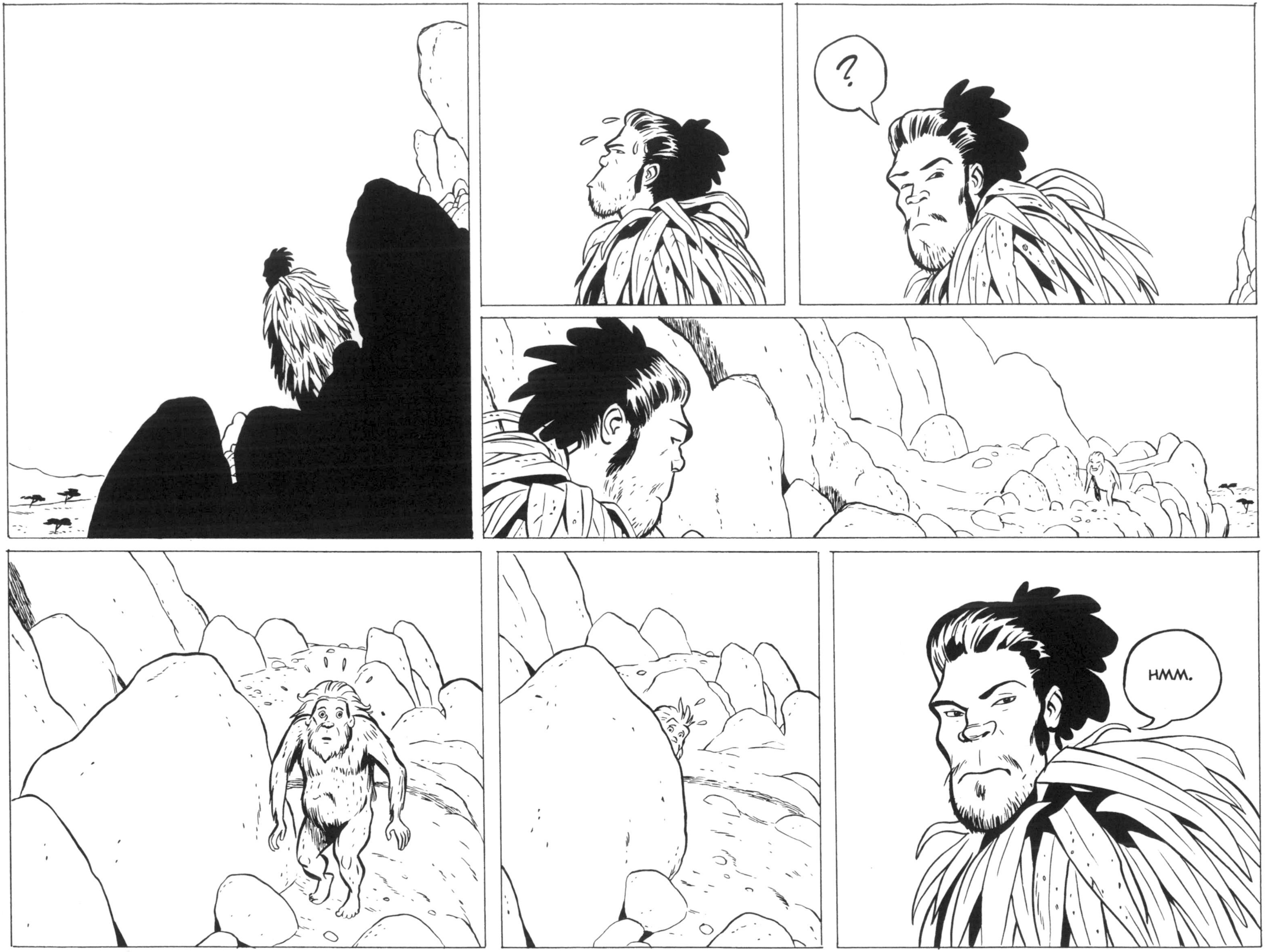
?
HMM.

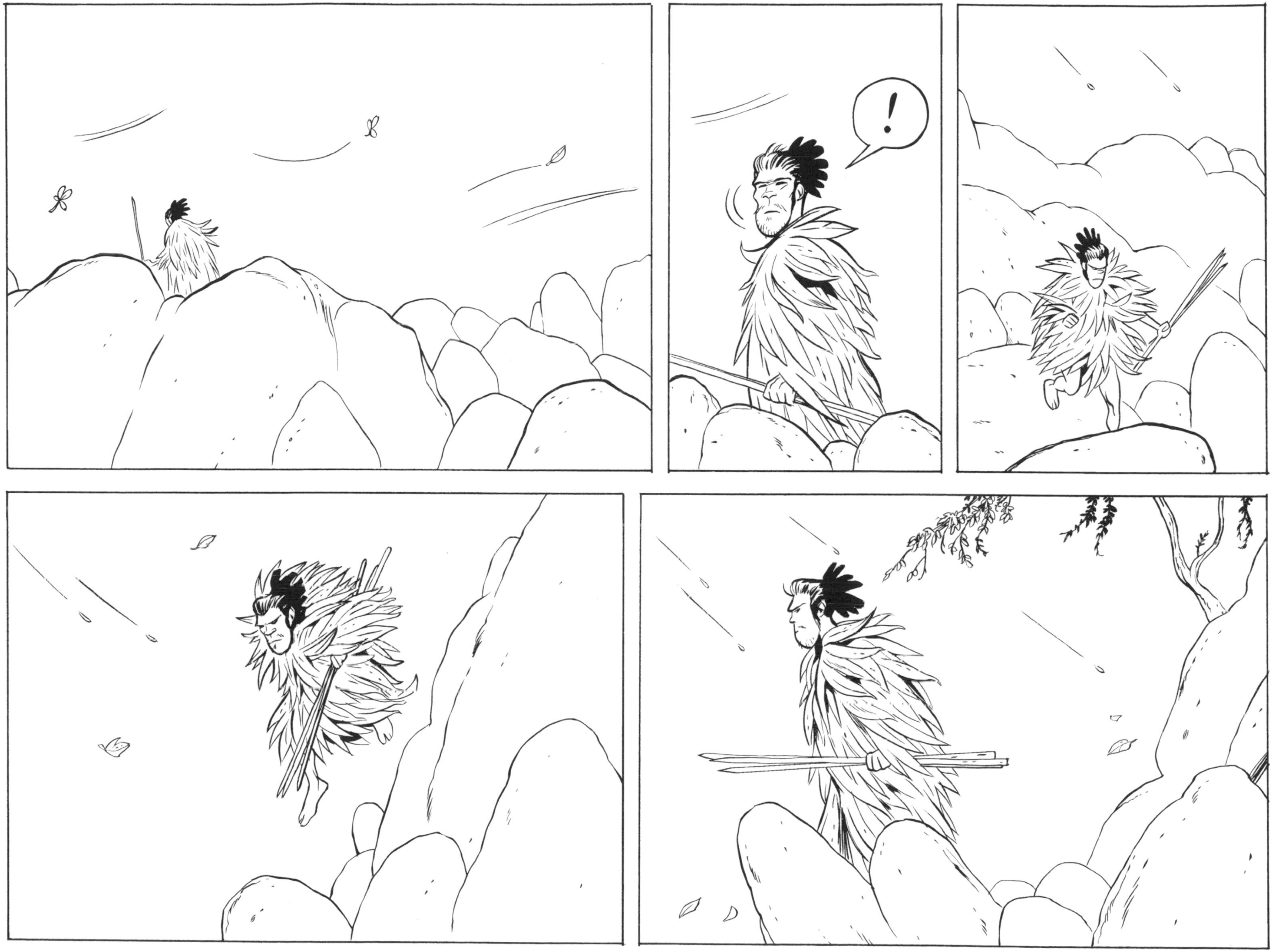
!

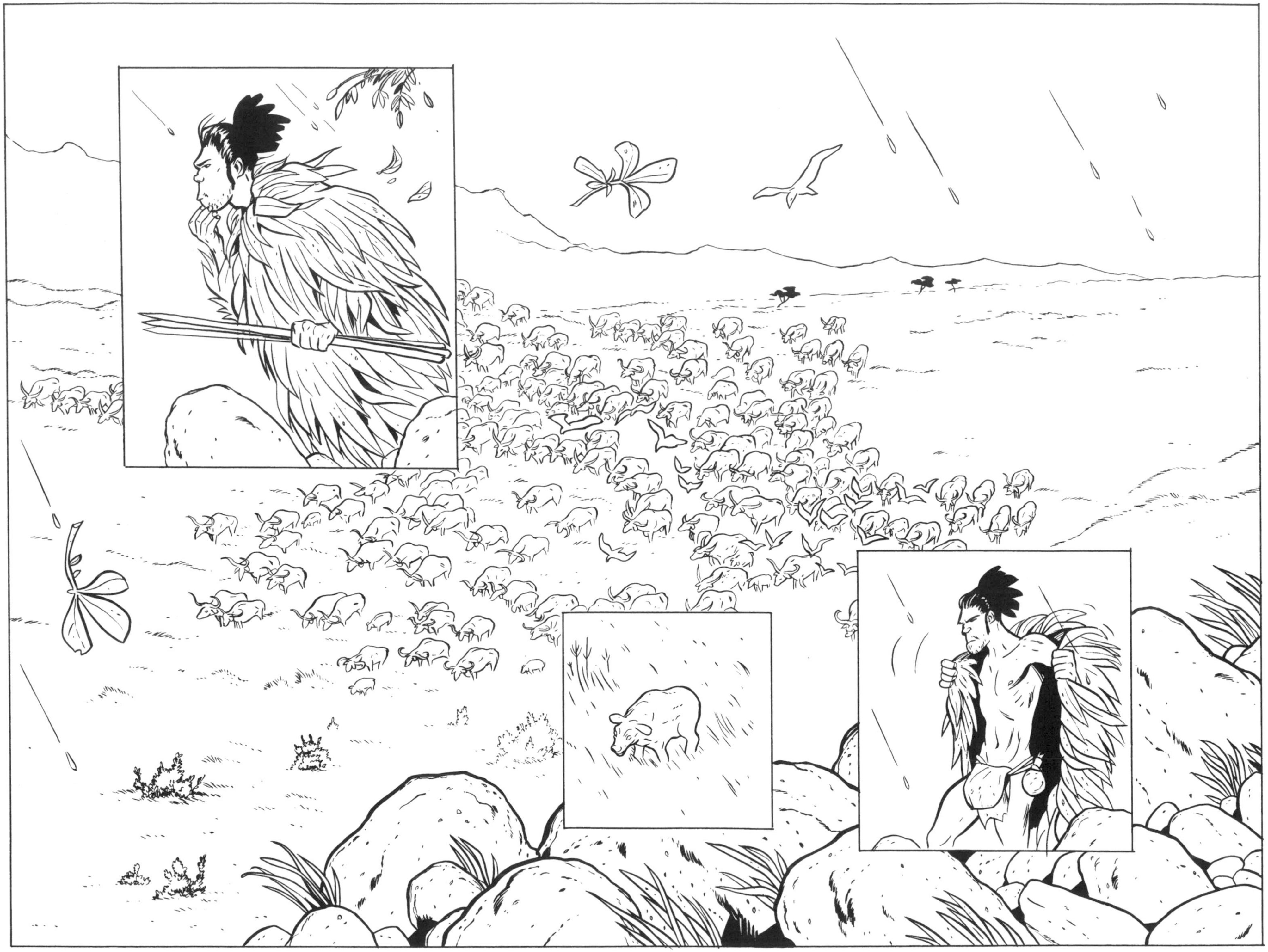

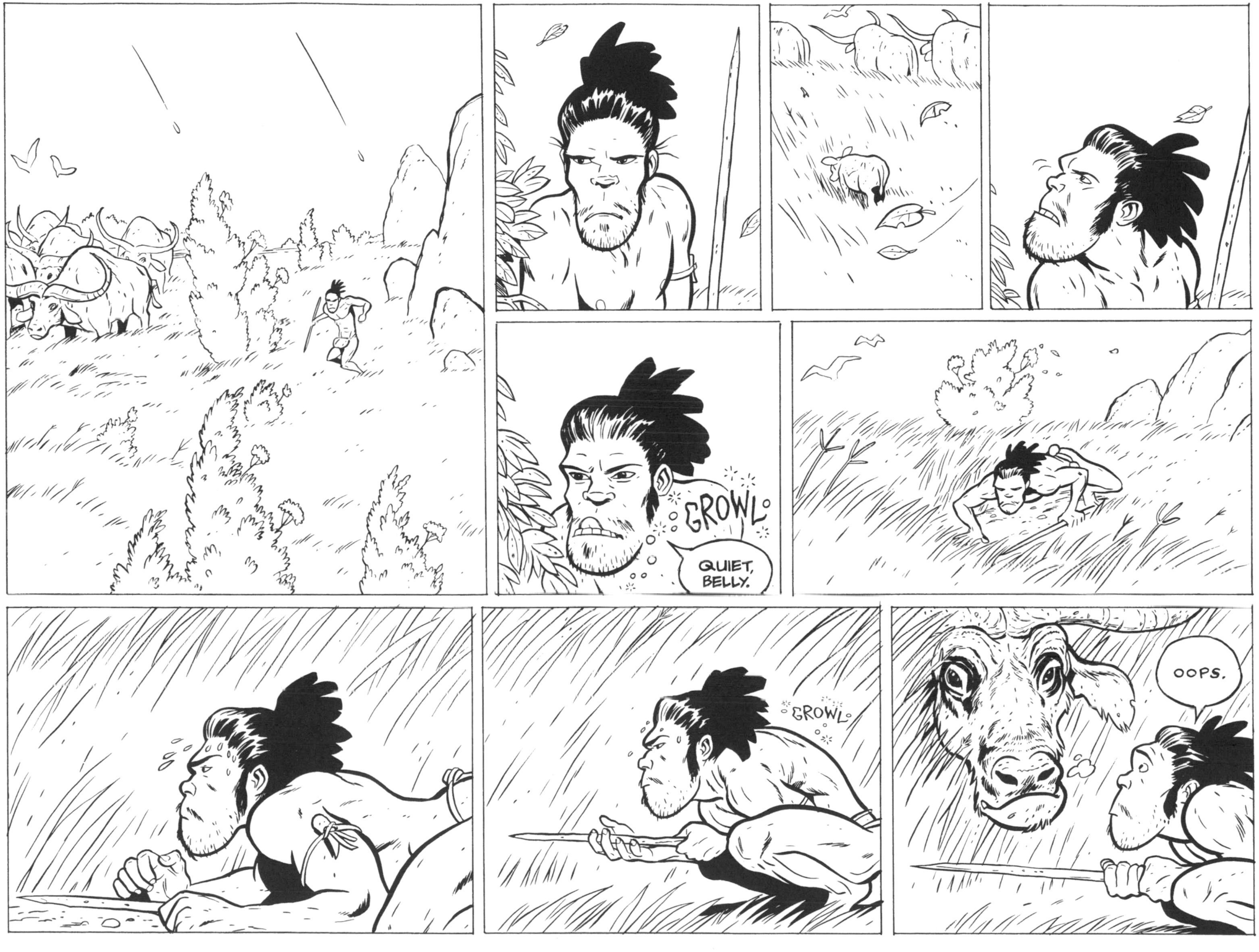
GROWL
QUIET, BELLY.
GROWL
OOPS.

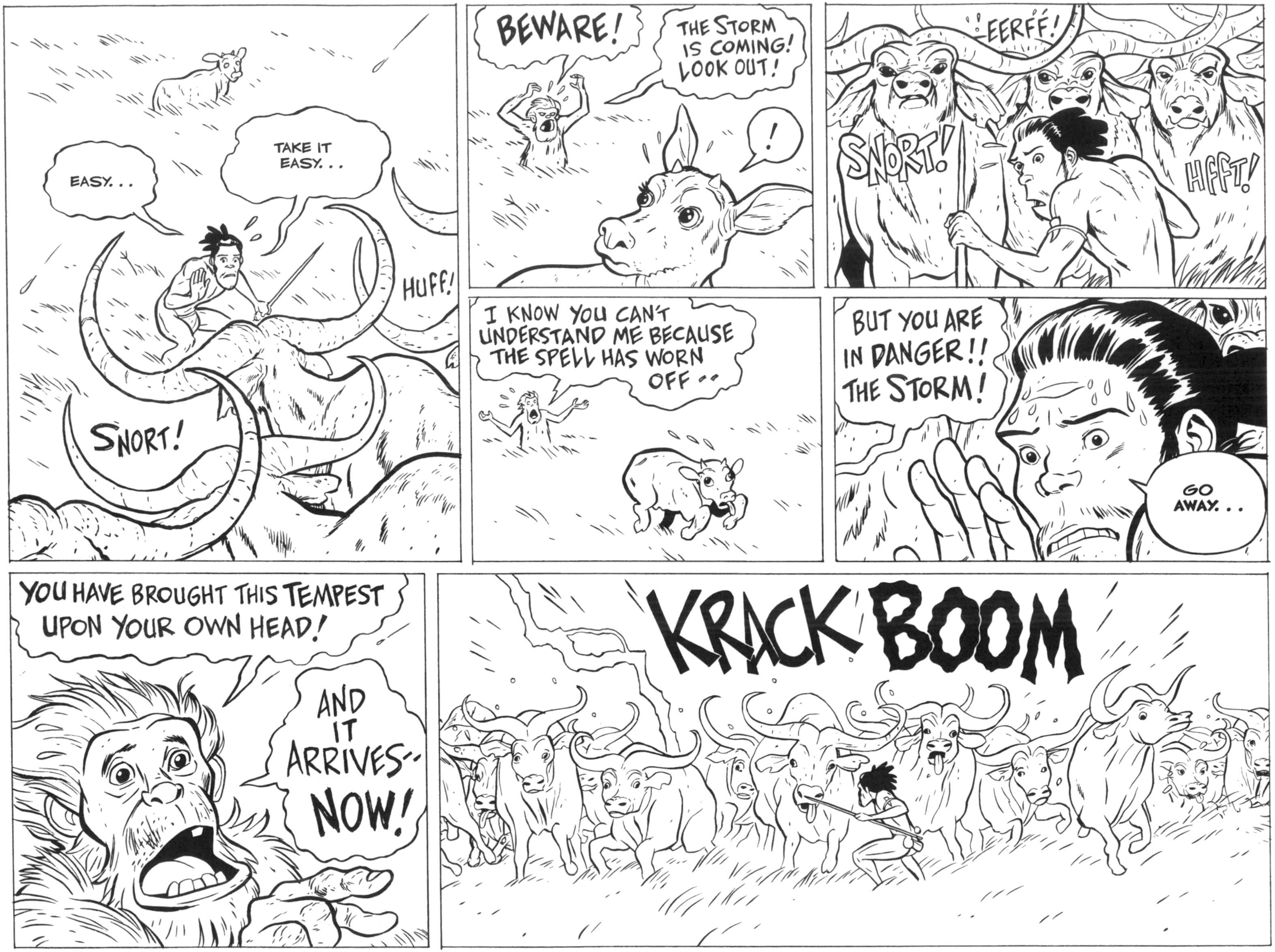
TAKE IT EASY...
EASY...
HUFF!
SNORT!
BEWARE!
THE STORM IS COMING! LOOK OUT!
!
EERFF!
SNORT!
HFFT!
I KNOW YOU CAN'T UNDERSTAND ME BECAUSE THE SPELL HAS WORN OFF..
BUT YOU ARE IN DANGER!! THE STORM!
GO AWAY...
YOU HAVE BROUGHT THIS TEMPEST UPON YOUR OWN HEAD!
AND IT ARRIVES-- NOW!
KRACK BOOM

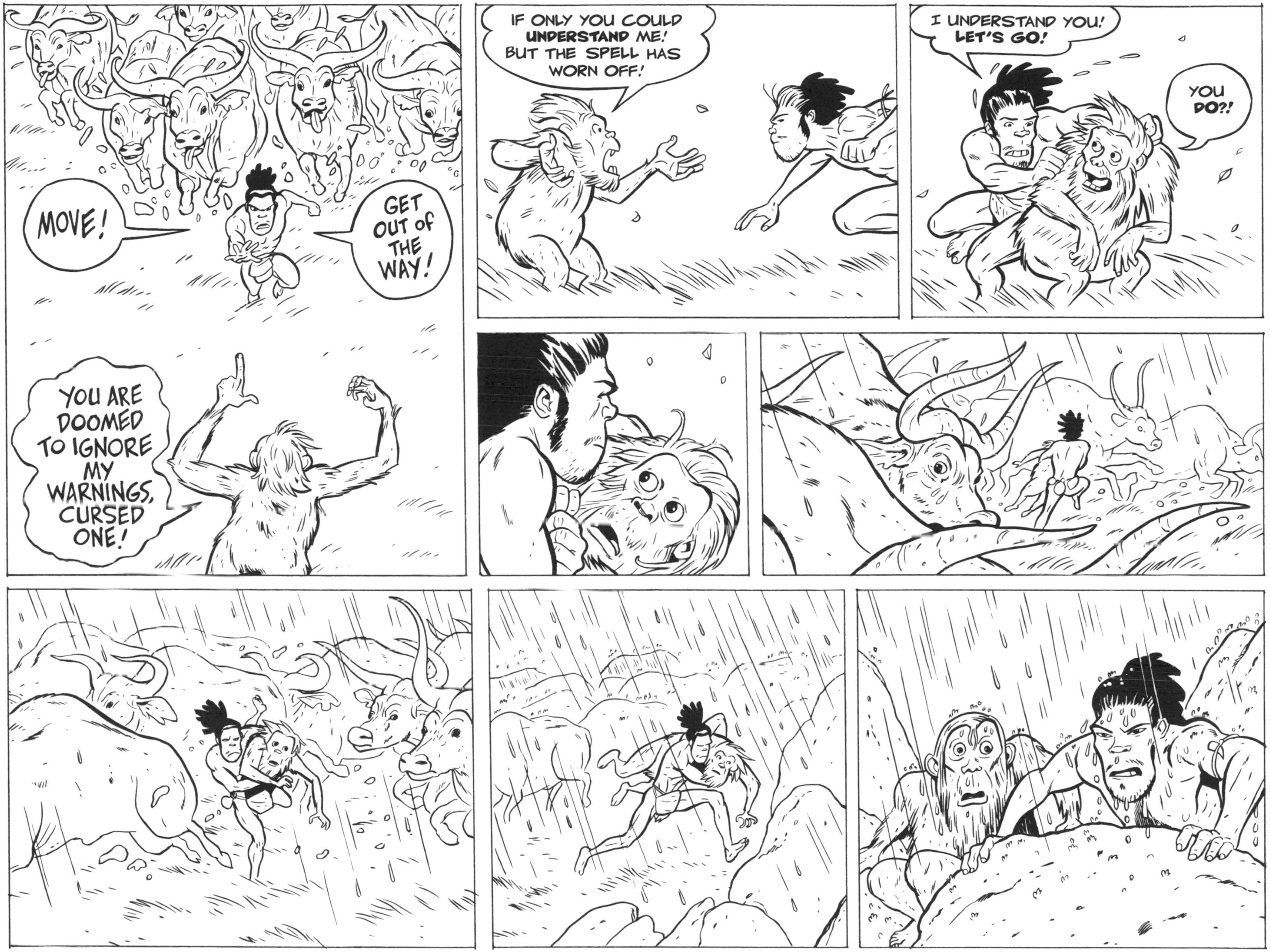
MOVE!
GET OUT of THE WAY!
YOU ARE DOOMED TO IGNORE MY WARNINGS, CURSED ONE!
IF ONLY YOU COULD UNDERSTAND ME! BUT THE SPELL HAS WORN OFF!
I UNDERSTAND YOU! LET'S GO!
YOU DO?!

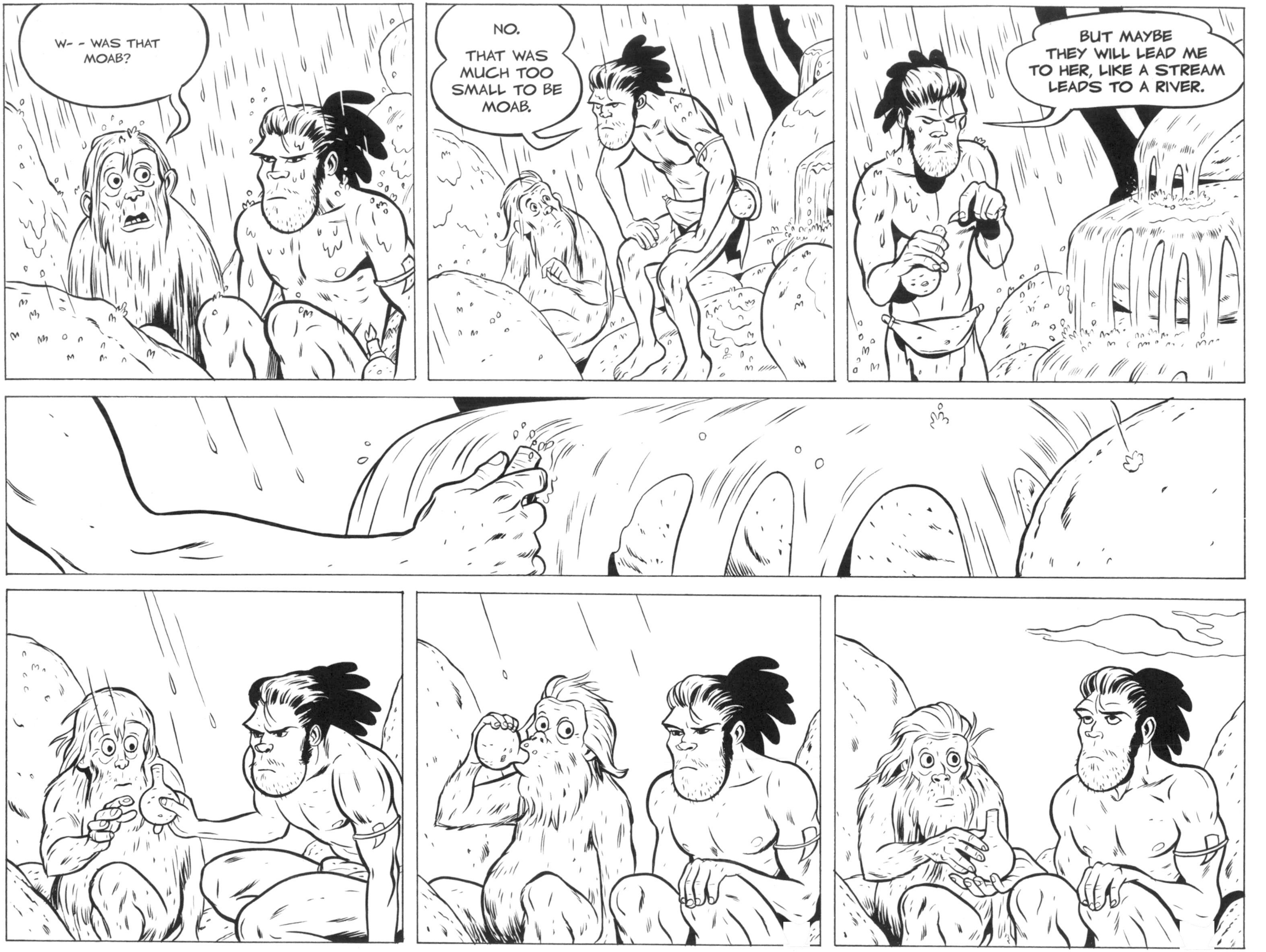
W- - WAS THAT MOAB?
NO.
THAT WAS MUCH TOO SMALL TO BE MOAB.
BUT MAYBE THEY WILL LEAD ME TO HER, LIKE A STREAM LEADS TO A RIVER.

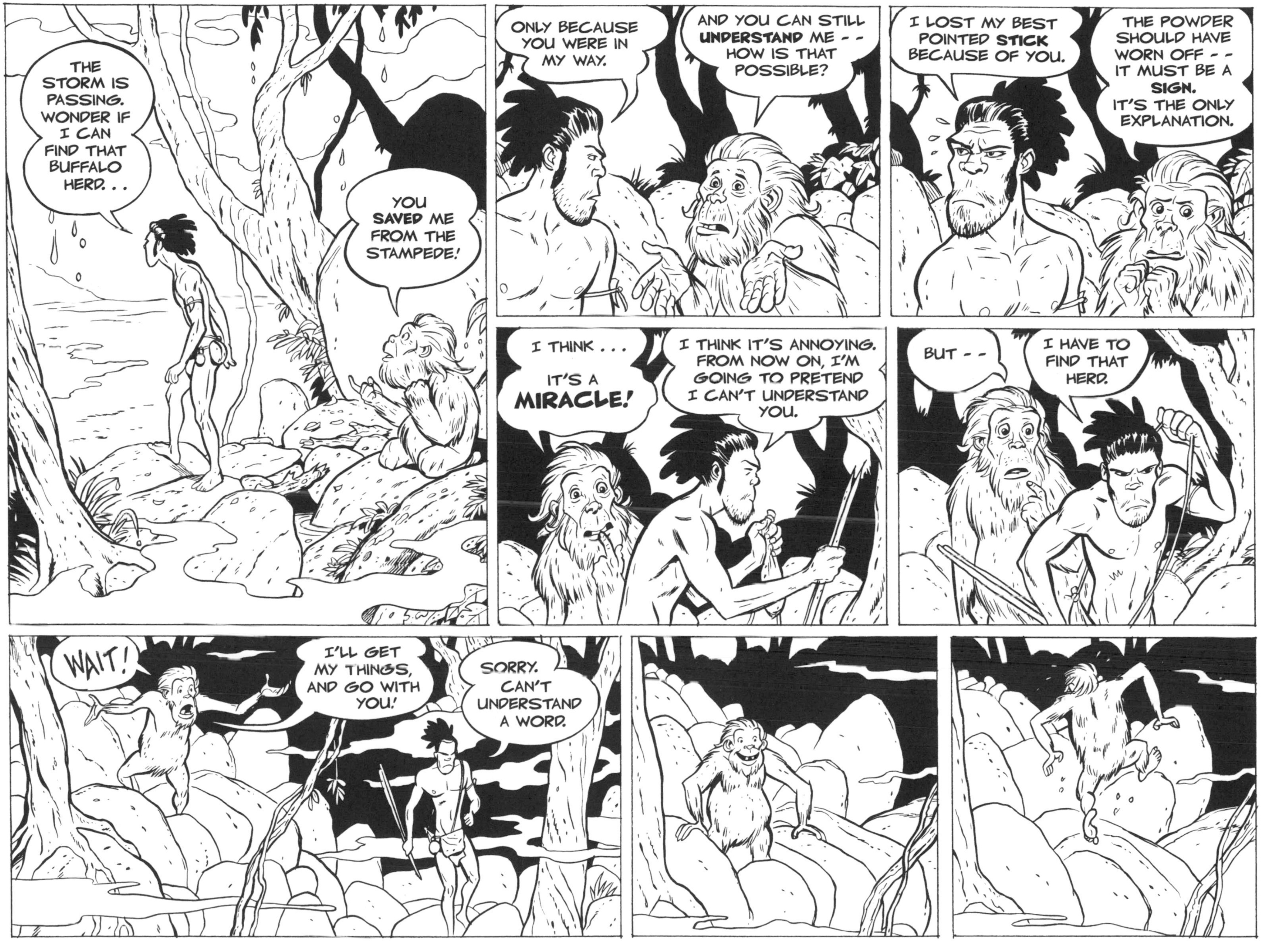
THE STORM IS PASSING. WONDER IF I CAN FIND THAT BUFFALO HERD. . .
YOU SAVED ME FROM THE STAMPEDE!
ONLY BECAUSE YOU WERE IN MY WAY.
AND YOU CAN STILL UNDERSTAND ME - - HOW IS THAT POSSIBLE?
I LOST MY BEST POINTED STICK BECAUSE OF YOU.
THE POWDER SHOULD HAVE WORN OFF - - IT MUST BE A SIGN. IT'S THE ONLY EXPLANATION.
I THINK . . . IT'S A MIRACLE!
I THINK IT'S ANNOYING. FROM NOW ON, I'M GOING TO PRETEND I CAN'T UNDERSTAND YOU.
BUT - -
I HAVE TO FIND THAT HERD.
WAIT!
I'LL GET MY THINGS, AND GO WITH YOU!
SORRY. CAN'T UNDERSTAND A WORD.

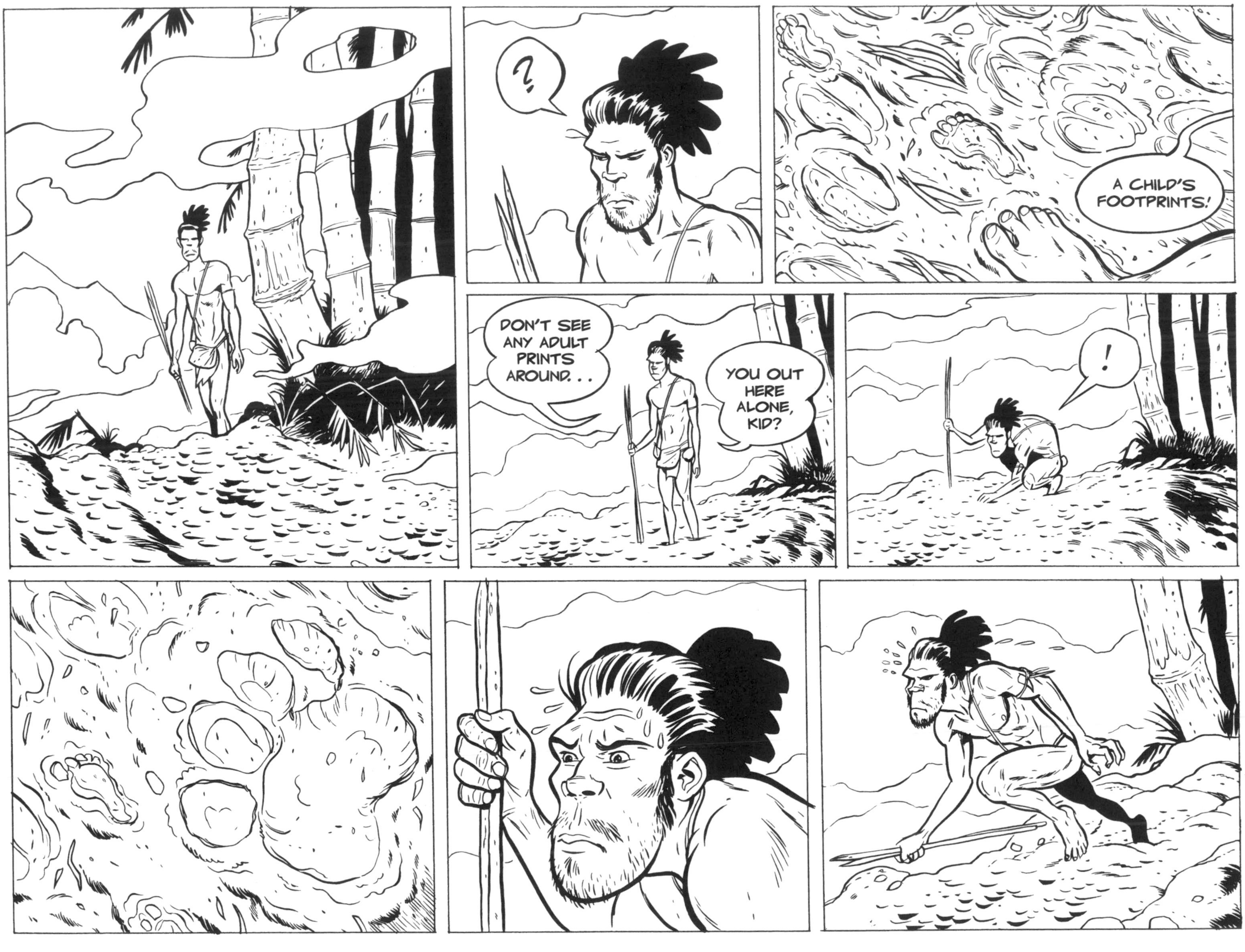
?
A CHILD'S FOOTPRINTS!
DON'T SEE ANY ADULT PRINTS AROUND. . .
YOU OUT HERE ALONE, KID?
!

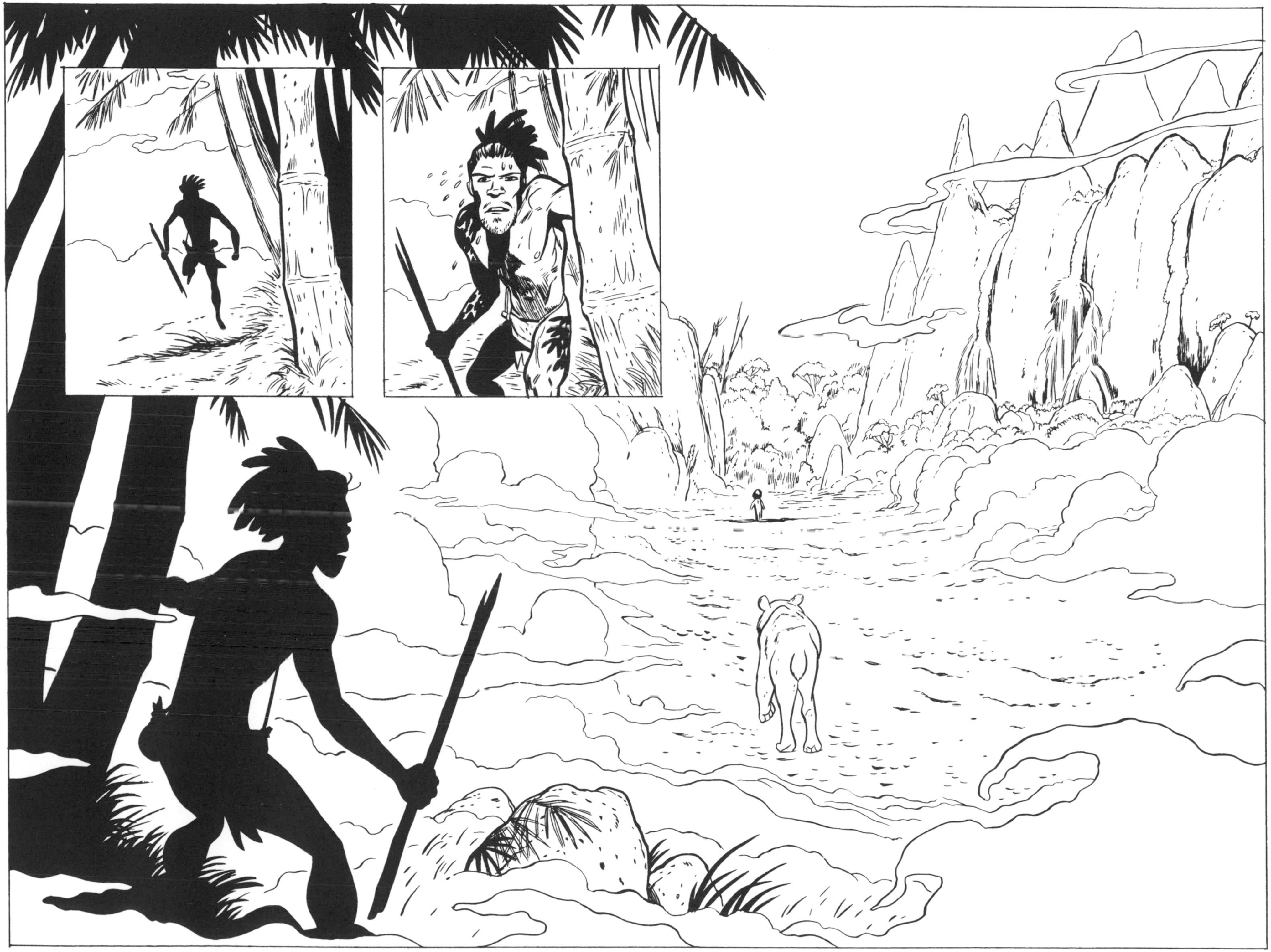

Three

The Three Waterfalls

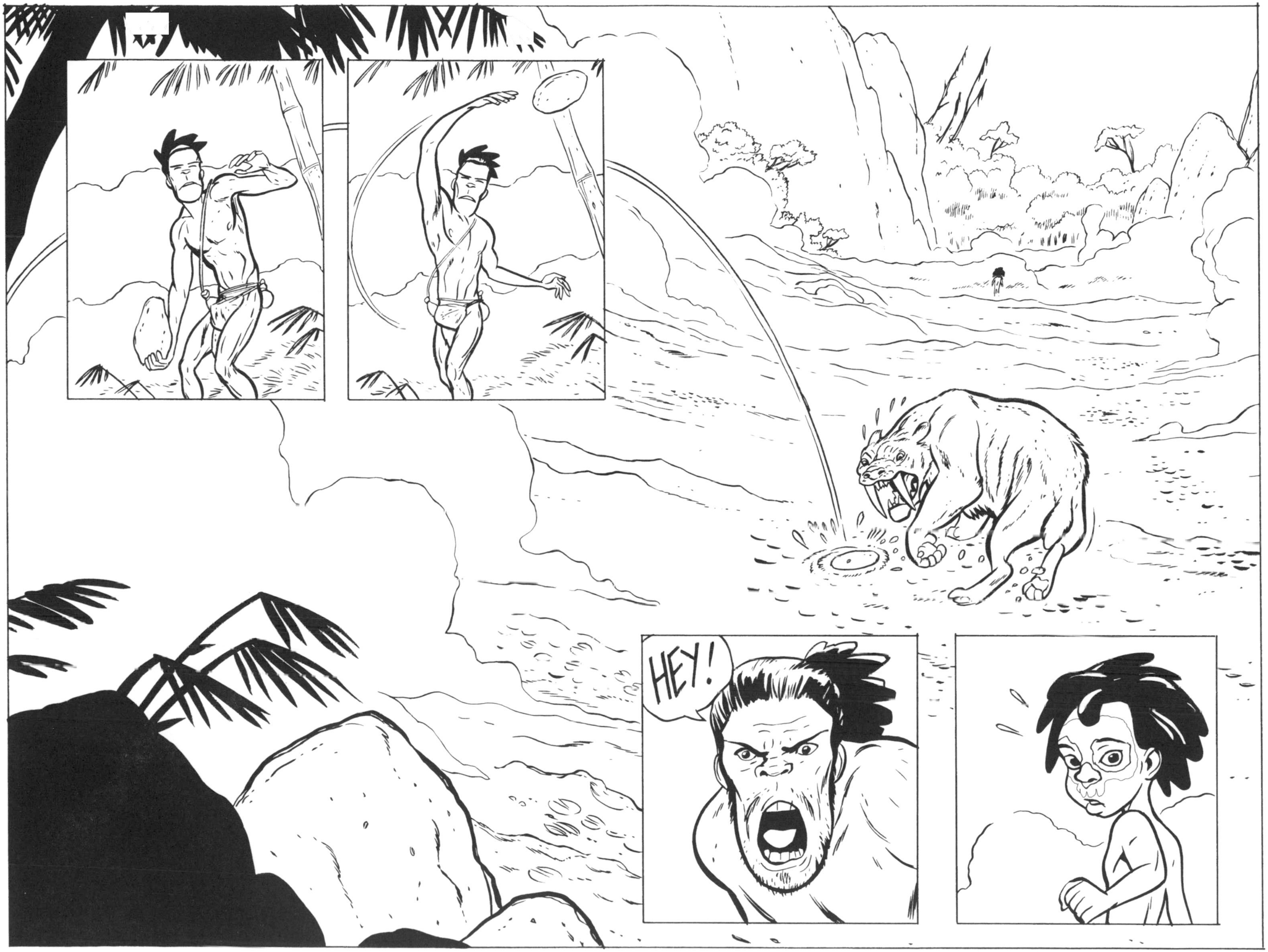
HEY!

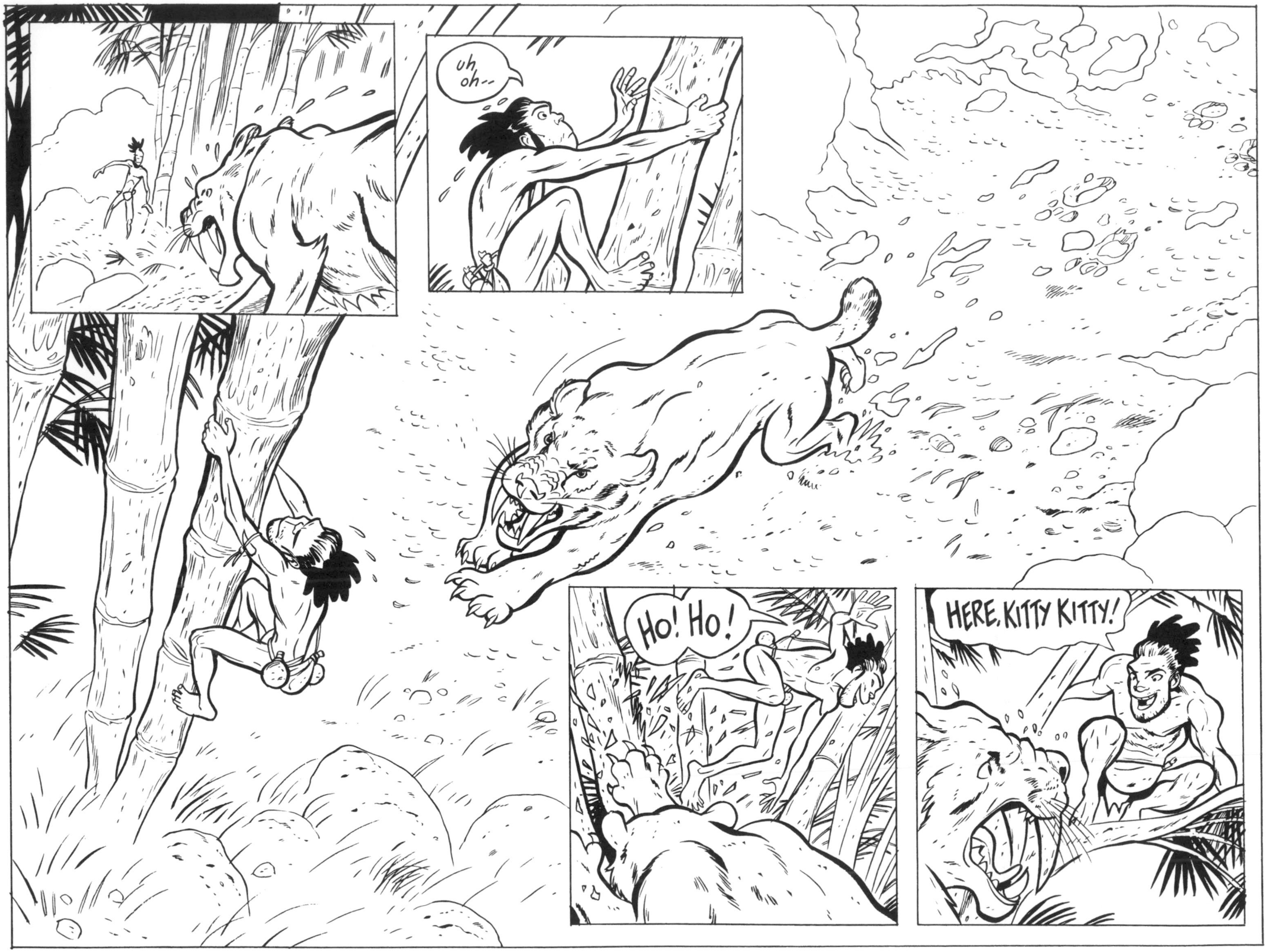
uh oh--
Ho! Ho!
HERE, KITTY KITTY!

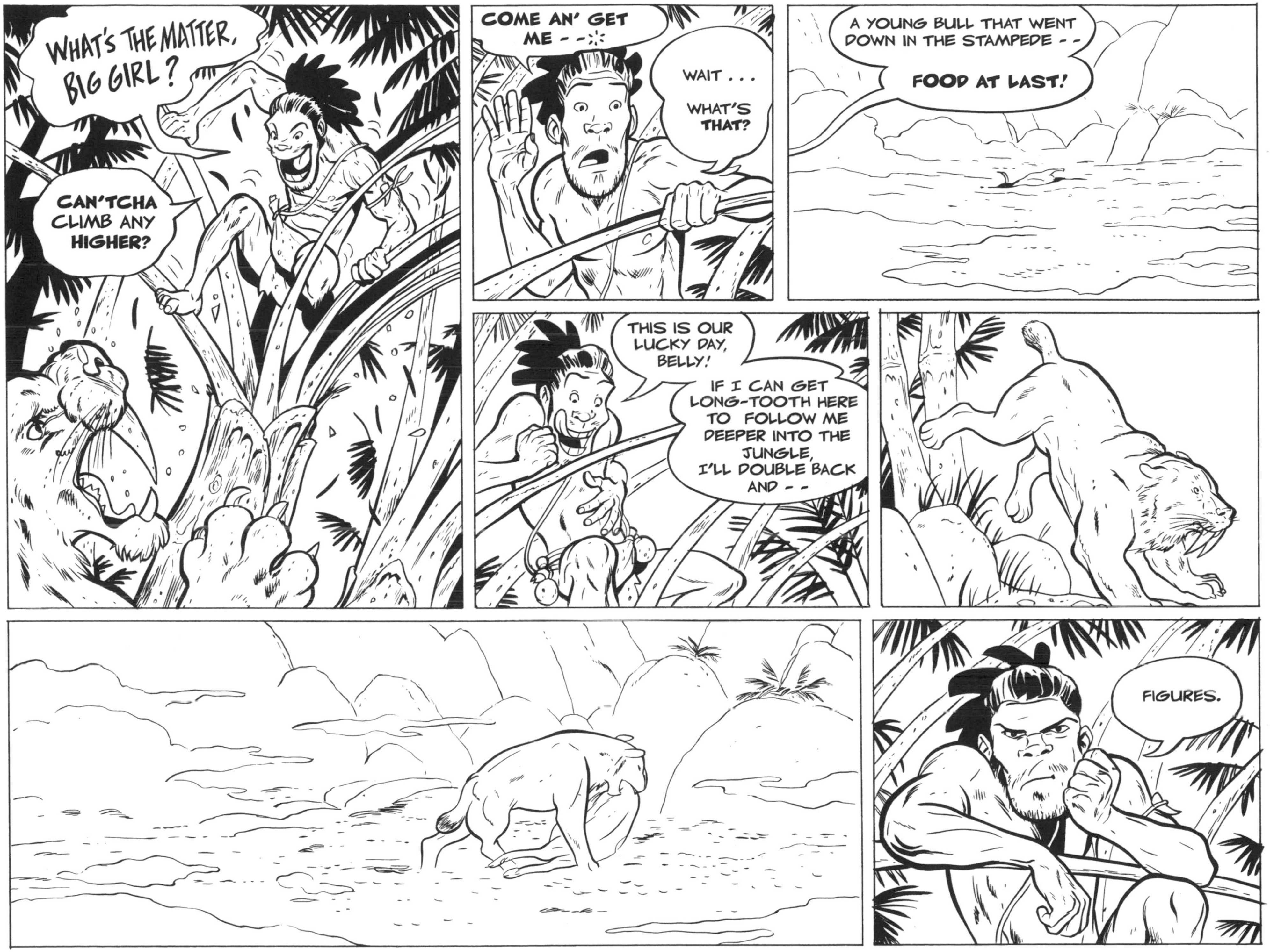
WHAT'S THE MATTER, BIG GIRL?
CAN'TCHA CLIMB ANY HIGHER?
COME AN' GET ME - - !
WAIT . . . WHAT'S THAT?
A YOUNG BULL THAT WENT DOWN IN THE STAMPEDE - -
FOOD AT LAST!
THIS IS OUR LUCKY DAY, BELLY!
IF I CAN GET LONG-TOOTH HERE TO FOLLOW ME DEEPER INTO THE JUNGLE, I'LL DOUBLE BACK AND - -
FIGURES.

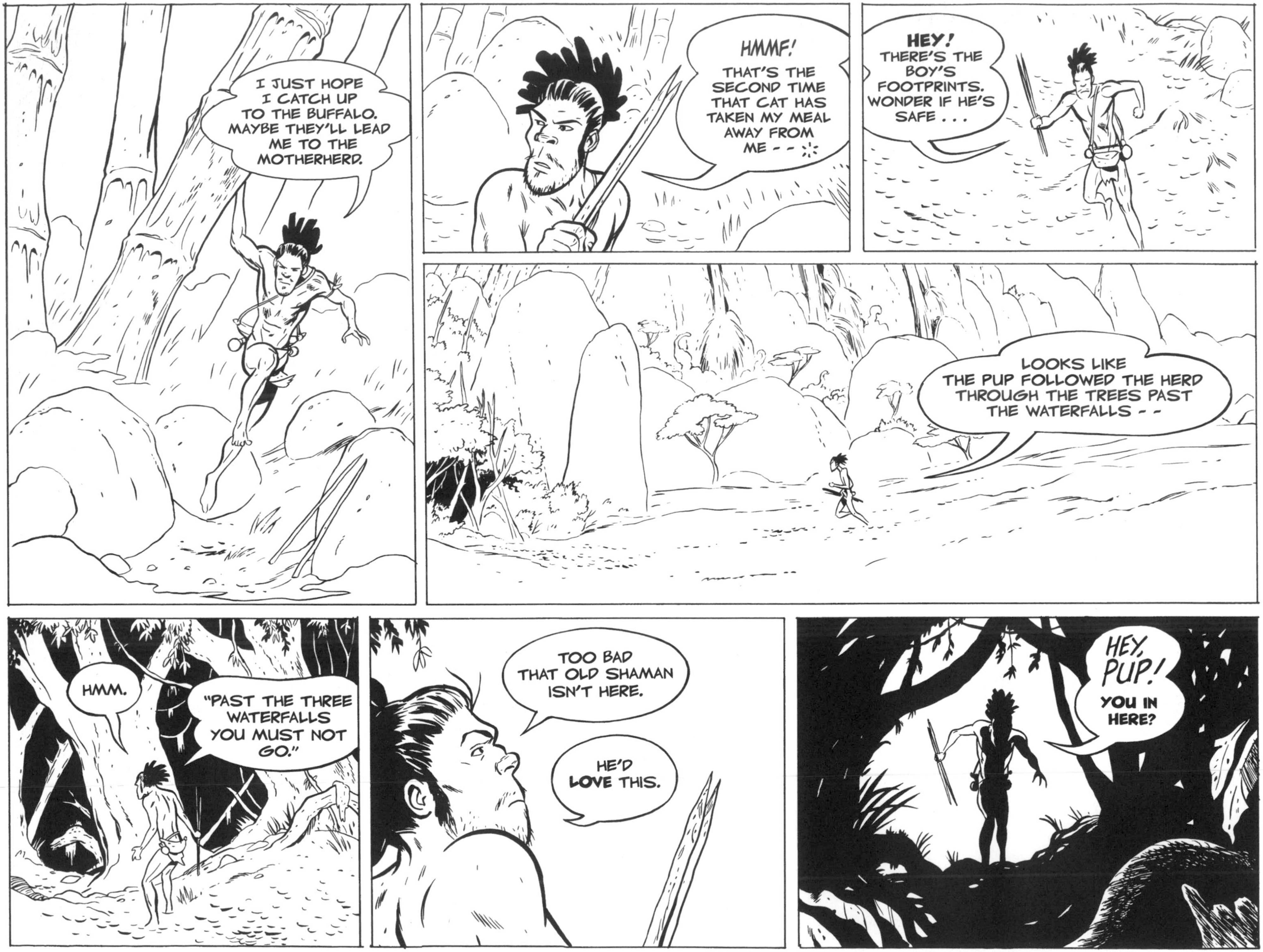

I JUST HOPE I CATCH UP TO THE BUFFALO. MAYBE THEY'LL LEAD ME TO THE MOTHERHERD.
HMMF!
THAT'S THE SECOND TIME THAT CAT HAS TAKEN MY MEAL AWAY FROM ME - -
HEY!
THERE'S THE BOY'S FOOTPRINTS. WONDER IF HE'S SAFE . . .
LOOKS LIKE THE PUP FOLLOWED THE HERD THROUGH THE TREES PAST THE WATERFALLS - -
HMM.
"PAST THE THREE WATERFALLS YOU MUST NOT GO."
TOO BAD THAT OLD SHAMAN ISN'T HERE.
HE'D LOVE THIS.
HEY, PUP!
YOU IN HERE?

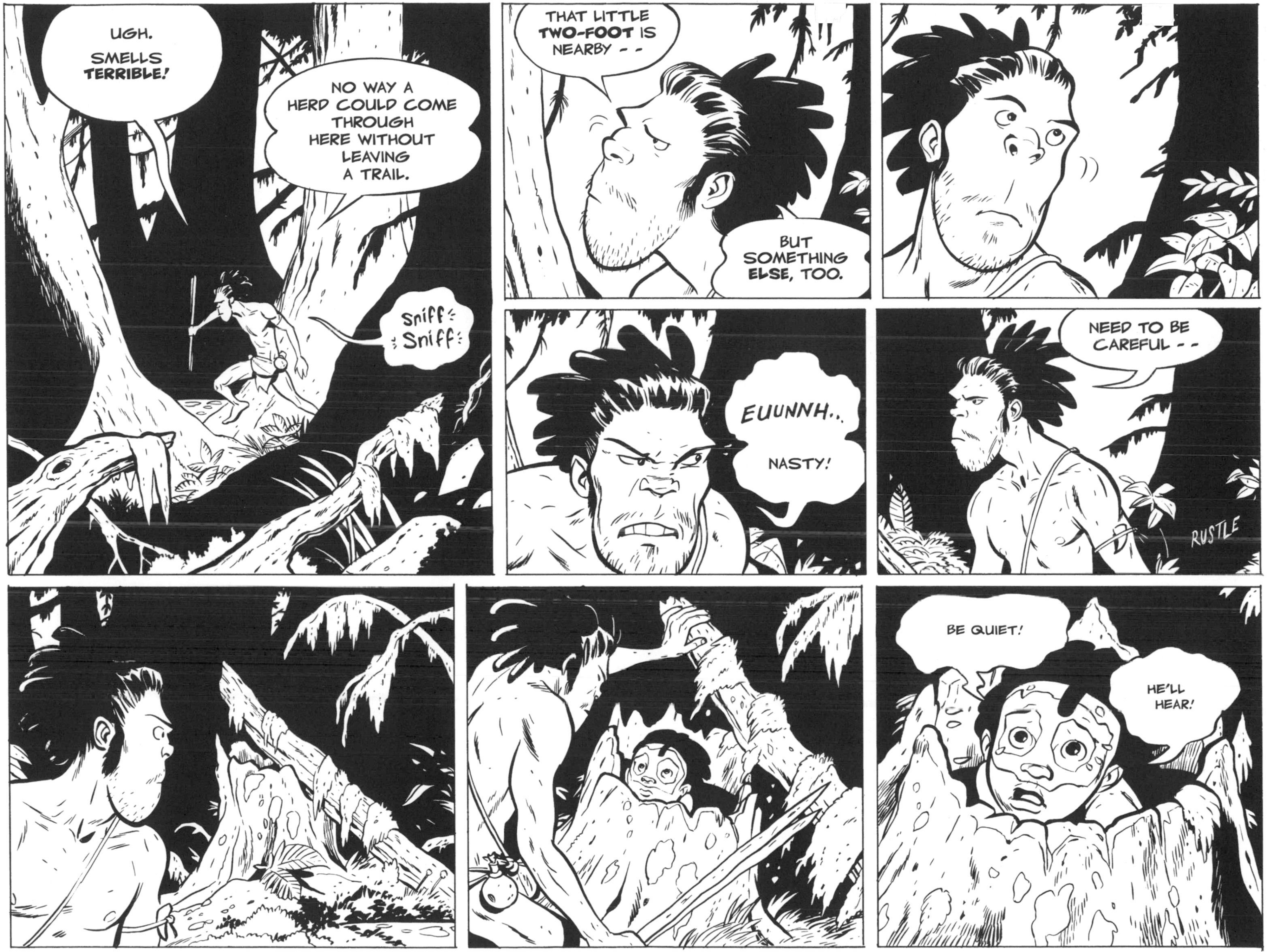
UGH.
SMELLS TERRIBLE!
NO WAY A HERD COULD COME THROUGH HERE WITHOUT LEAVING A TRAIL.
Sniff Sniff
THAT LITTLE TWO-FOOT IS NEARBY --
BUT SOMETHING ELSE, TOO.
EUUNNH..
NASTY!
NEED TO BE CAREFUL --
RUSTLE
BE QUIET!
HE'LL HEAR!

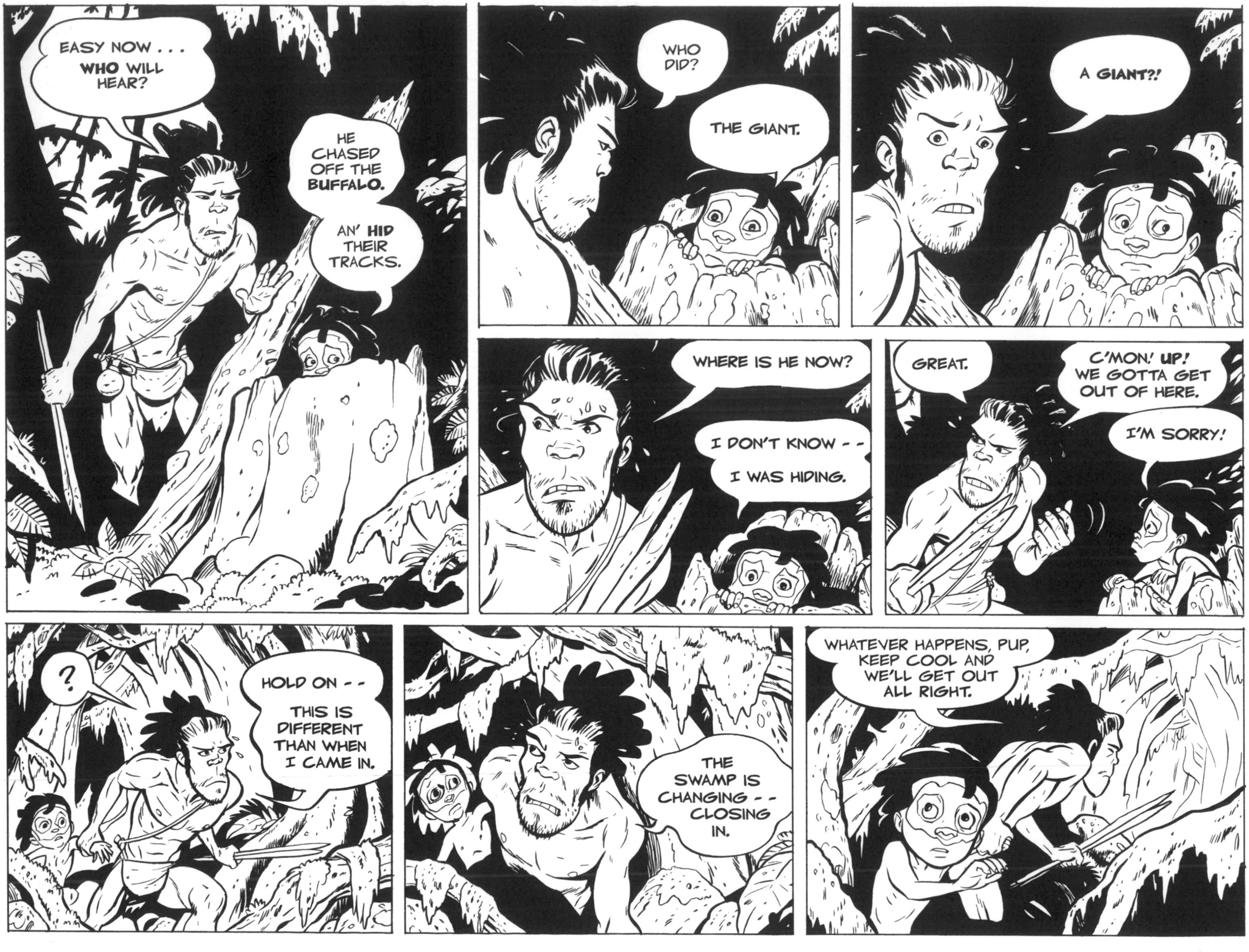
EASY NOW . . . WHO WILL HEAR?
HE CHASED OFF THE BUFFALO.
AN' HID THEIR TRACKS.
WHO DID?
THE GIANT.
A GIANT?!
WHERE IS HE NOW?
I DON'T KNOW - -
I WAS HIDING.
GREAT.
C'MON! UP! WE GOTTA GET OUT OF HERE.
I'M SORRY!
?
HOLD ON - -
THIS IS DIFFERENT THAN WHEN I CAME IN.
THE SWAMP IS CHANGING - - CLOSING IN.
WHATEVER HAPPENS, PUP, KEEP COOL AND WE'LL GET OUT ALL RIGHT.

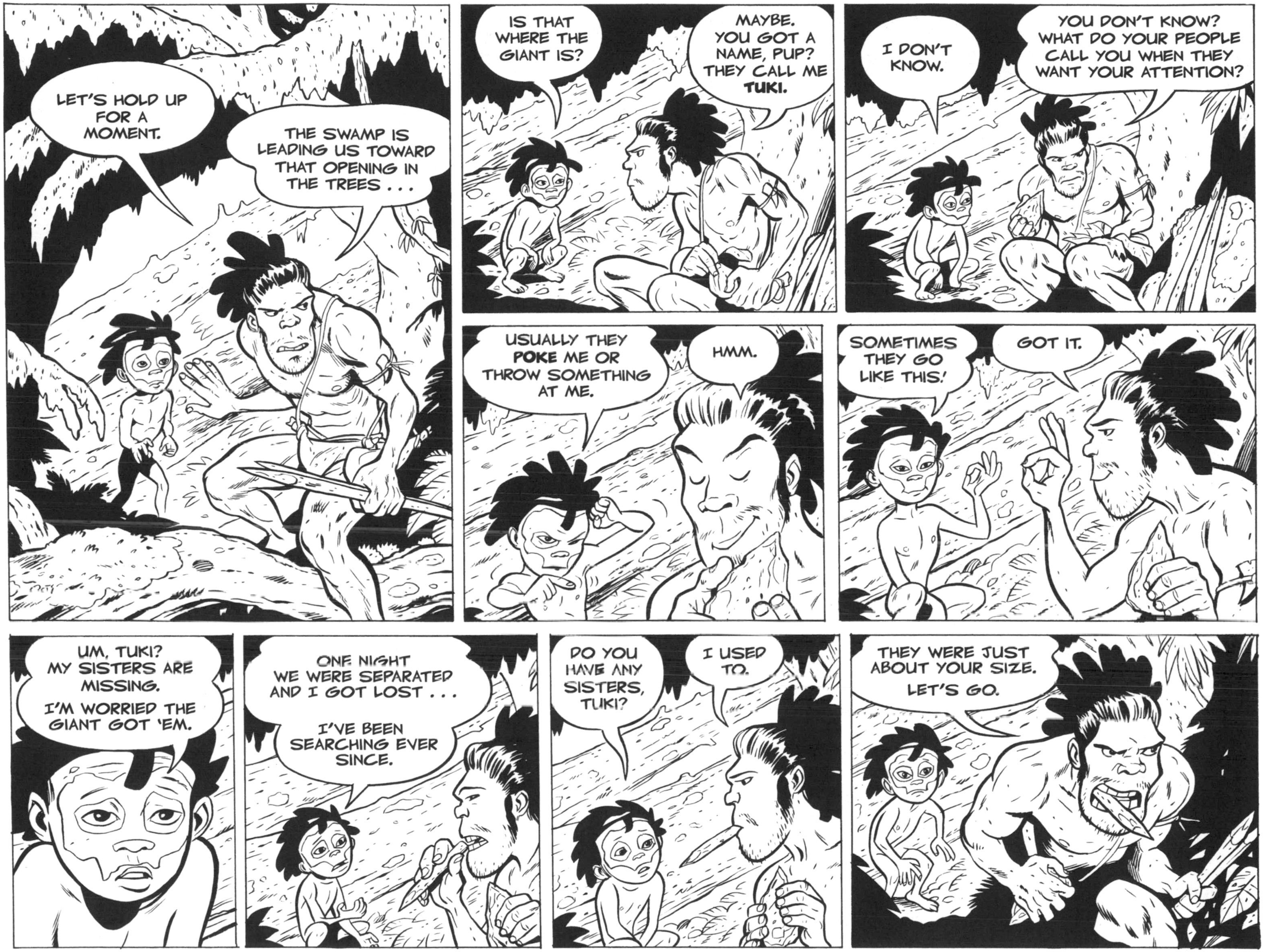
LET'S HOLD UP FOR A MOMENT.
THE SWAMP IS LEADING US TOWARD THAT OPENING IN THE TREES . . .
IS THAT WHERE THE GIANT IS?
MAYBE. YOU GOT A NAME, PUP? THEY CALL ME **TUKI.**
I DON'T KNOW.
YOU DON'T KNOW? WHAT DO YOUR PEOPLE CALL YOU WHEN THEY WANT YOUR ATTENTION?
USUALLY THEY **POKE** ME OR THROW SOMETHING AT ME.
HMM.
SOMETIMES THEY GO LIKE THIS!
GOT IT.
UM, TUKI? MY SISTERS ARE MISSING.
I'M WORRIED THE GIANT GOT 'EM.
ONE NIGHT WE WERE SEPARATED AND I GOT LOST . . .
I'VE BEEN SEARCHING EVER SINCE.
DO YOU HAVE ANY SISTERS, TUKI?
I USED TO.
THEY WERE JUST ABOUT YOUR SIZE.
LET'S GO.

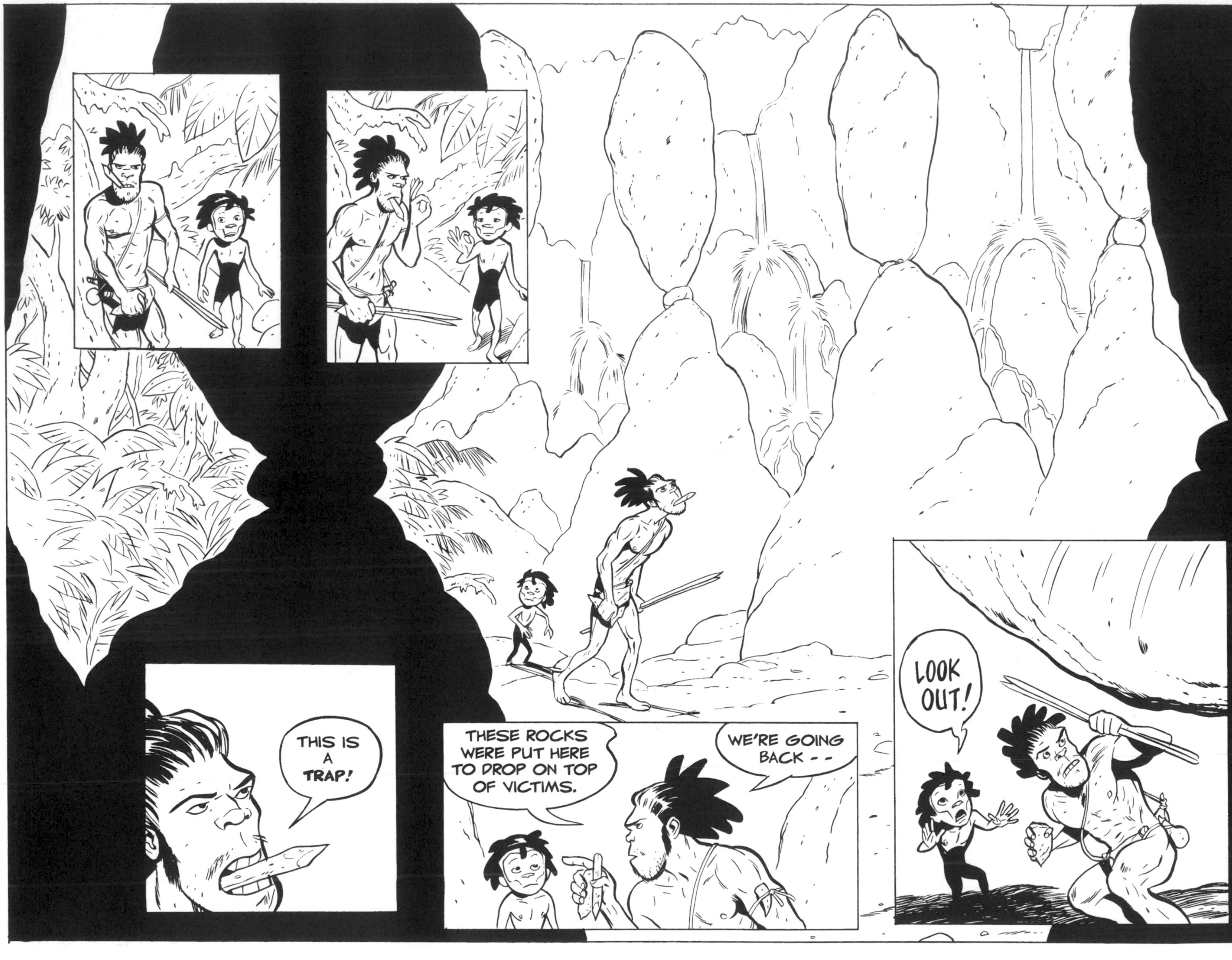
THIS IS A TRAP!
THESE ROCKS WERE PUT HERE TO DROP ON TOP OF VICTIMS.
WE'RE GOING BACK - -
LOOK OUT!

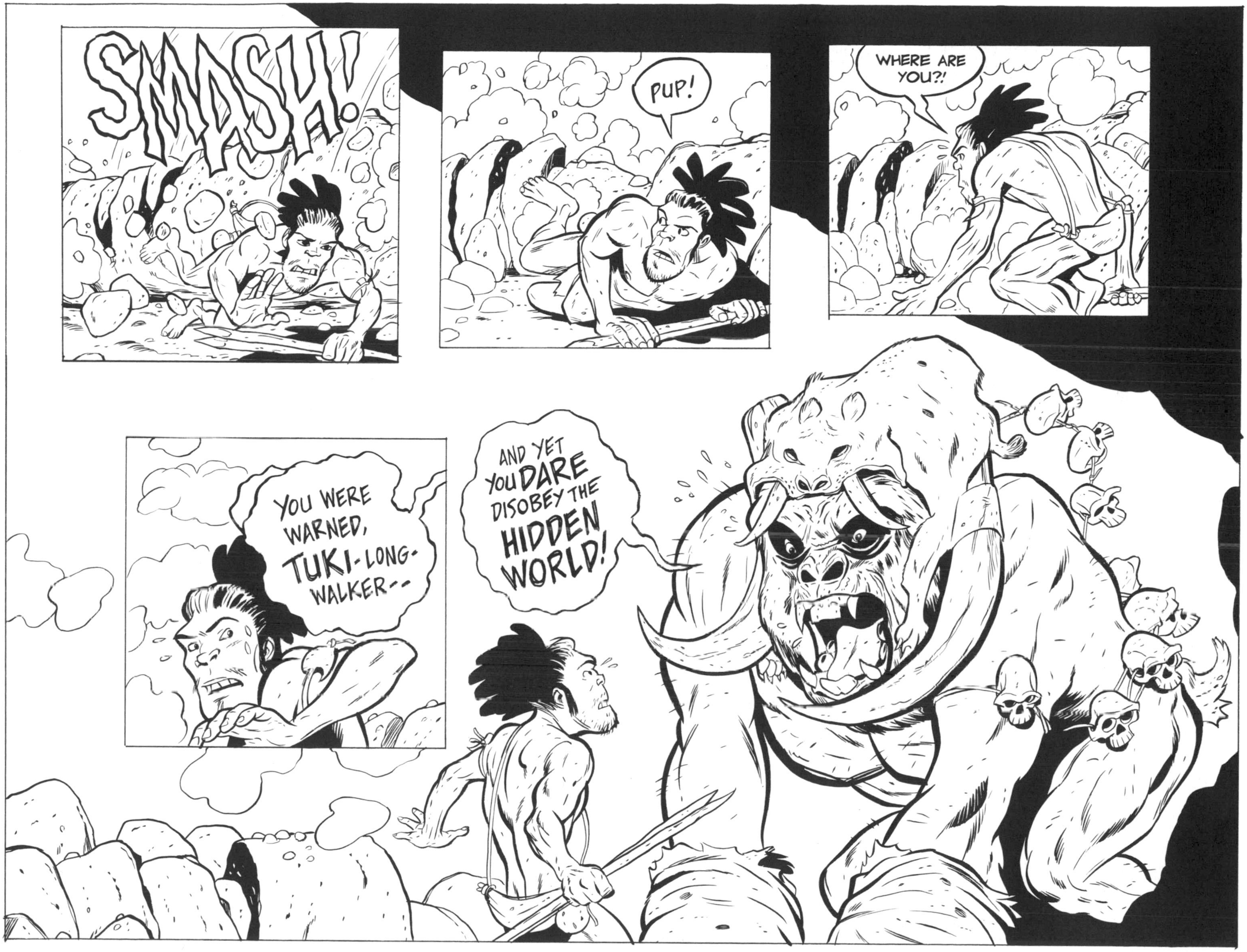
SMASH!
PUP!
WHERE ARE YOU?!
YOU WERE WARNED, TUKI-LONG-WALKER--
AND YET YOU DARE DISOBEY THE HIDDEN WORLD!

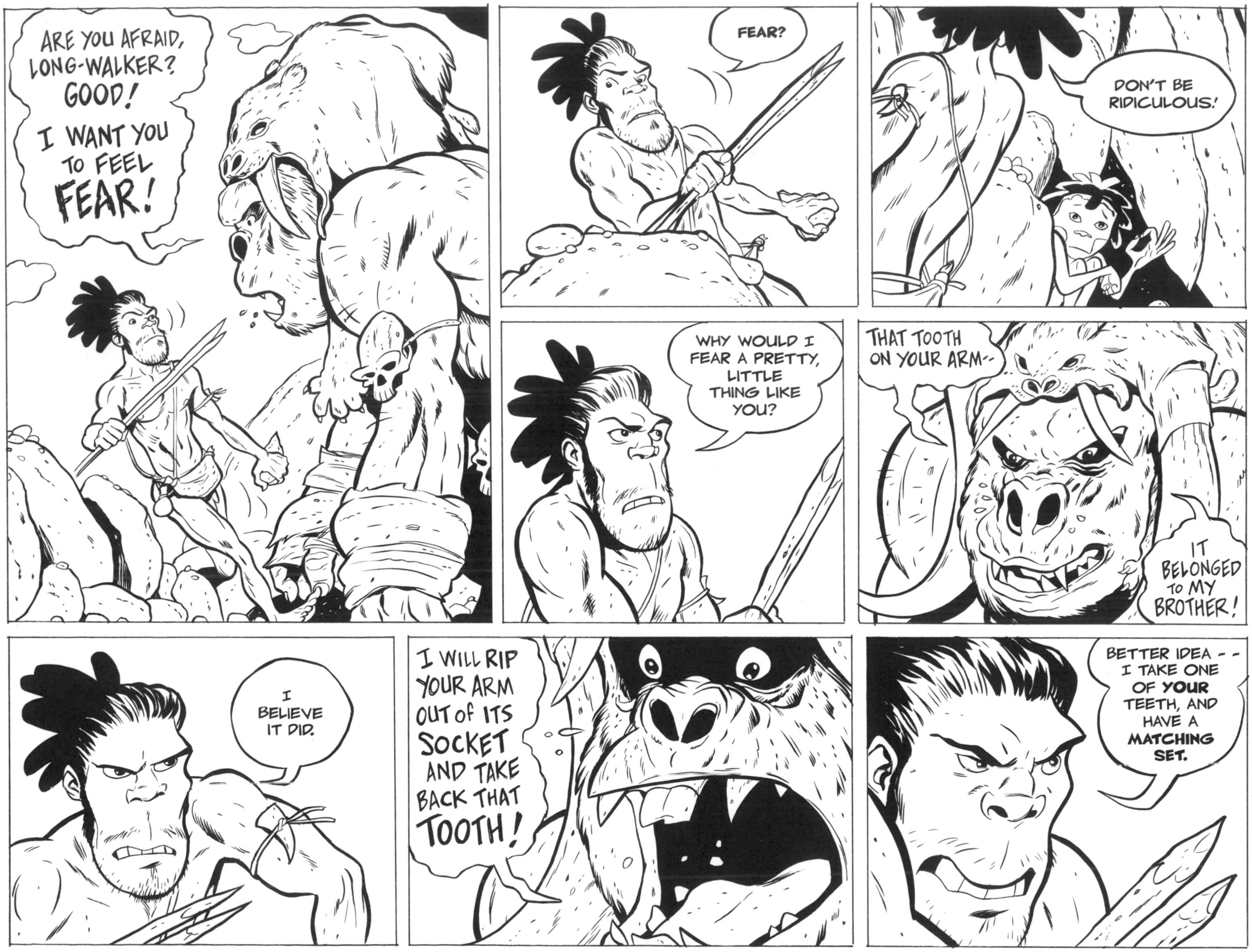
ARE YOU AFRAID, LONG-WALKER? GOOD!
I WANT YOU TO FEEL FEAR!
FEAR?
DON'T BE RIDICULOUS!
WHY WOULD I FEAR A PRETTY, LITTLE THING LIKE YOU?
THAT TOOTH ON YOUR ARM--
IT BELONGED TO MY BROTHER!
I BELIEVE IT DID.
I WILL RIP YOUR ARM OUT OF ITS SOCKET AND TAKE BACK THAT TOOTH!
BETTER IDEA -- I TAKE ONE OF YOUR TEETH, AND HAVE A MATCHING SET.

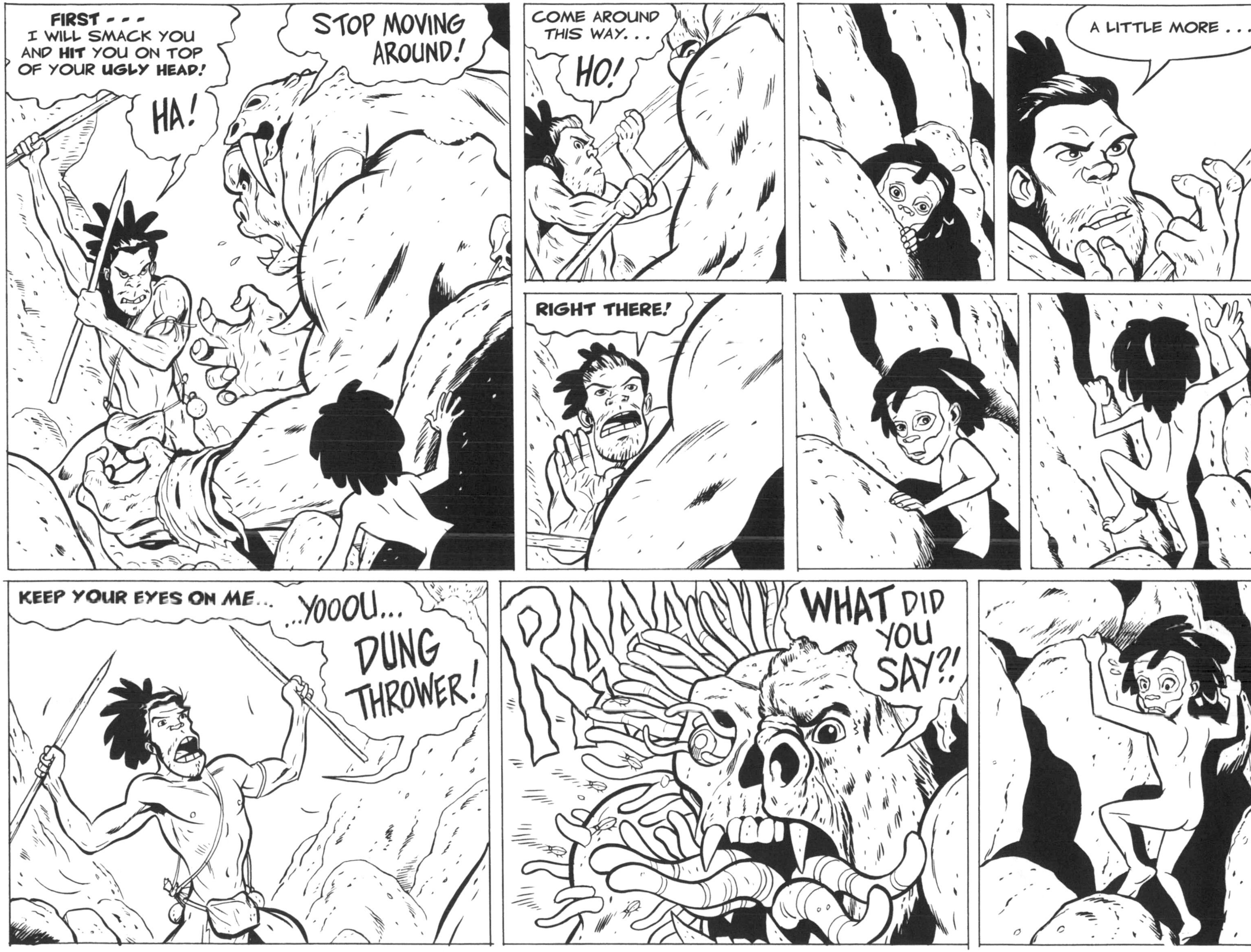
FIRST - - -
I WILL SMACK YOU AND HIT YOU ON TOP OF YOUR UGLY HEAD!
HA!
STOP MOVING AROUND!
COME AROUND THIS WAY...
HO!
A LITTLE MORE . . .
RIGHT THERE!
KEEP YOUR EYES ON ME...
...YOOOU... DUNG THROWER!
WHAT DID YOU SAY?!

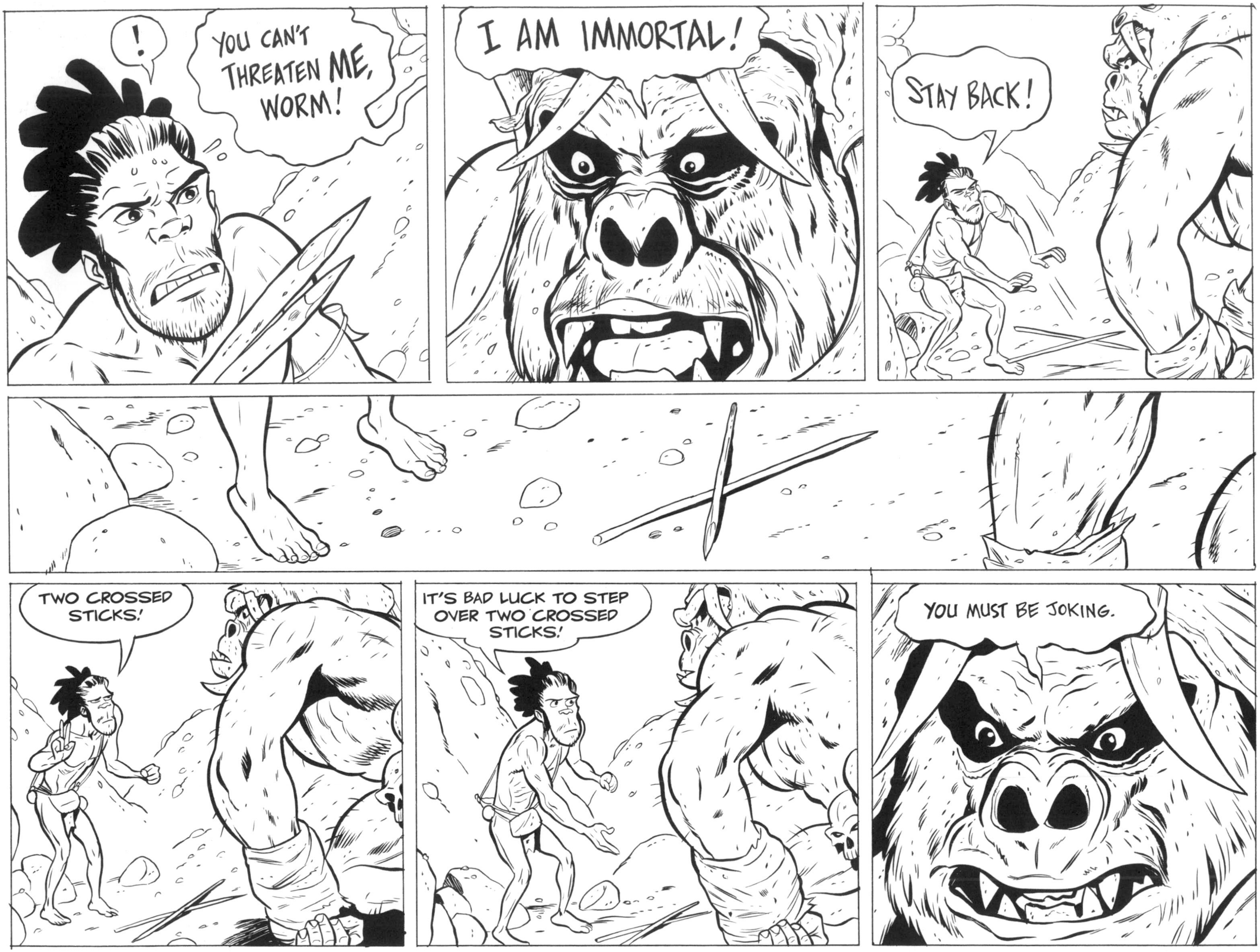
!
YOU CAN'T THREATEN ME, WORM!
I AM IMMORTAL!
STAY BACK!
TWO CROSSED STICKS!
IT'S BAD LUCK TO STEP OVER TWO CROSSED STICKS!
YOU MUST BE JOKING.

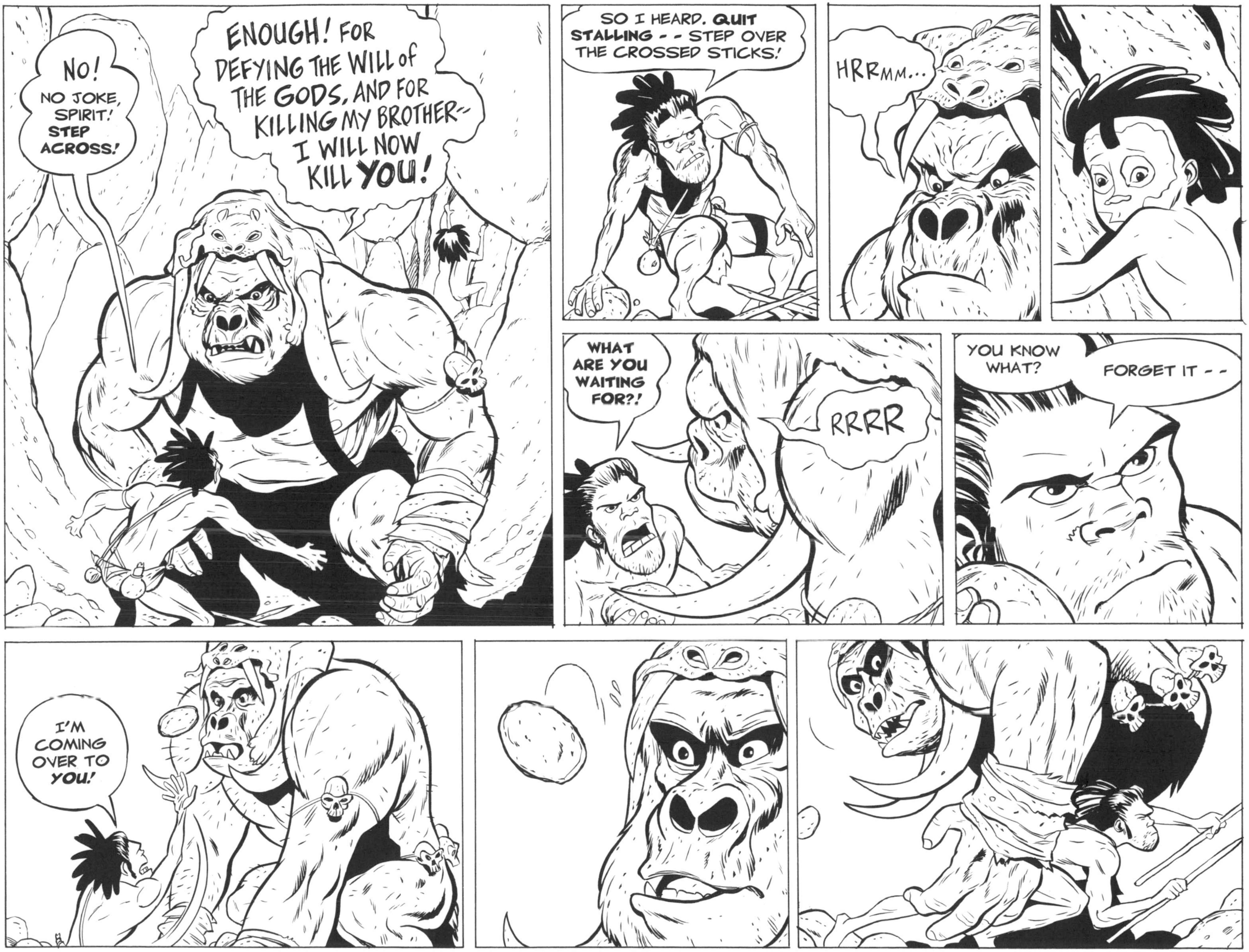
NO! NO JOKE, SPIRIT! STEP ACROSS!
ENOUGH! FOR DEFYING THE WILL OF THE GODS, AND FOR KILLING MY BROTHER-- I WILL NOW KILL YOU!
SO I HEARD. QUIT STALLING - - STEP OVER THE CROSSED STICKS!
HRRMM...
WHAT ARE YOU WAITING FOR?!
RRRR
YOU KNOW WHAT?
FORGET IT - -
I'M COMING OVER TO YOU!

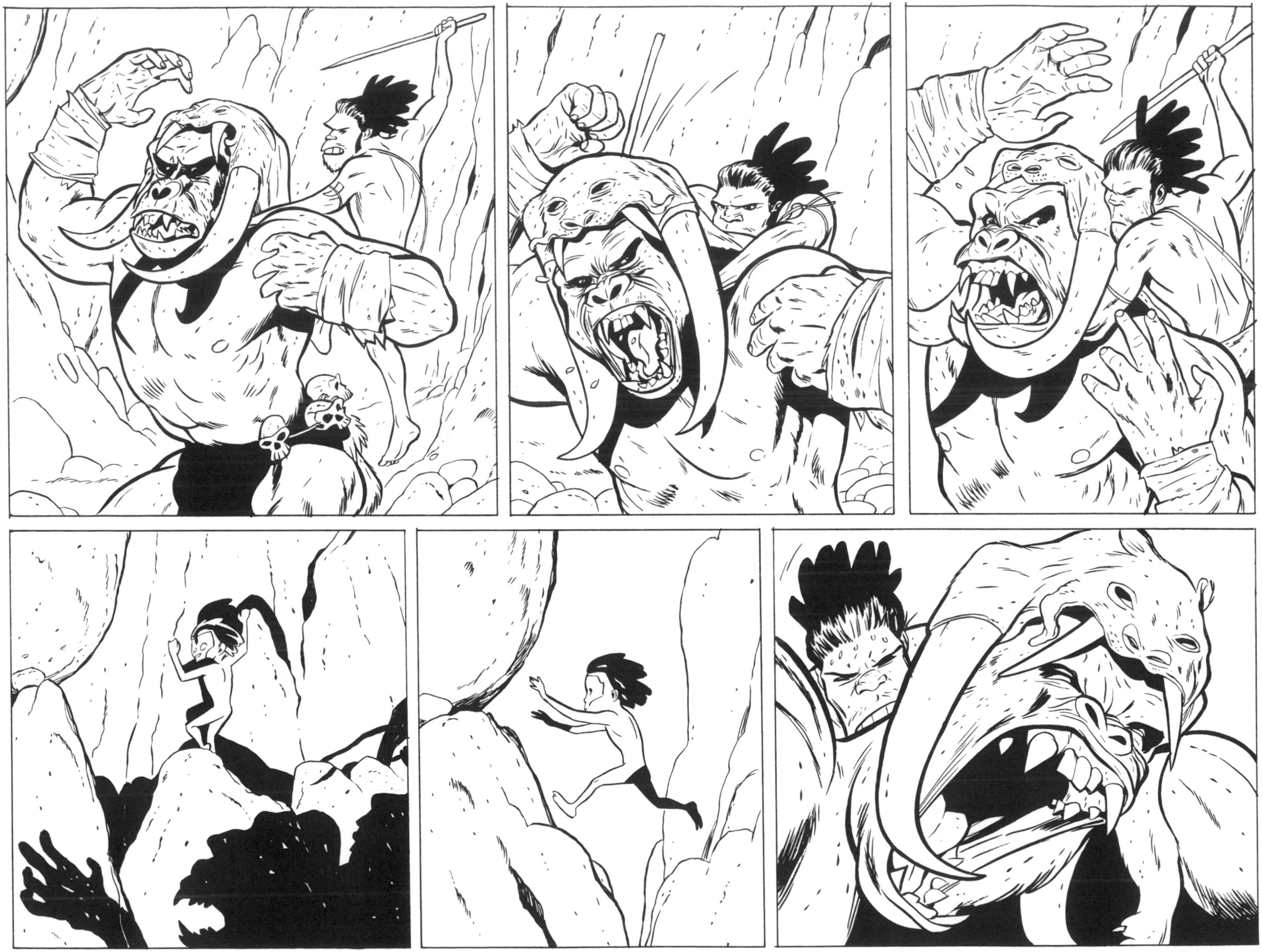

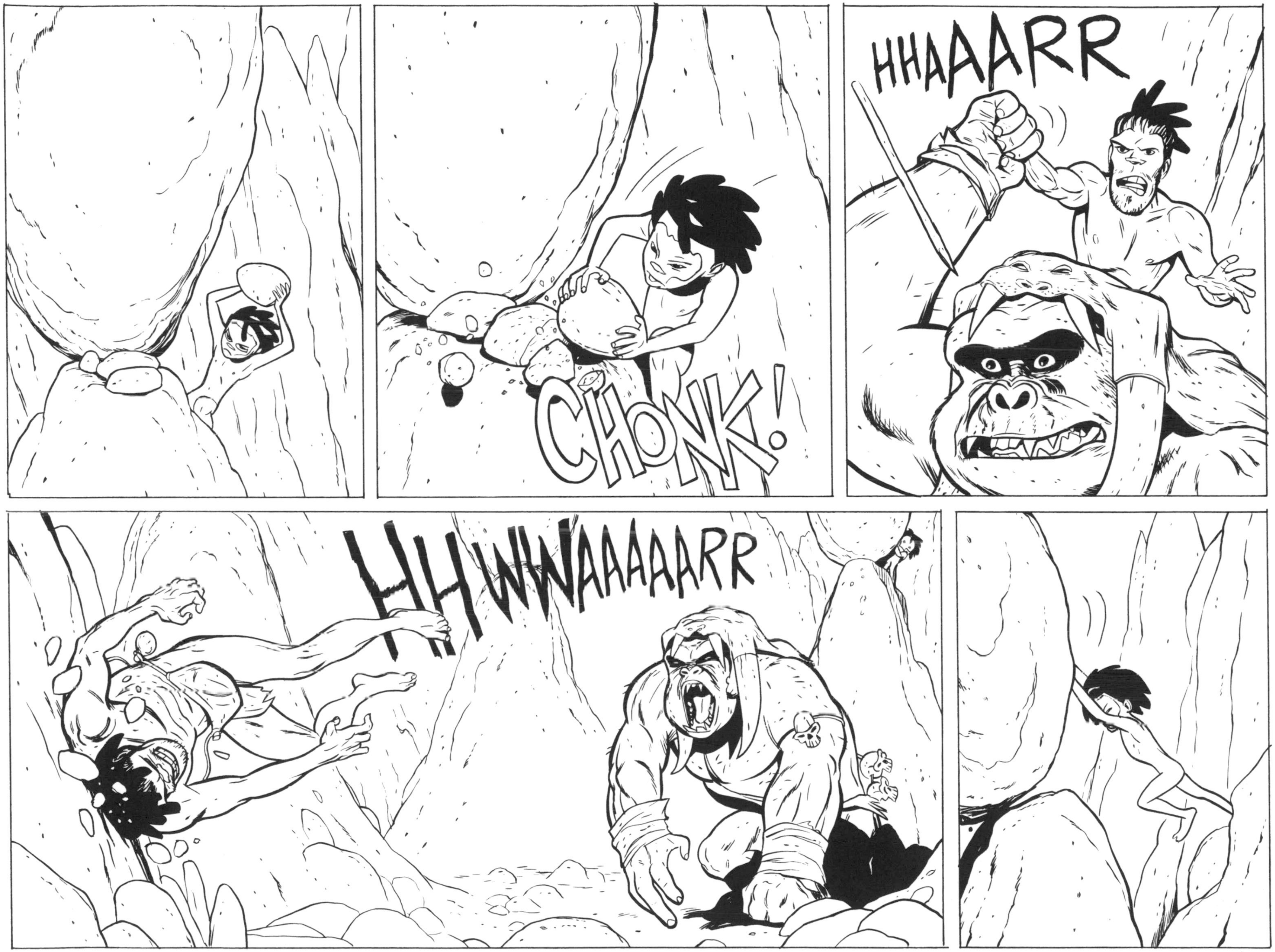
CHONK!
HHAAARR
HHWWAAAAARR

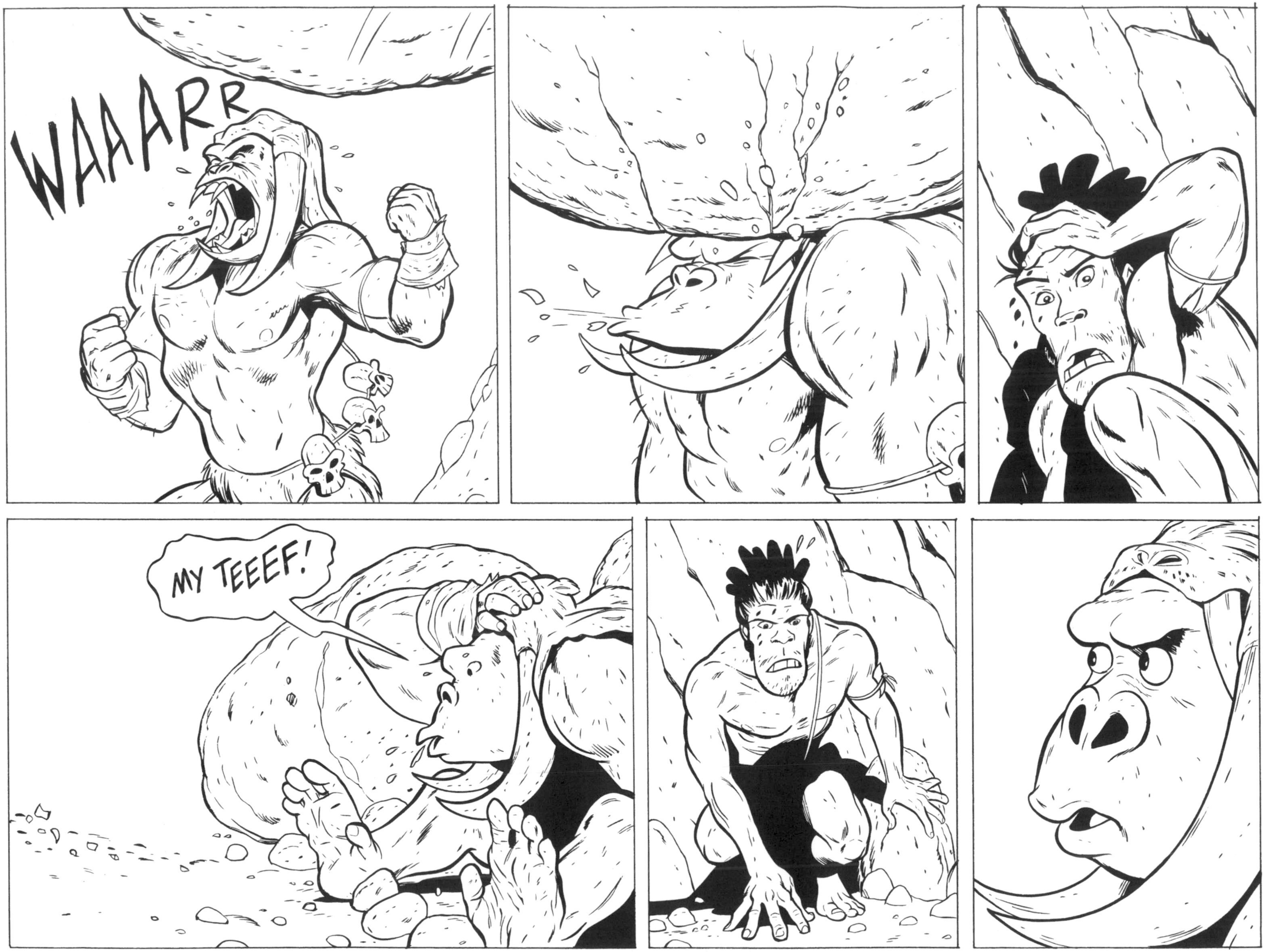
WAAARR
MY TEEEF!

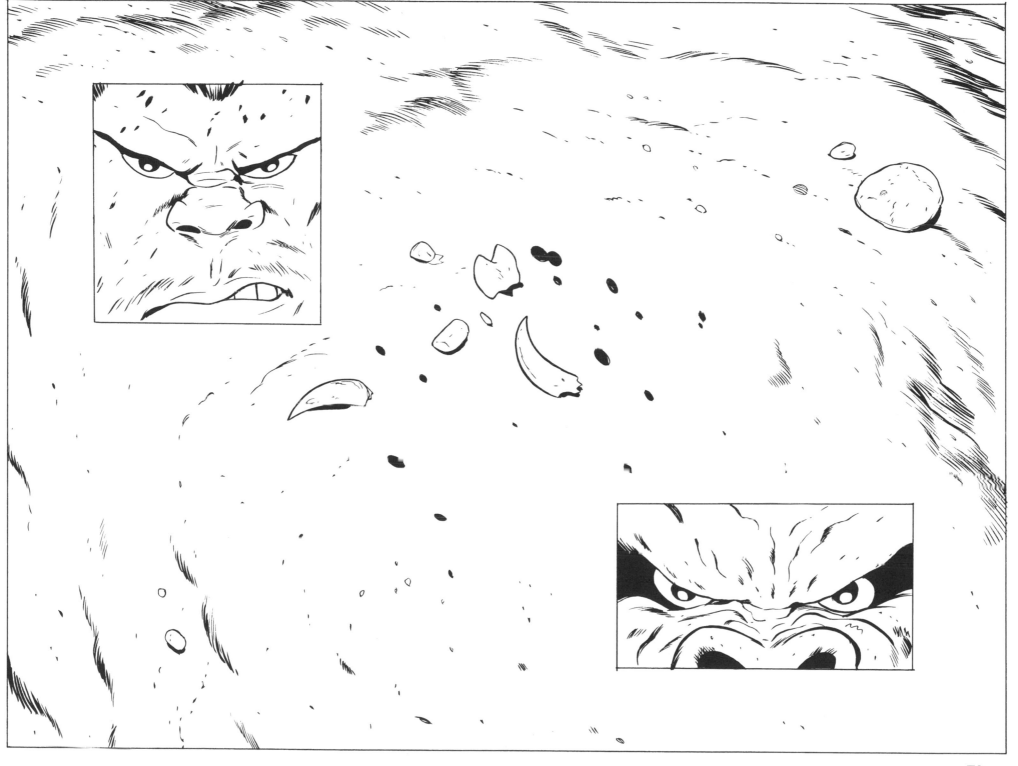

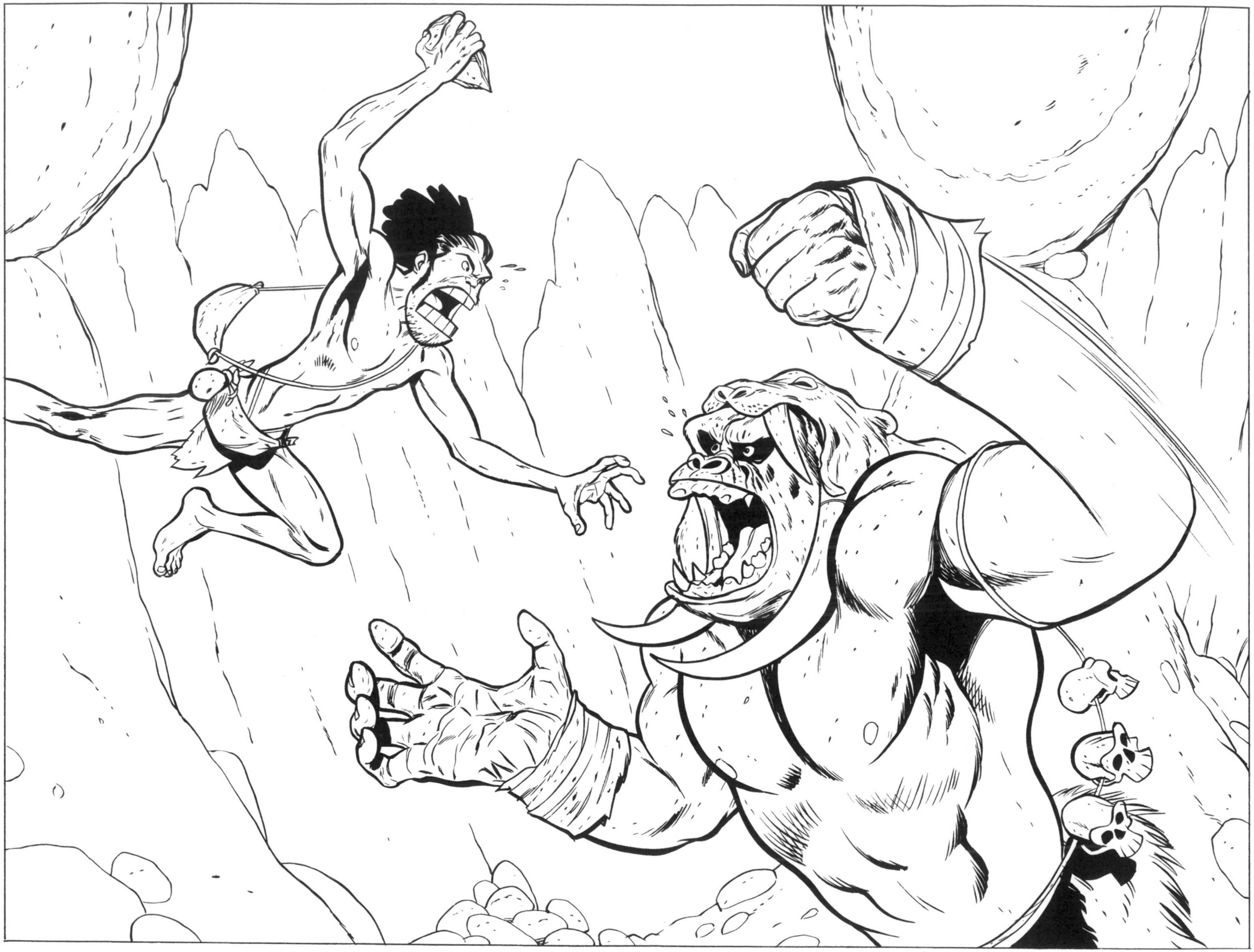

Four

Kwarell

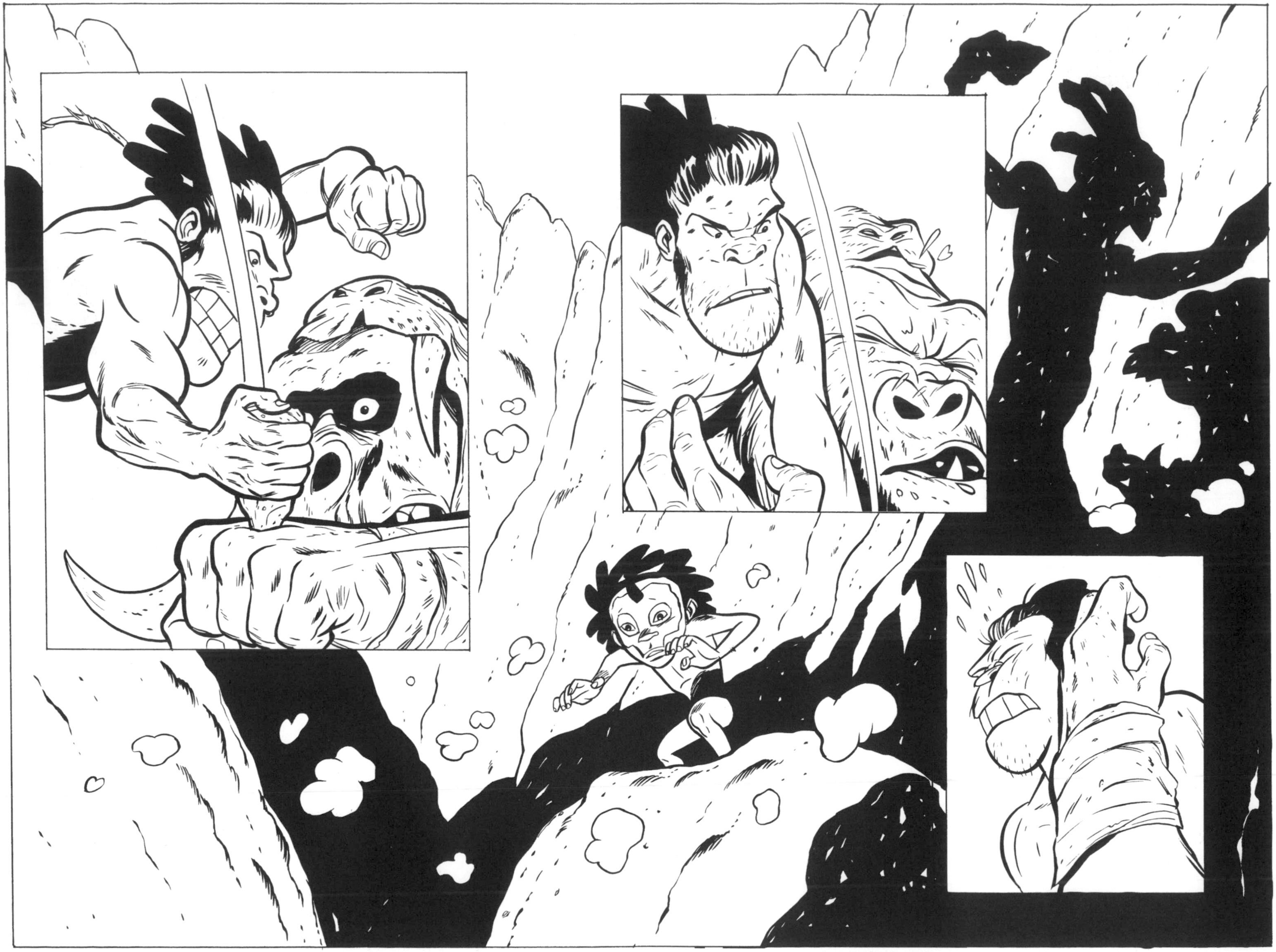

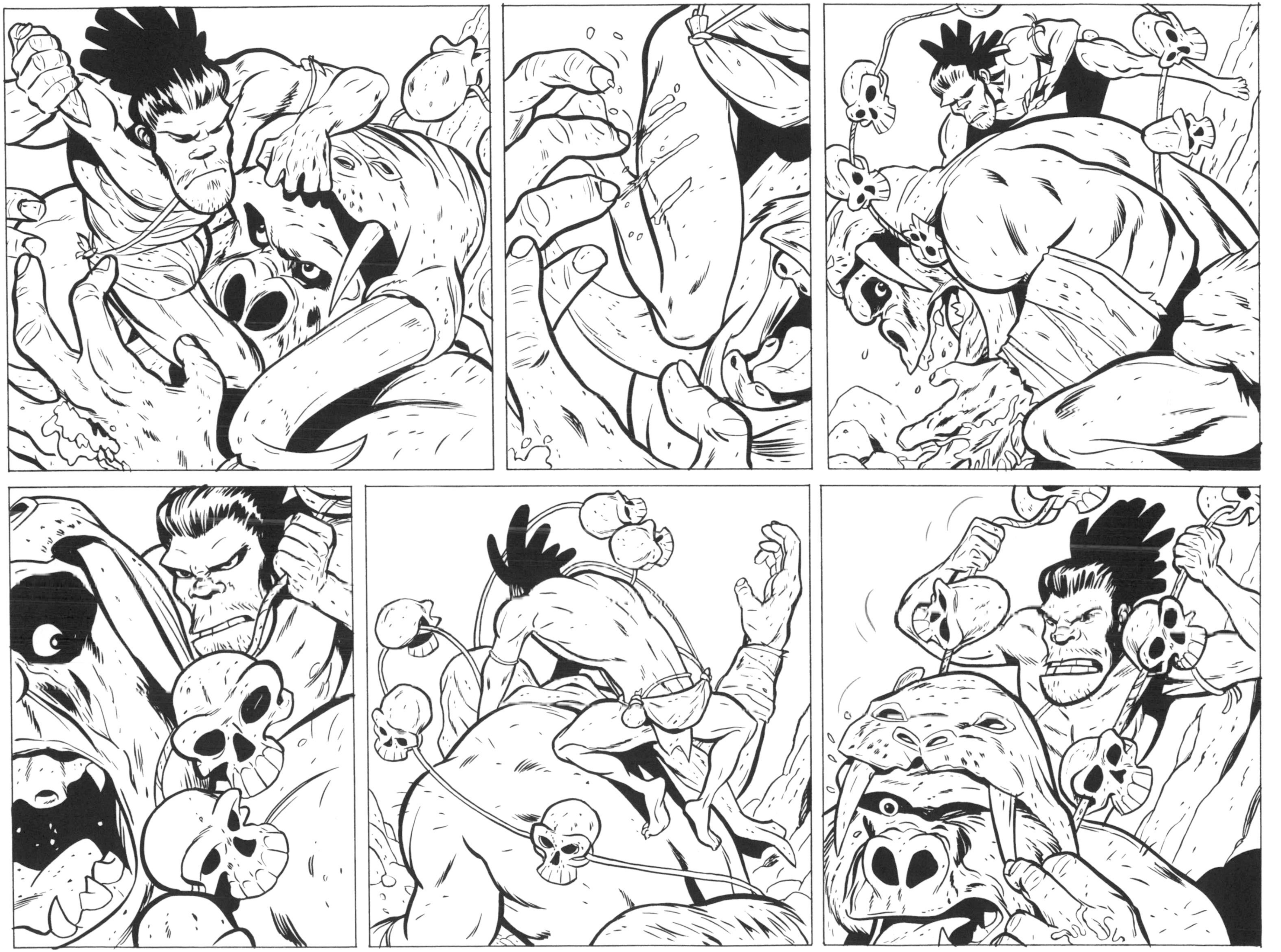

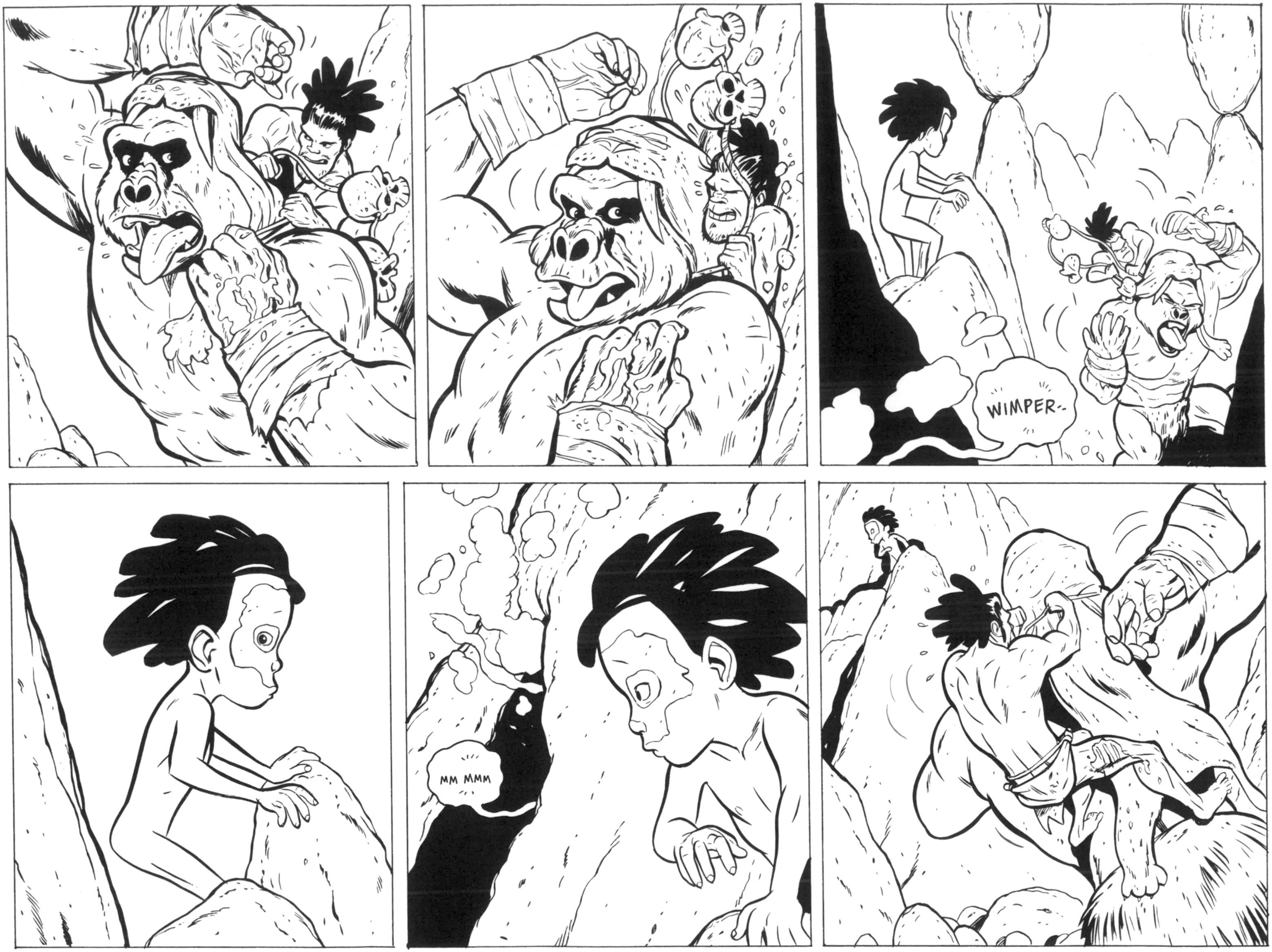
WIMPER
MM MMM

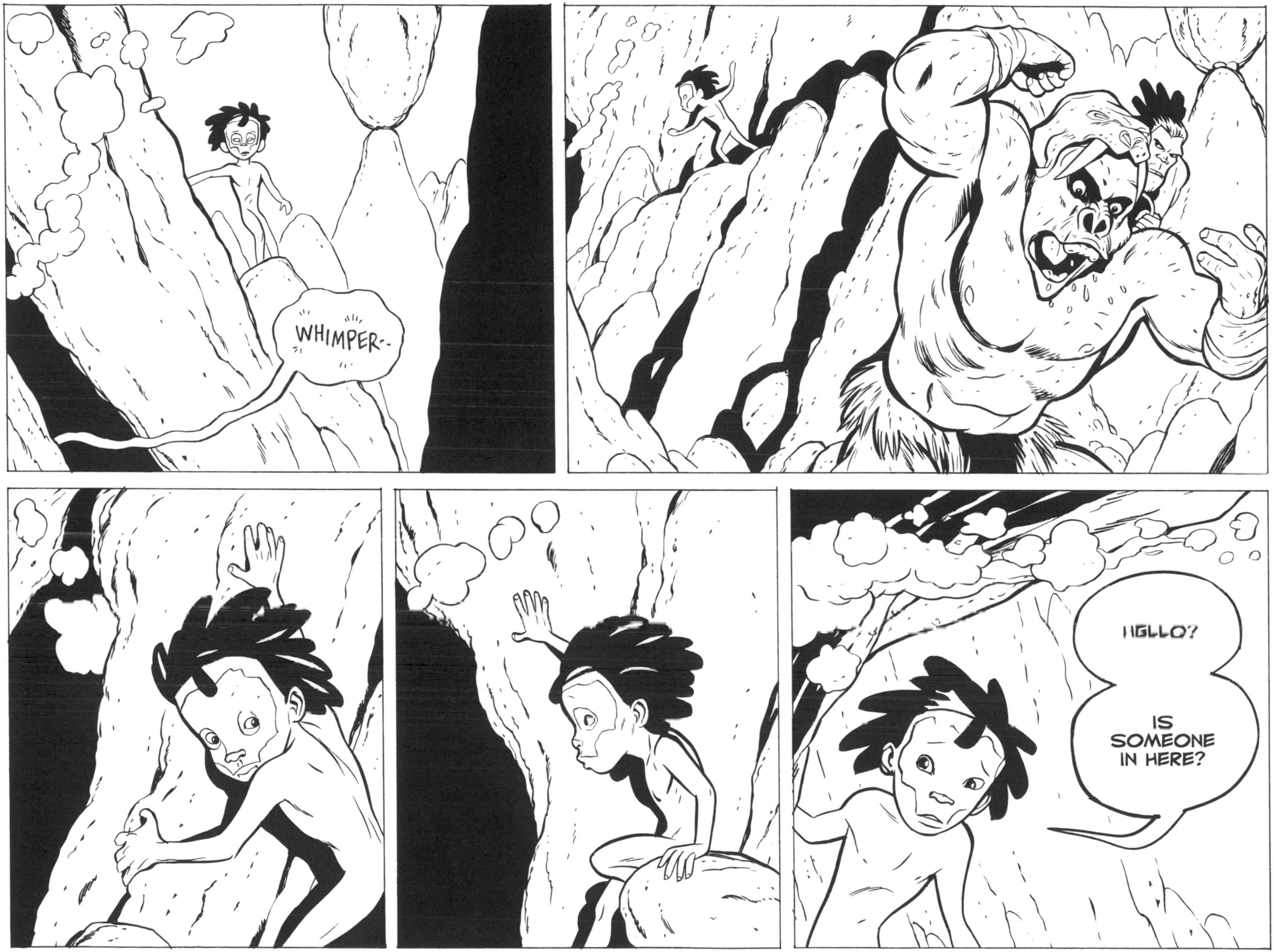
WHIMPER--
HELLO?
IS SOMEONE IN HERE?

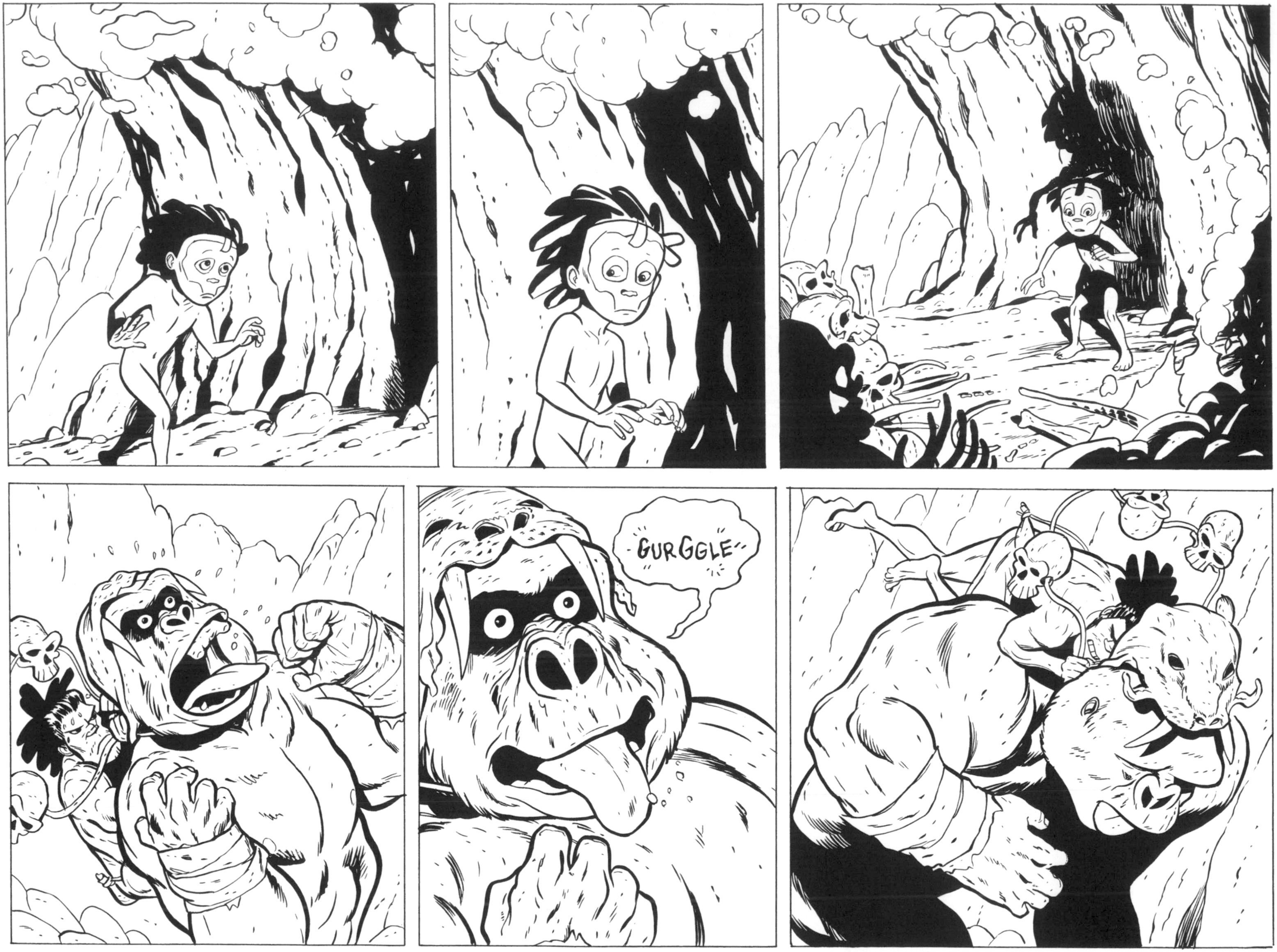
GURGGLE

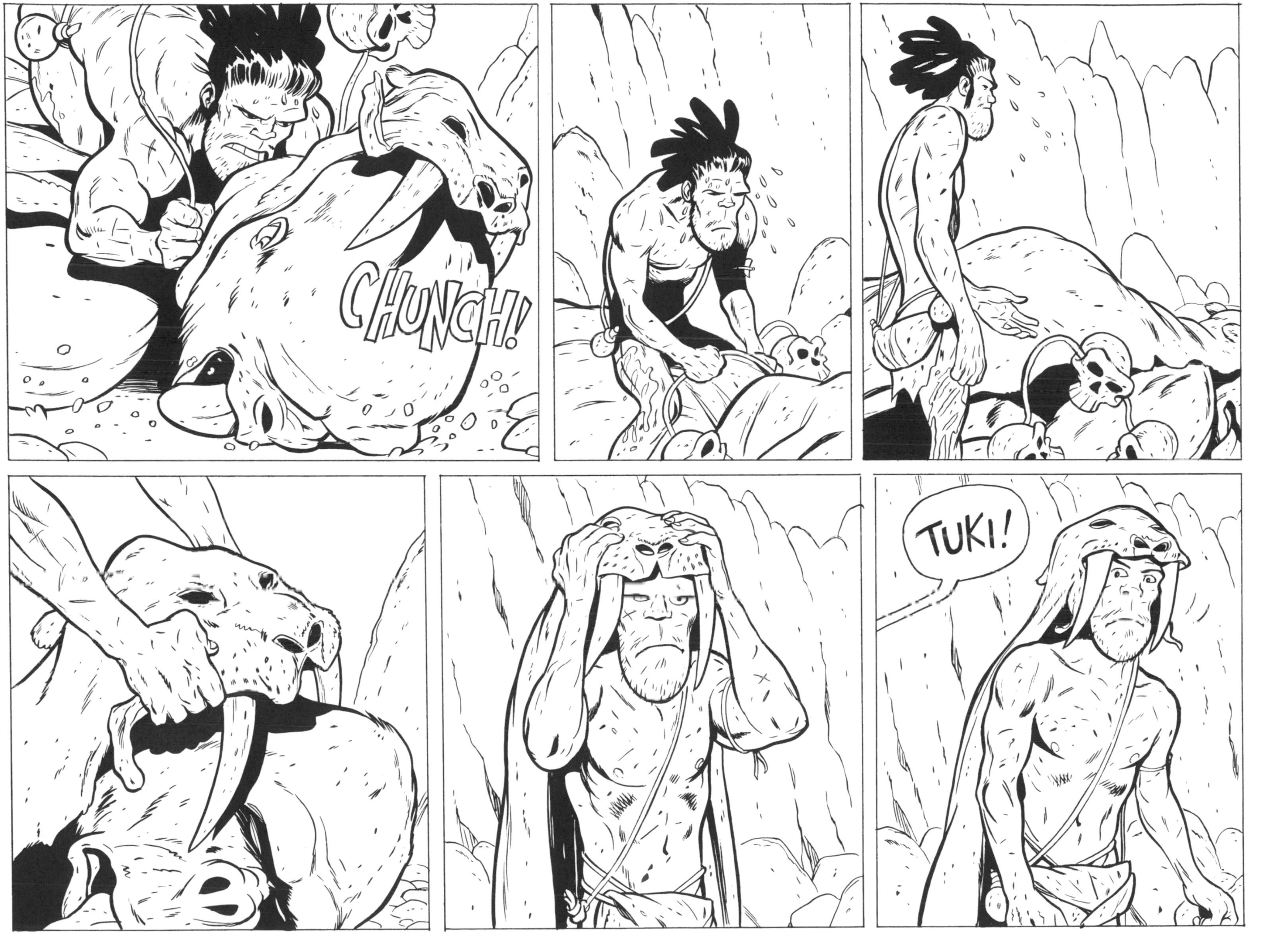
CHUNCH!
TUKI!

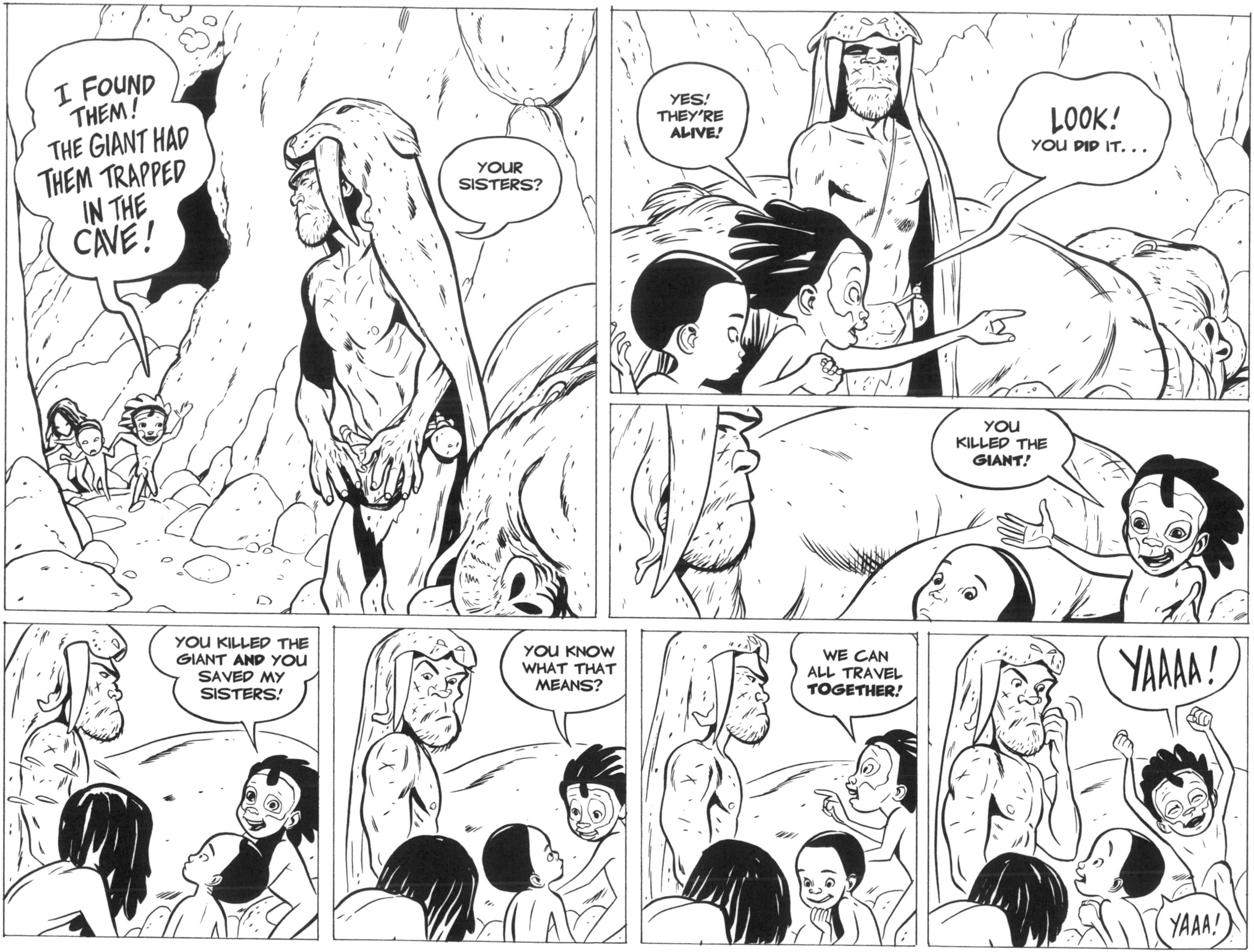
I FOUND THEM! THE GIANT HAD THEM TRAPPED IN THE CAVE!
YOUR SISTERS?
YES! THEY'RE ALIVE!
LOOK! YOU DID IT...
YOU KILLED THE GIANT!
YOU KILLED THE GIANT AND YOU SAVED MY SISTERS!
YOU KNOW WHAT THAT MEANS?
WE CAN ALL TRAVEL TOGETHER!
YAAAA!
YAAA!

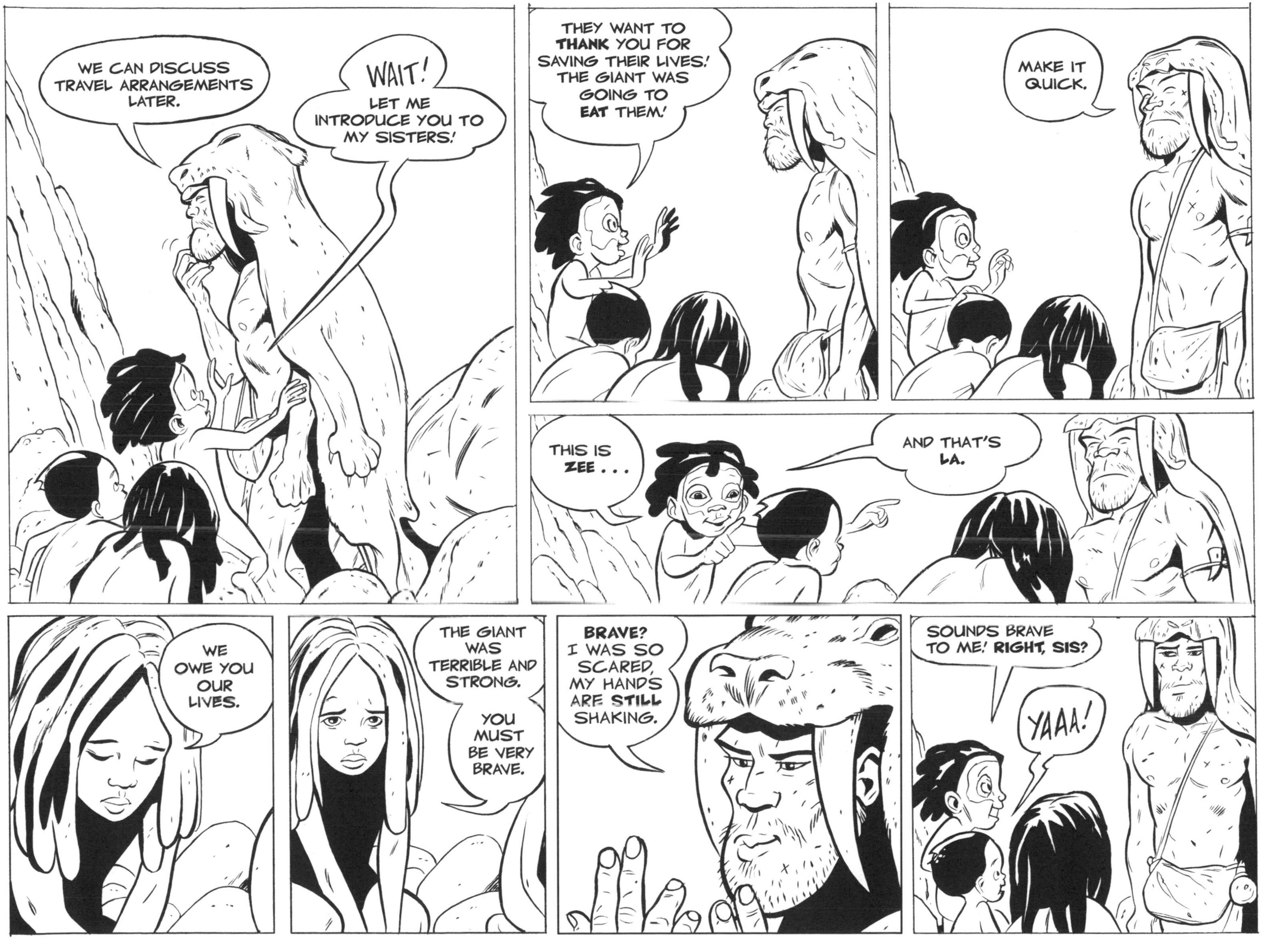

WE CAN DISCUSS TRAVEL ARRANGEMENTS LATER.
WAIT!
LET ME INTRODUCE YOU TO MY SISTERS!
THEY WANT TO **THANK** YOU FOR SAVING THEIR LIVES! THE GIANT WAS GOING TO **EAT** THEM!
MAKE IT QUICK.
THIS IS **ZEE** . . .
AND THAT'S **LA.**
WE OWE YOU OUR **LIVES.**
THE GIANT WAS TERRIBLE AND STRONG.
YOU MUST BE VERY BRAVE.
BRAVE? I WAS SO SCARED, MY HANDS ARE **STILL** SHAKING.
SOUNDS BRAVE TO ME! **RIGHT, SIS?**
YAAA!

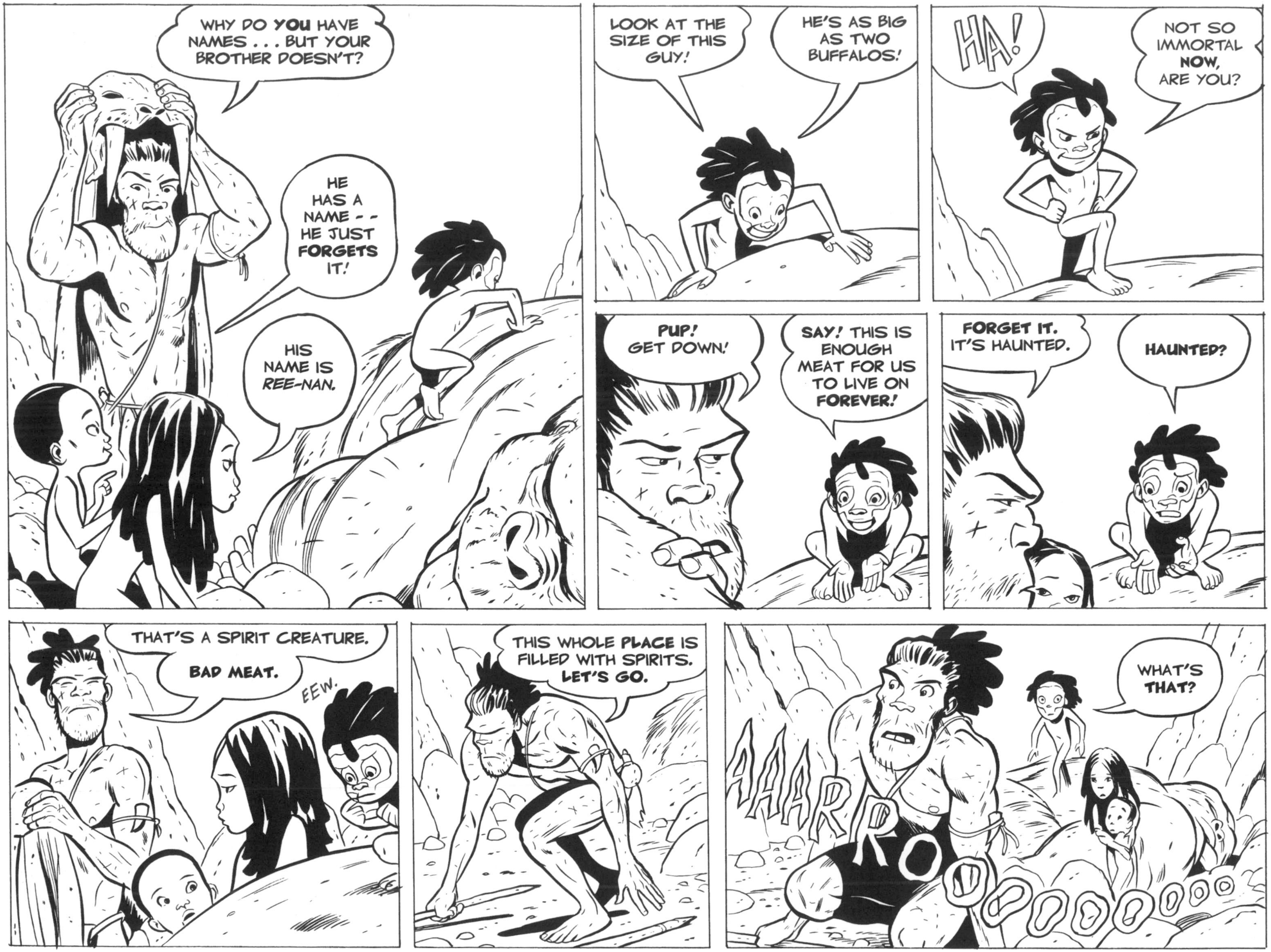
WHY DO YOU HAVE NAMES . . . BUT YOUR BROTHER DOESN'T?
HE HAS A NAME - - HE JUST FORGETS IT!
HIS NAME IS REE-NAN.
LOOK AT THE SIZE OF THIS GUY!
HE'S AS BIG AS TWO BUFFALOS!
HA!
NOT SO IMMORTAL NOW, ARE YOU?
PUP! GET DOWN!
SAY! THIS IS ENOUGH MEAT FOR US TO LIVE ON FOREVER!
FORGET IT. IT'S HAUNTED.
HAUNTED?
THAT'S A SPIRIT CREATURE.
BAD MEAT.
EEW.
THIS WHOLE PLACE IS FILLED WITH SPIRITS. LET'S GO.
WHAT'S THAT?
AAARROOOOOOOOOOO

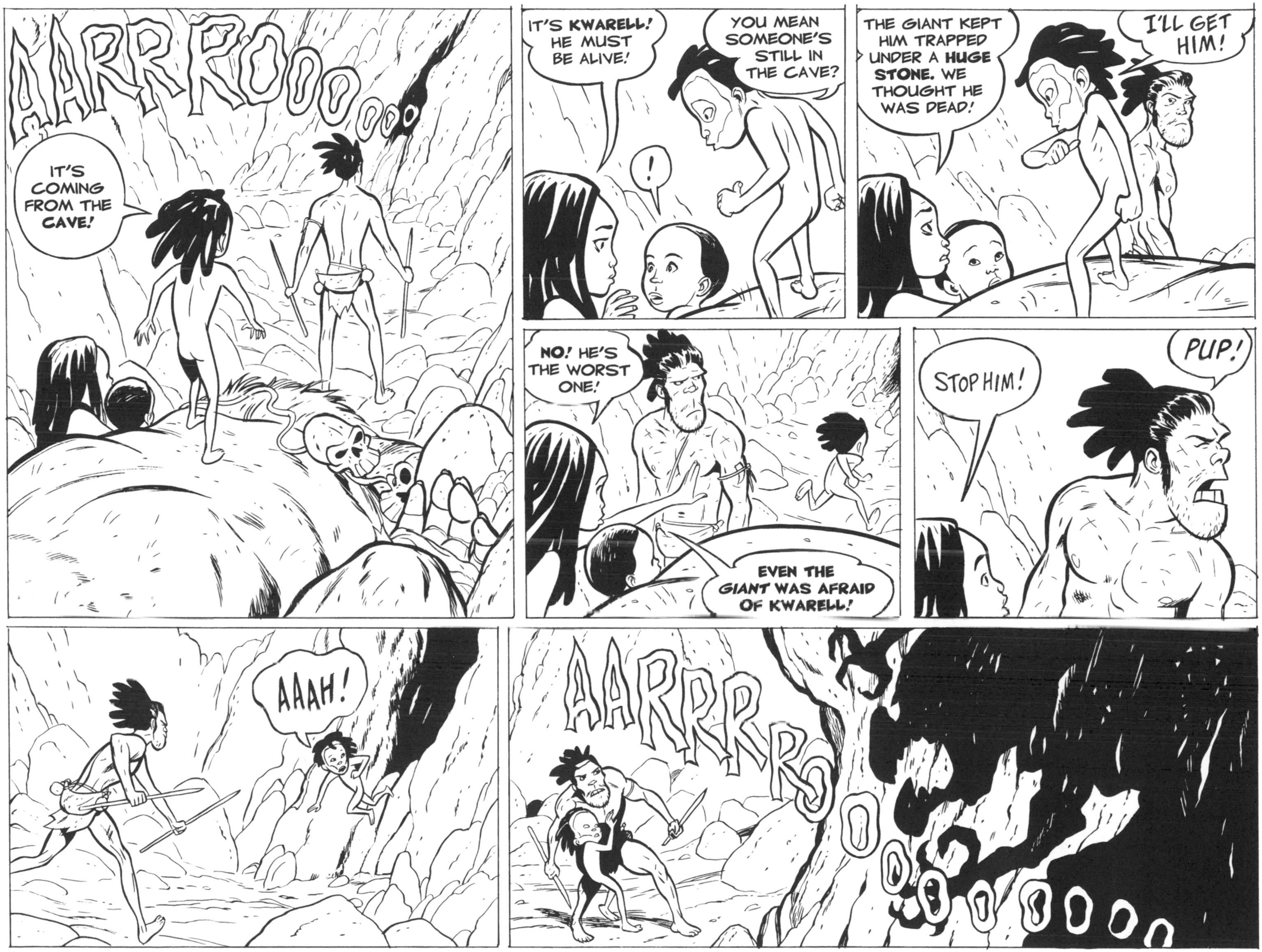
AARROOOOOO
IT'S COMING FROM THE CAVE!
IT'S KWARELL! HE MUST BE ALIVE!
YOU MEAN SOMEONE'S STILL IN THE CAVE?
!
THE GIANT KEPT HIM TRAPPED UNDER A HUGE STONE. WE THOUGHT HE WAS DEAD!
I'LL GET HIM!
NO! HE'S THE WORST ONE!
EVEN THE GIANT WAS AFRAID OF KWARELL!
STOP HIM!
PUP!
AAAH!
AARRRROOOOOOOOO

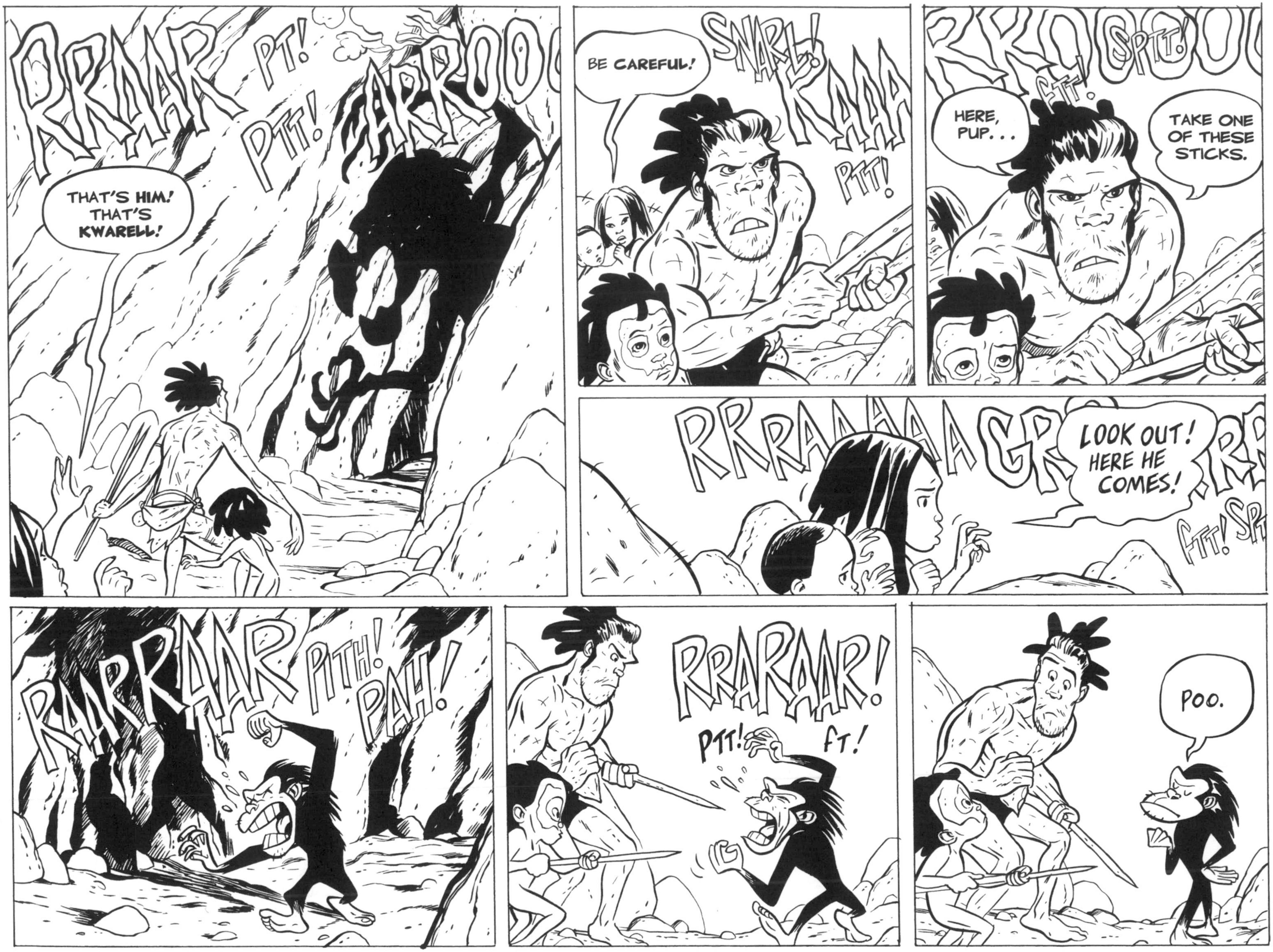

RRAAR
PT!
PTT!
ARROOO
THAT'S HIM! THAT'S KWARELL!
BE CAREFUL!
SNARL!
KAAA
PTT!
RROO
SPIT!
FT!
HERE, PUP...
TAKE ONE OF THESE STICKS.
RRRAAAAAAGR
LOOK OUT! HERE HE COMES!
FTT! SPT
RAARRAAR
PITH!
PAH!
RRARAAR!
PTT!
FT!
POO.

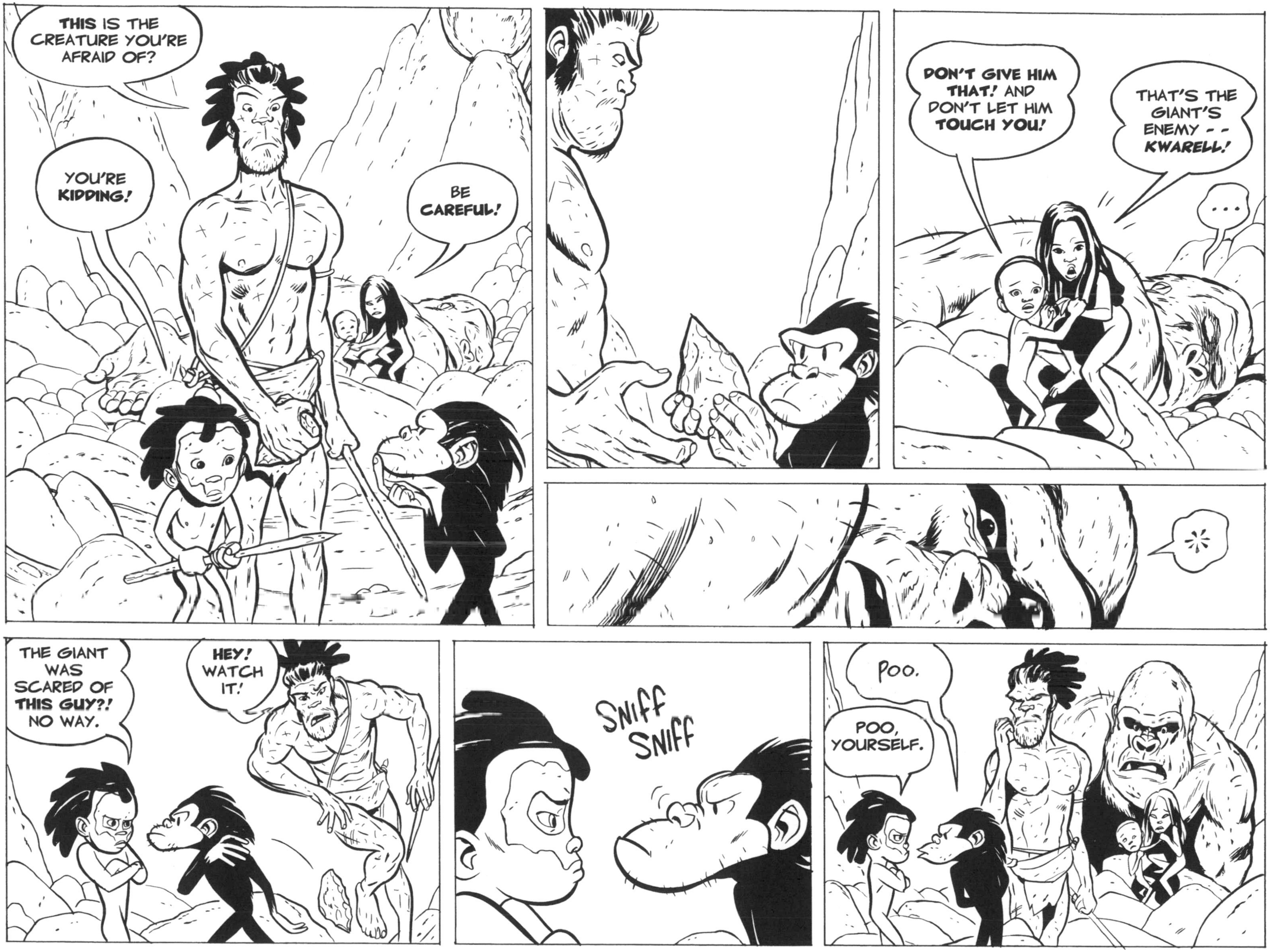
THIS IS THE CREATURE YOU'RE AFRAID OF?
YOU'RE KIDDING!
BE CAREFUL!
DON'T GIVE HIM THAT! AND DON'T LET HIM TOUCH YOU!
THAT'S THE GIANT'S ENEMY -- KWARELL!
...
THE GIANT WAS SCARED OF THIS GUY?! NO WAY.
HEY! WATCH IT!
SNIFF SNIFF
POO.
POO, YOURSELF.

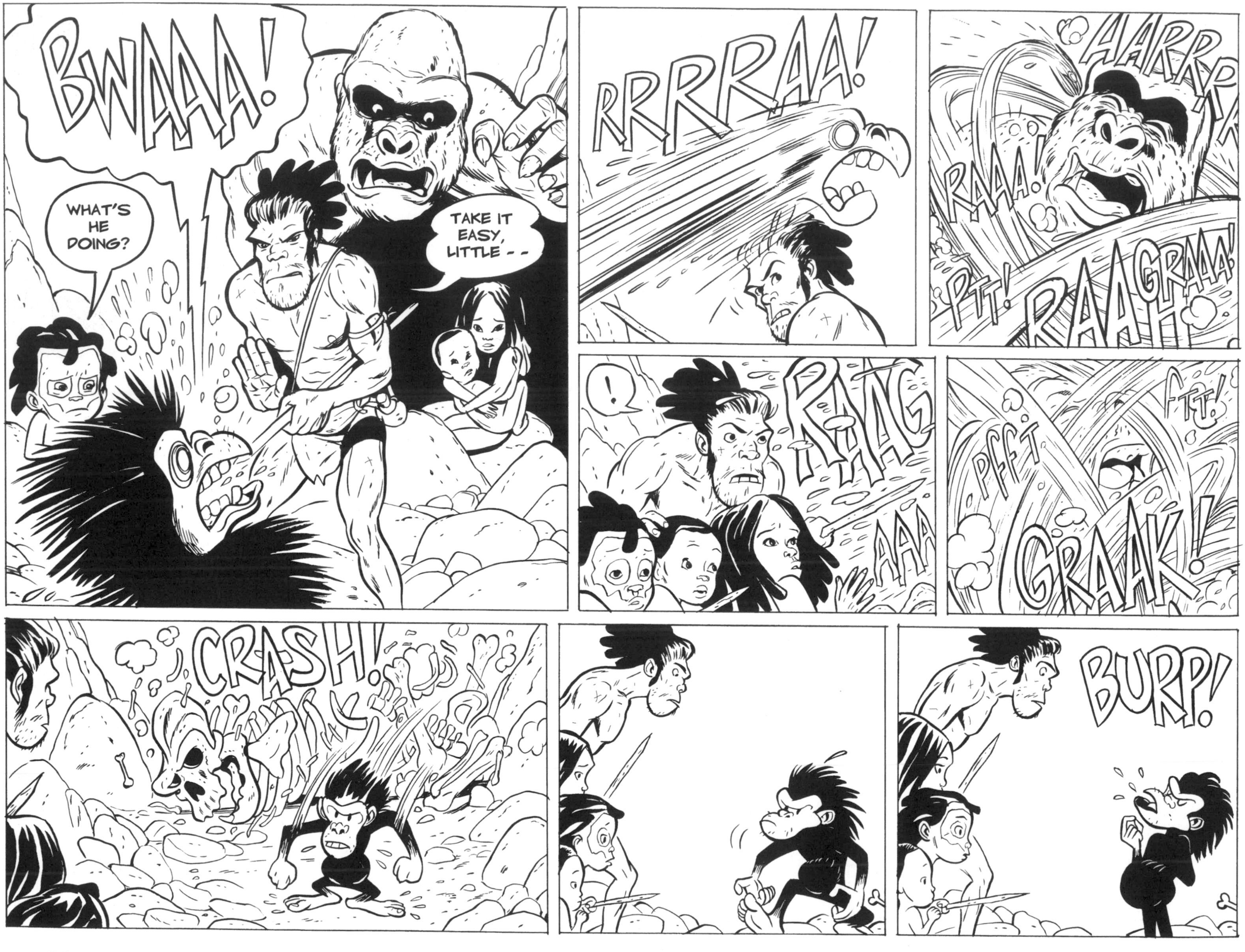

BWAAAA!
WHAT'S HE DOING?
TAKE IT EASY, LITTLE - -
RRRRAA!
AARRRRR
RAAA!
PTT!
RAAGRAAA!
RAAAH
!
RAAG
AAA
PFFT
FTT!
GRAAK!
CRASH!
BURP!

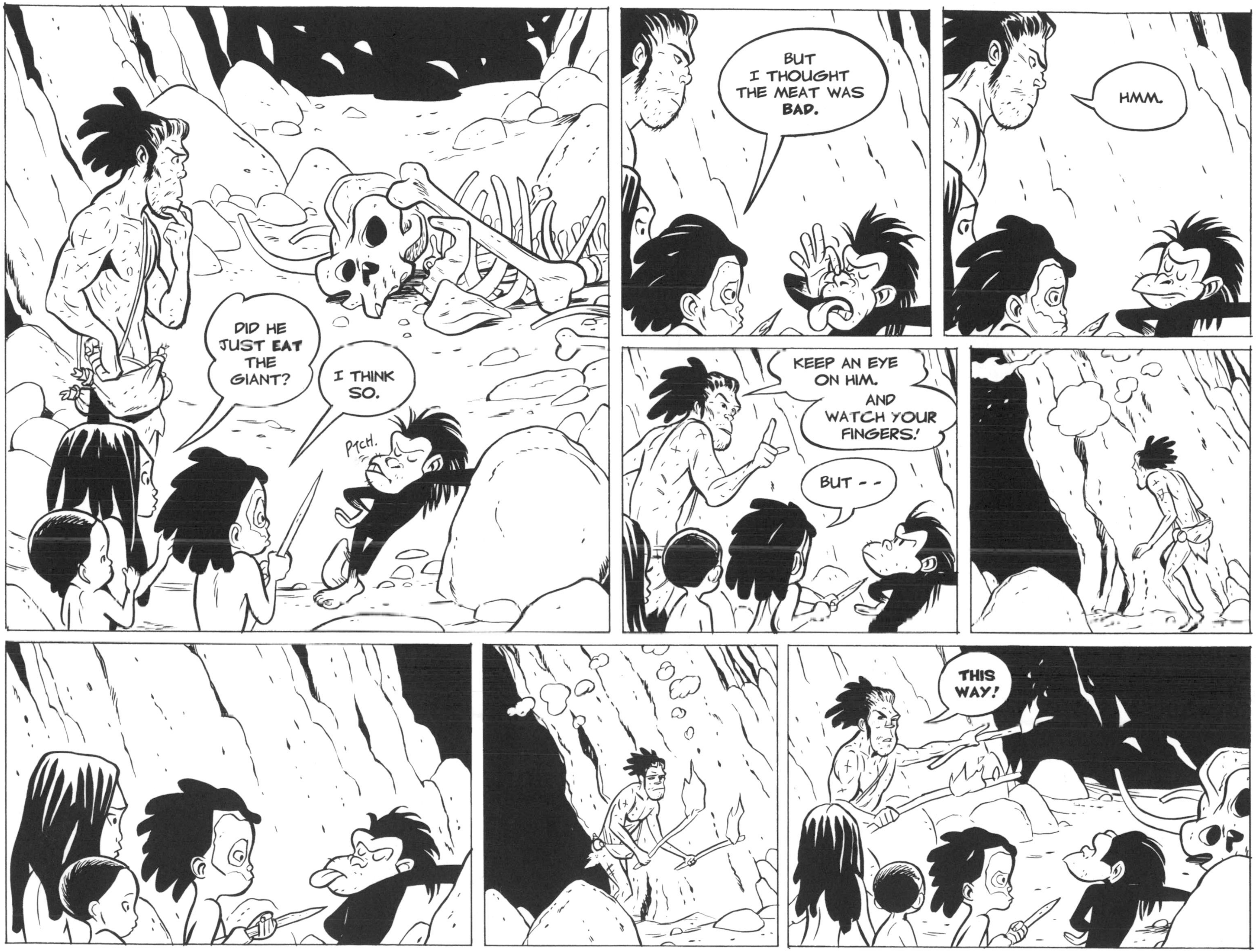
DID HE JUST EAT THE GIANT?
I THINK SO.
PTCH.
BUT I THOUGHT THE MEAT WAS BAD.
HMM.
KEEP AN EYE ON HIM.
AND WATCH YOUR FINGERS!
BUT --
THIS WAY!

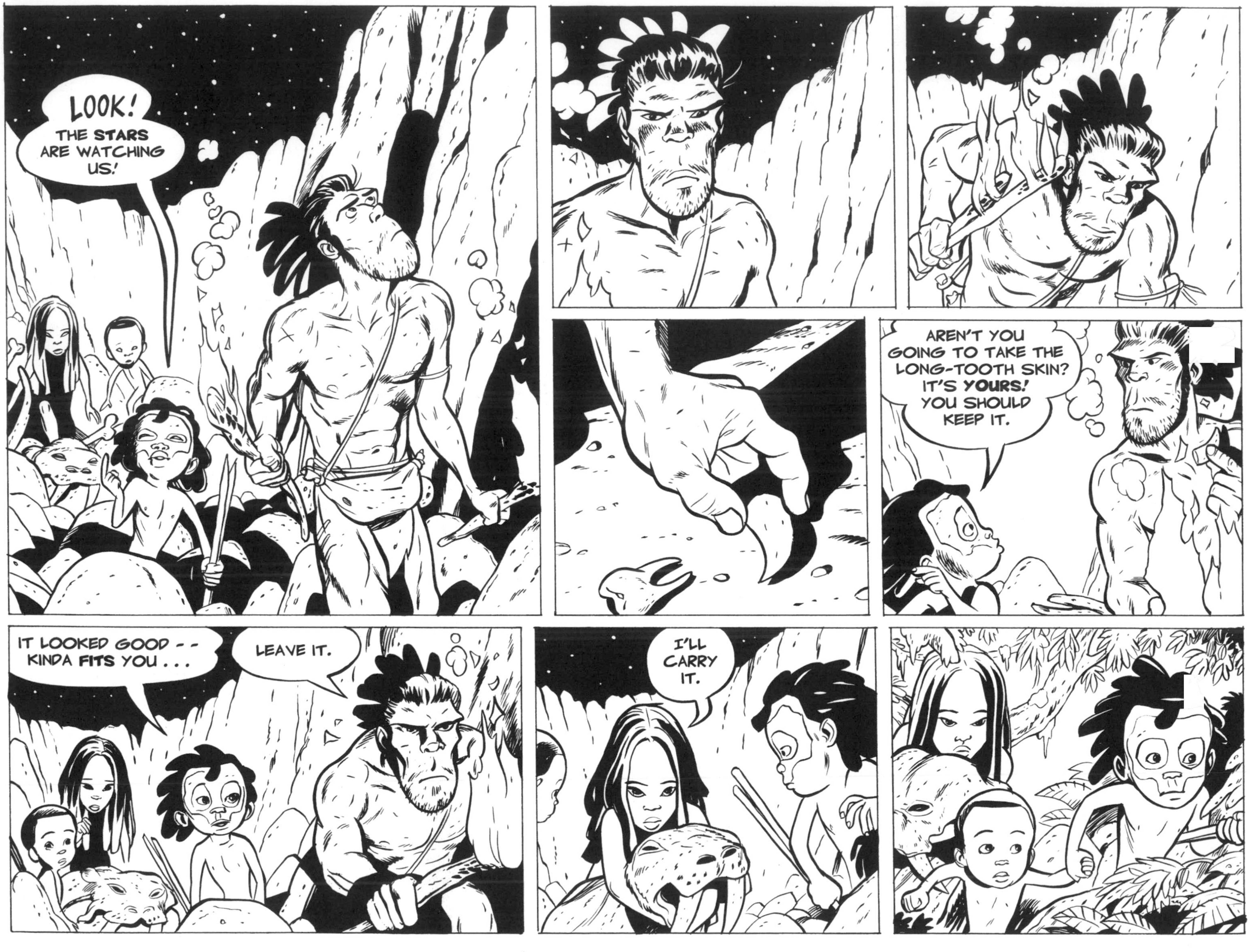
LOOK! THE STARS ARE WATCHING US!
AREN'T YOU GOING TO TAKE THE LONG-TOOTH SKIN? IT'S YOURS! YOU SHOULD KEEP IT.
IT LOOKED GOOD -- KINDA FITS YOU . . .
LEAVE IT.
I'LL CARRY IT.

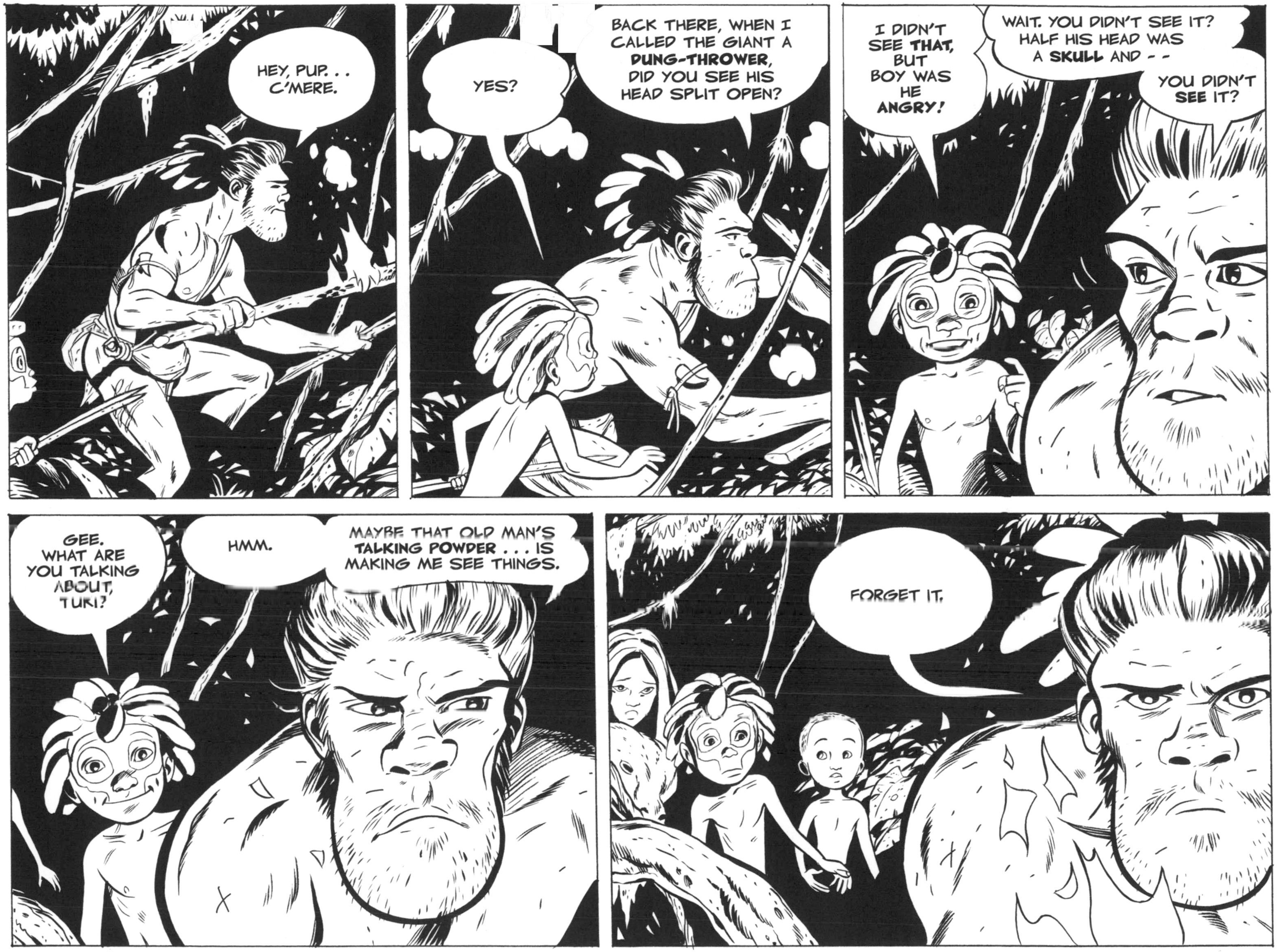
HEY, PUP. . .
C'MERE.
YES?
BACK THERE, WHEN I CALLED THE GIANT A **DUNG-THROWER**, DID YOU SEE HIS HEAD SPLIT OPEN?
I DIDN'T SEE **THAT**, BUT BOY WAS HE **ANGRY!**
WAIT. YOU DIDN'T SEE IT? HALF HIS HEAD WAS A **SKULL** AND - -
YOU DIDN'T **SEE** IT?
GEE. WHAT ARE YOU TALKING ABOUT, TURI?
HMM.
MAYBE THAT OLD MAN'S **TALKING POWDER** . . . IS MAKING ME SEE THINGS.
FORGET IT.

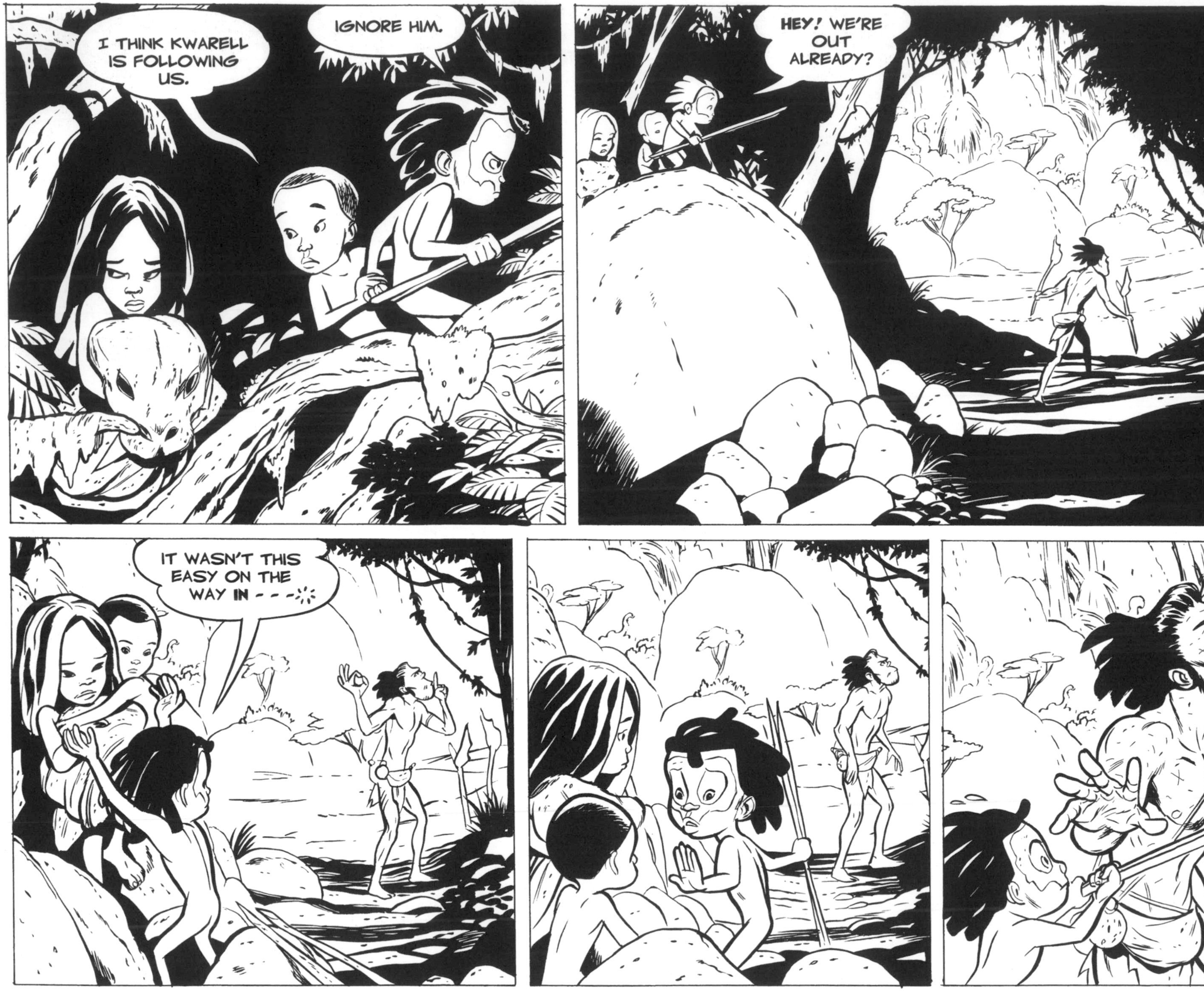
I THINK KWARELL IS FOLLOWING US.
IGNORE HIM.
HEY! WE'RE OUT ALREADY?
IT WASN'T THIS EASY ON THE WAY IN - - -

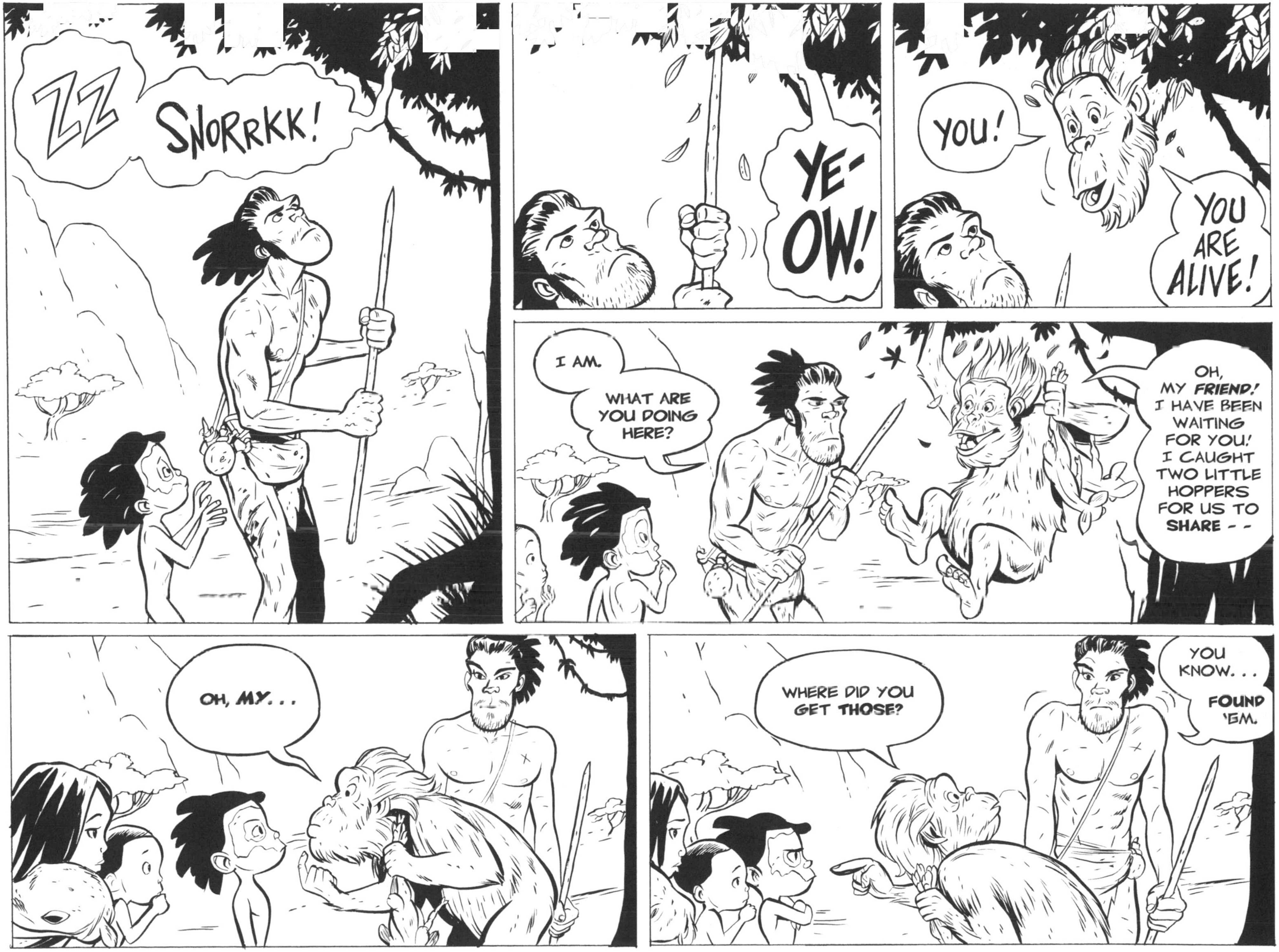
ZZ
SNORRKK!
YE-OW!
YOU!
YOU ARE ALIVE!
I AM.
WHAT ARE YOU DOING HERE?
OH, MY FRIEND! I HAVE BEEN WAITING FOR YOU! I CAUGHT TWO LITTLE HOPPERS FOR US TO SHARE --
OH, MY...
WHERE DID YOU GET THOSE?
YOU KNOW...
FOUND 'EM.

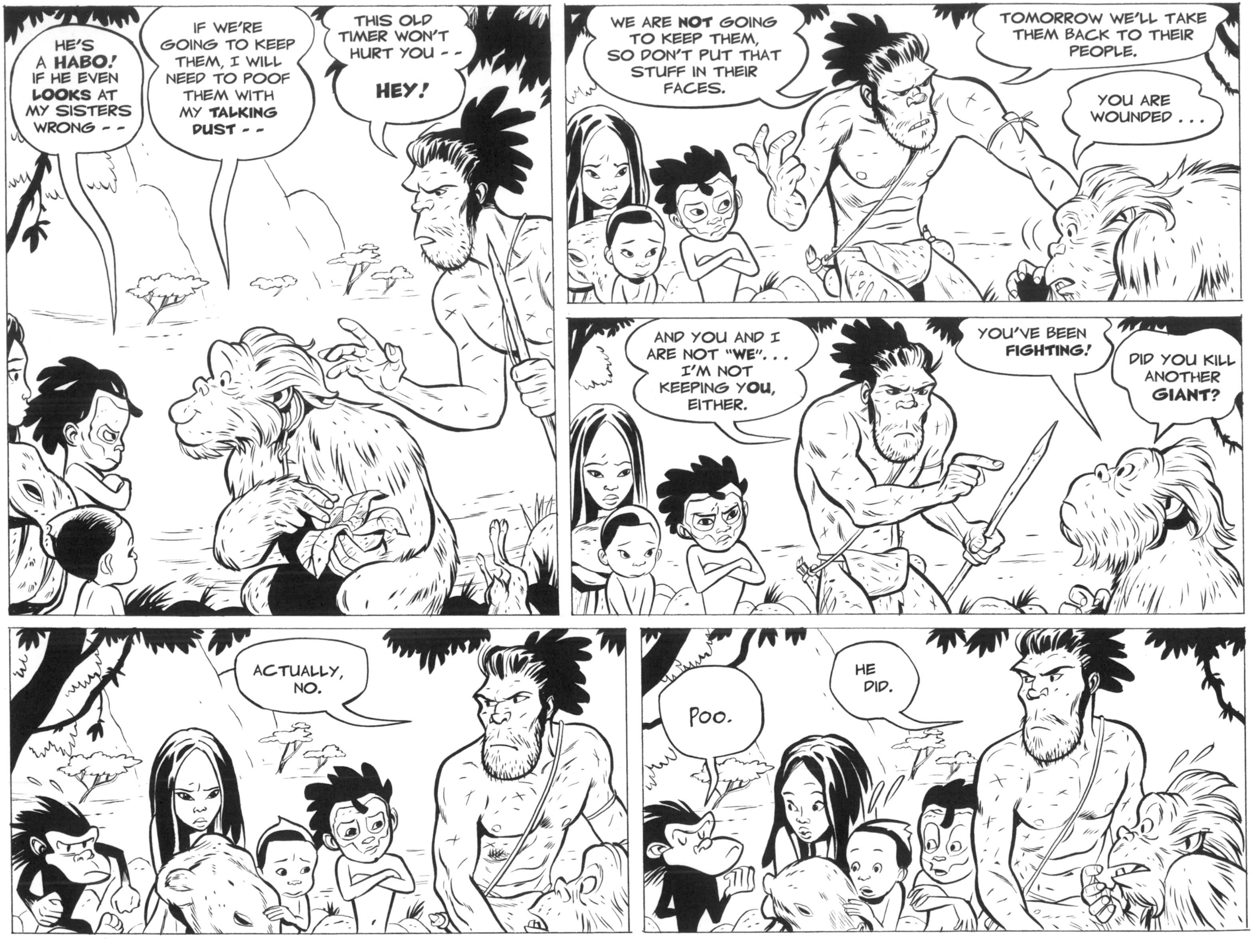
HE'S A **HABO!** IF HE EVEN **LOOKS** AT MY SISTERS WRONG - -
IF WE'RE GOING TO KEEP THEM, I WILL NEED TO POOF THEM WITH MY **TALKING DUST** - -
THIS OLD TIMER WON'T HURT YOU - -
HEY!
WE ARE **NOT** GOING TO KEEP THEM, SO DON'T PUT THAT STUFF IN THEIR FACES.
TOMORROW WE'LL TAKE THEM BACK TO THEIR PEOPLE.
YOU ARE WOUNDED . . .
AND YOU AND I ARE NOT "**WE**". . . I'M NOT KEEPING Y**OU**, EITHER.
YOU'VE BEEN **FIGHTING!**
DID YOU KILL ANOTHER **GIANT?**
ACTUALLY, NO.
POO.
HE DID.

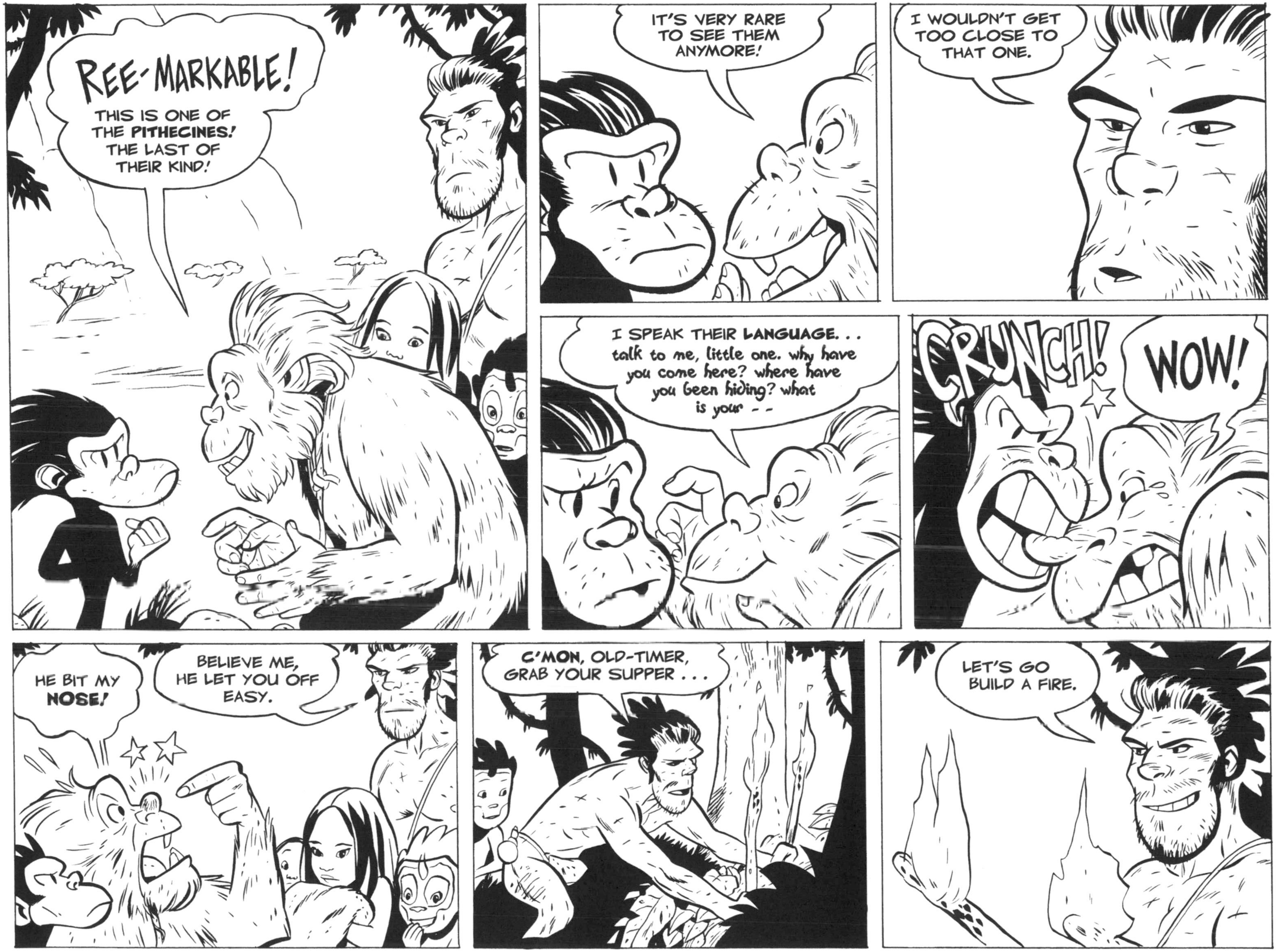

REE-MARKABLE! THIS IS ONE OF THE **PITHECINES!** THE LAST OF THEIR KIND!
IT'S VERY RARE TO SEE THEM ANYMORE!
I WOULDN'T GET TOO CLOSE TO THAT ONE.
I SPEAK THEIR **LANGUAGE**... talk to me, little one. why have you come here? where have you been hiding? what is your --
CRUNCH!
WOW!
HE BIT MY **NOSE!**
BELIEVE ME, HE LET YOU OFF EASY.
C'MON, OLD-TIMER, GRAB YOUR SUPPER...
LET'S GO BUILD A FIRE.

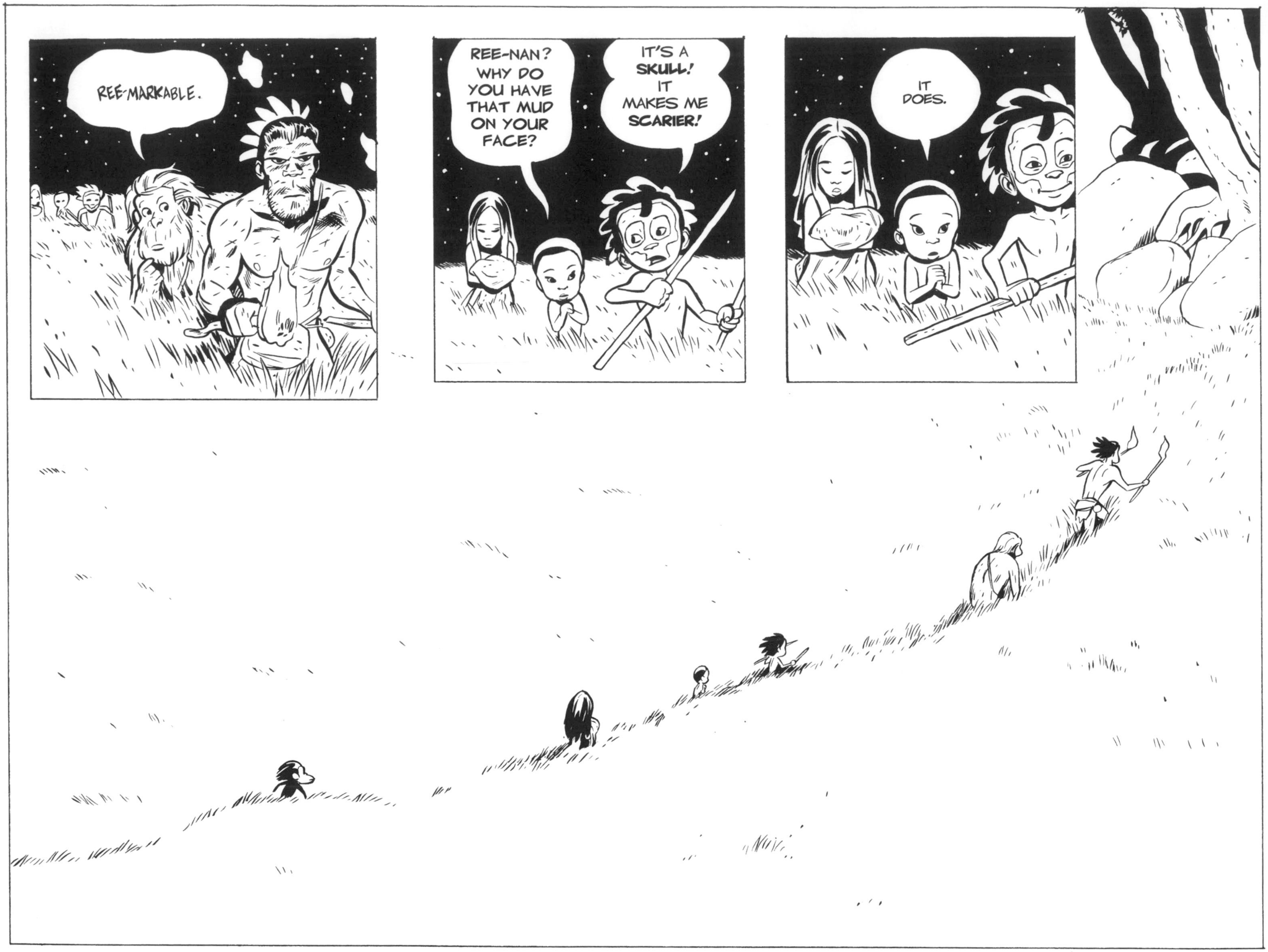
REE-MARKABLE.
REE-NAN? WHY DO YOU HAVE THAT MUD ON YOUR FACE?
IT'S A **SKULL!** IT MAKES ME **SCARIER!**
IT DOES.

Five

Fire

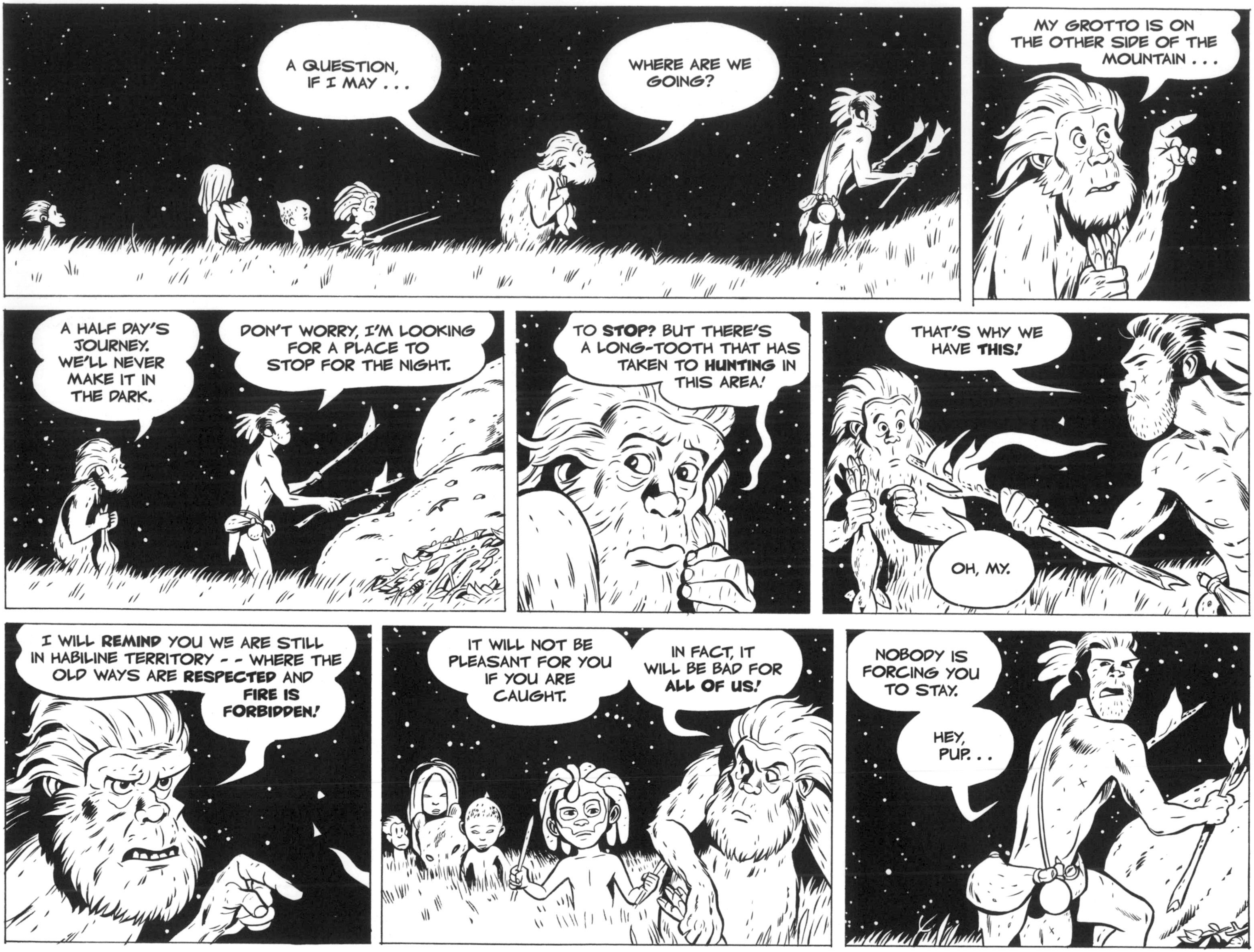
A QUESTION, IF I MAY . . .
WHERE ARE WE GOING?
MY GROTTO IS ON THE OTHER SIDE OF THE MOUNTAIN . . .
A HALF DAY'S JOURNEY. WE'LL NEVER MAKE IT IN THE DARK.
DON'T WORRY, I'M LOOKING FOR A PLACE TO STOP FOR THE NIGHT.
TO **STOP**? BUT THERE'S A LONG-TOOTH THAT HAS TAKEN TO **HUNTING** IN THIS AREA!
THAT'S WHY WE HAVE **THIS!**
OH, MY.
I WILL **REMIND** YOU WE ARE STILL IN HABILINE TERRITORY - - WHERE THE OLD WAYS ARE **RESPECTED** AND **FIRE IS FORBIDDEN!**
IT WILL NOT BE PLEASANT FOR YOU IF YOU ARE CAUGHT.
IN FACT, IT WILL BE BAD FOR **ALL OF US!**
NOBODY IS FORCING YOU TO STAY.
HEY, PUP. . .

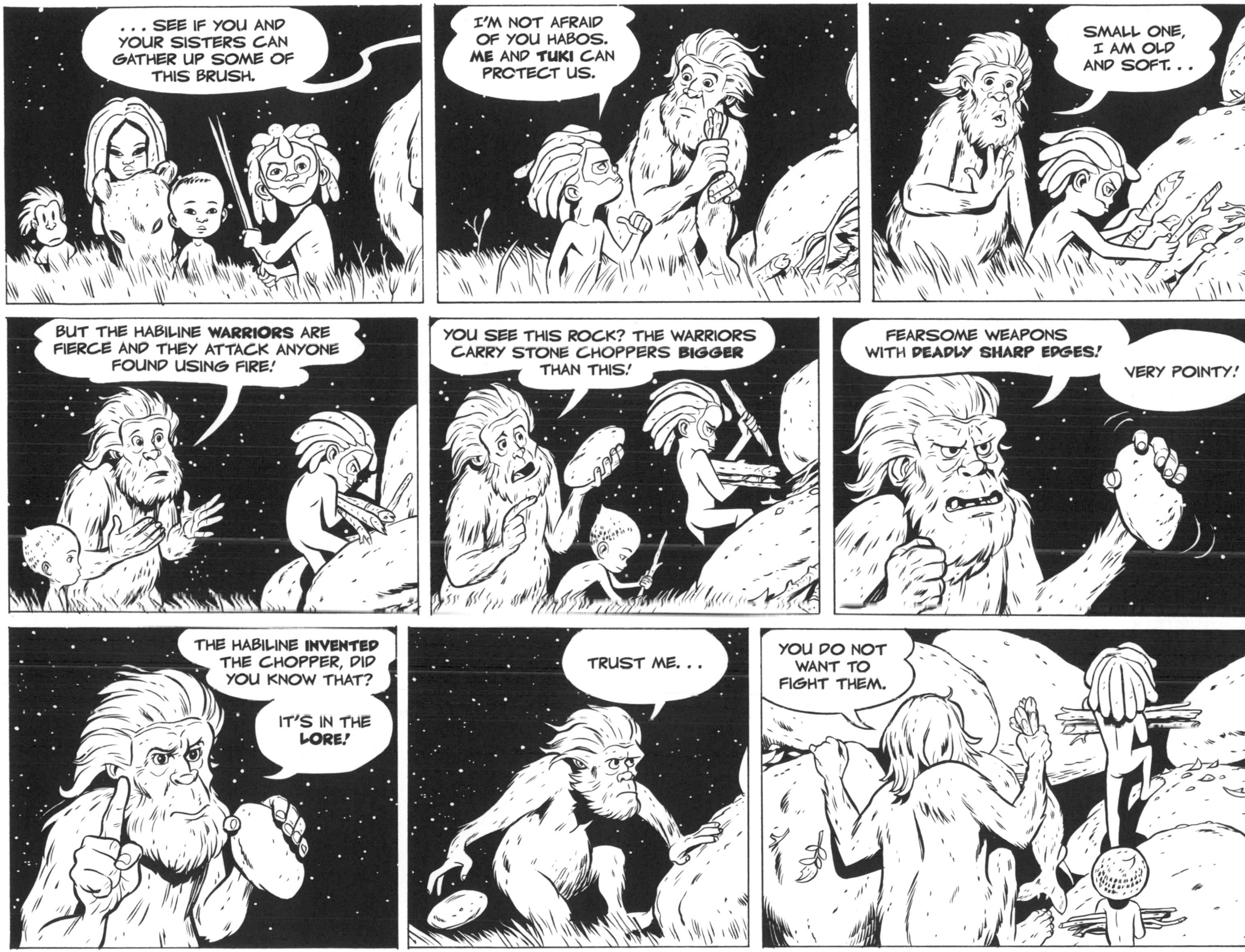
. . . SEE IF YOU AND YOUR SISTERS CAN GATHER UP SOME OF THIS BRUSH.
I'M NOT AFRAID OF YOU HABOS. ME AND TUKI CAN PROTECT US.
SMALL ONE, I AM OLD AND SOFT. . .
BUT THE HABILINE WARRIORS ARE FIERCE AND THEY ATTACK ANYONE FOUND USING FIRE!
YOU SEE THIS ROCK? THE WARRIORS CARRY STONE CHOPPERS BIGGER THAN THIS!
FEARSOME WEAPONS WITH DEADLY SHARP EDGES!
VERY POINTY!
THE HABILINE INVENTED THE CHOPPER, DID YOU KNOW THAT?
IT'S IN THE LORE!
TRUST ME. . .
YOU DO NOT WANT TO FIGHT THEM.

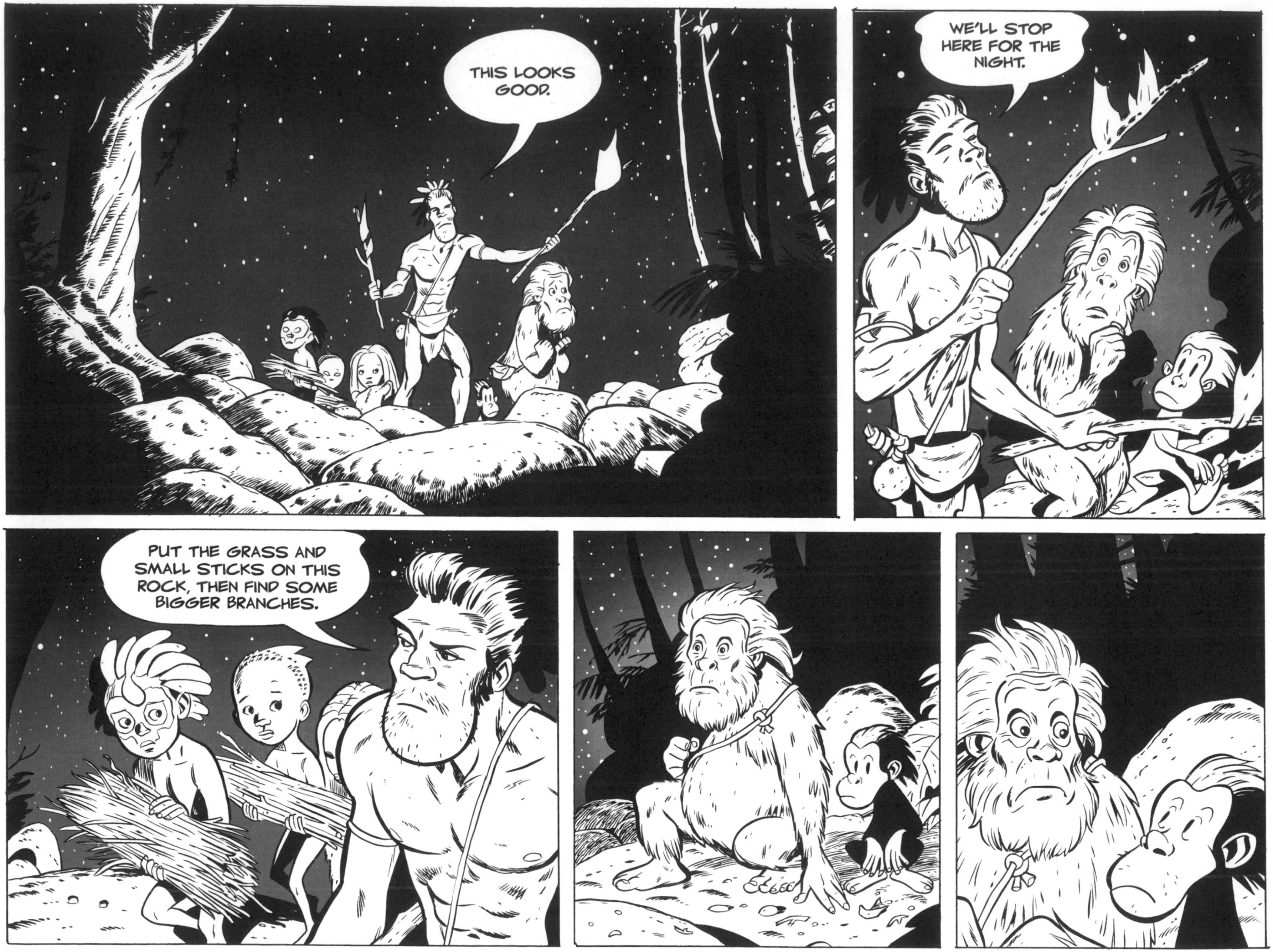
THIS LOOKS GOOD.
WE'LL STOP HERE FOR THE NIGHT.
PUT THE GRASS AND SMALL STICKS ON THIS ROCK, THEN FIND SOME BIGGER BRANCHES.

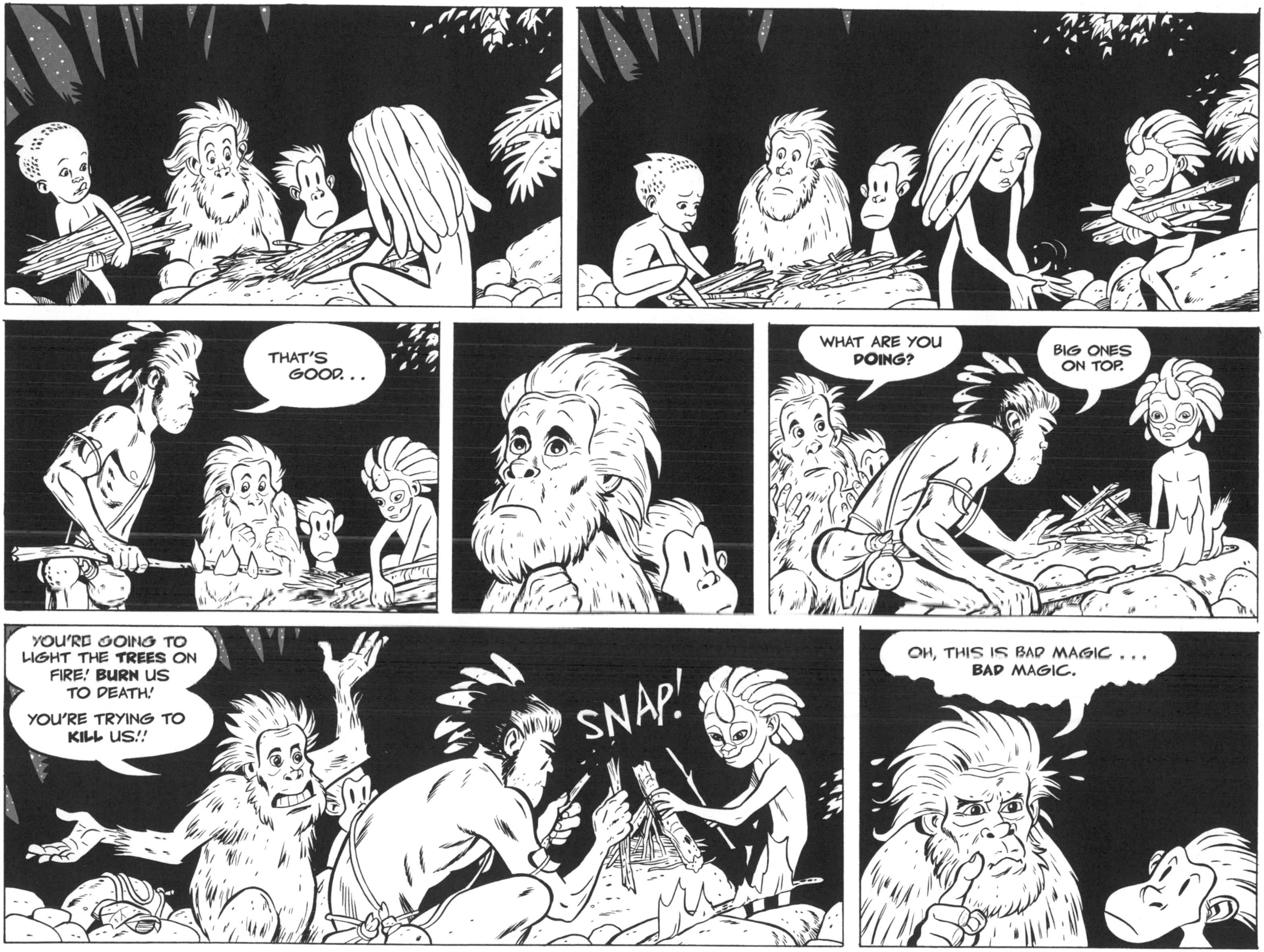
THAT'S GOOD. . .
WHAT ARE YOU **DOING?**
BIG ONES ON TOP.
YOU'RE GOING TO LIGHT THE **TREES** ON FIRE! **BURN** US TO DEATH!
YOU'RE TRYING TO **KILL** US!!
SNAP!
OH, THIS IS BAD MAGIC . . . **BAD MAGIC.**

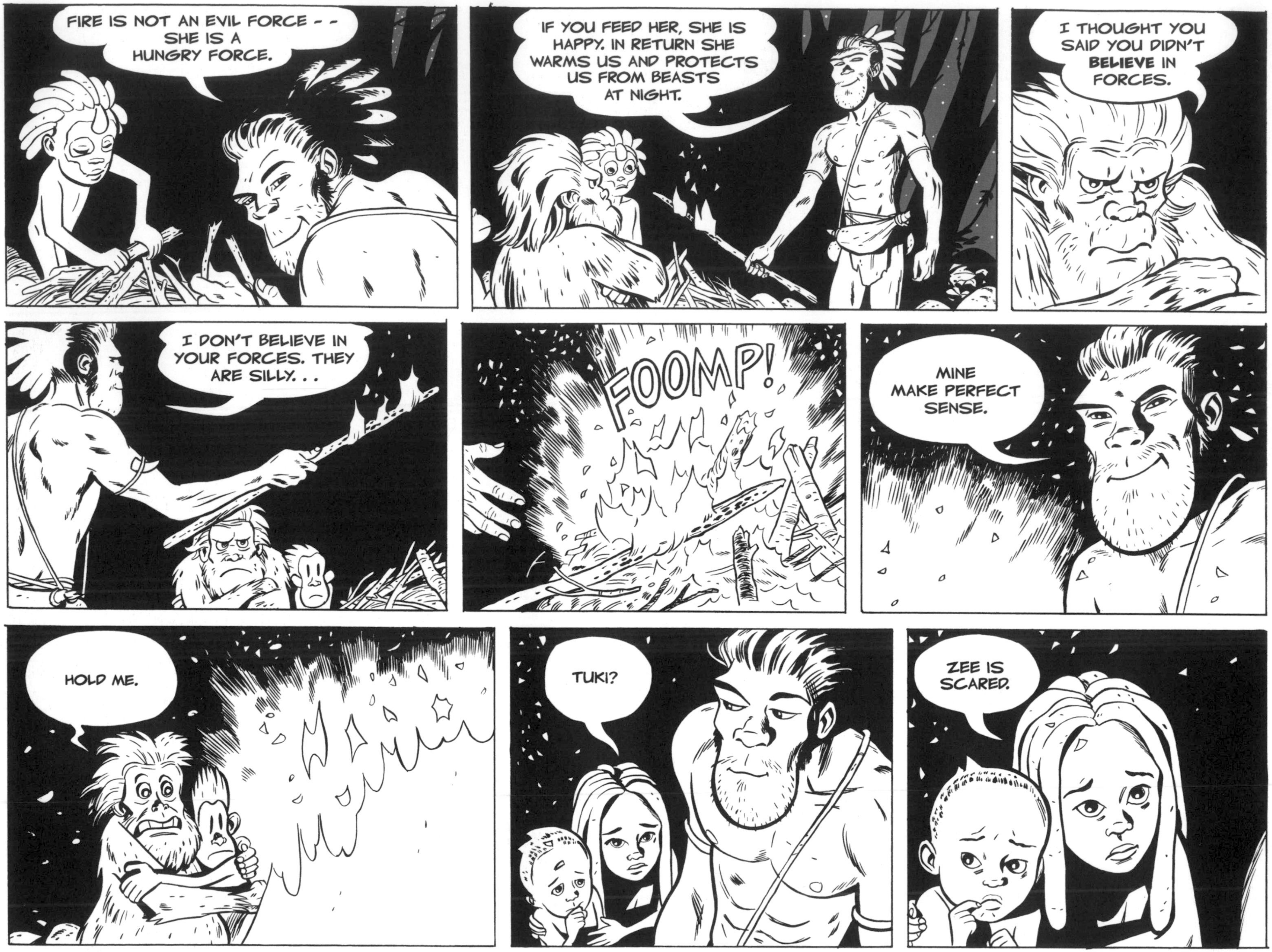
FIRE IS NOT AN EVIL FORCE - - SHE IS A HUNGRY FORCE.
IF YOU FEED HER, SHE IS HAPPY. IN RETURN SHE WARMS US AND PROTECTS US FROM BEASTS AT NIGHT.
I THOUGHT YOU SAID YOU DIDN'T **BELIEVE** IN FORCES.
I DON'T BELIEVE IN YOUR FORCES. THEY ARE SILLY. . .
FOOMP!
MINE MAKE PERFECT SENSE.
HOLD ME.
TUKI?
ZEE IS SCARED.

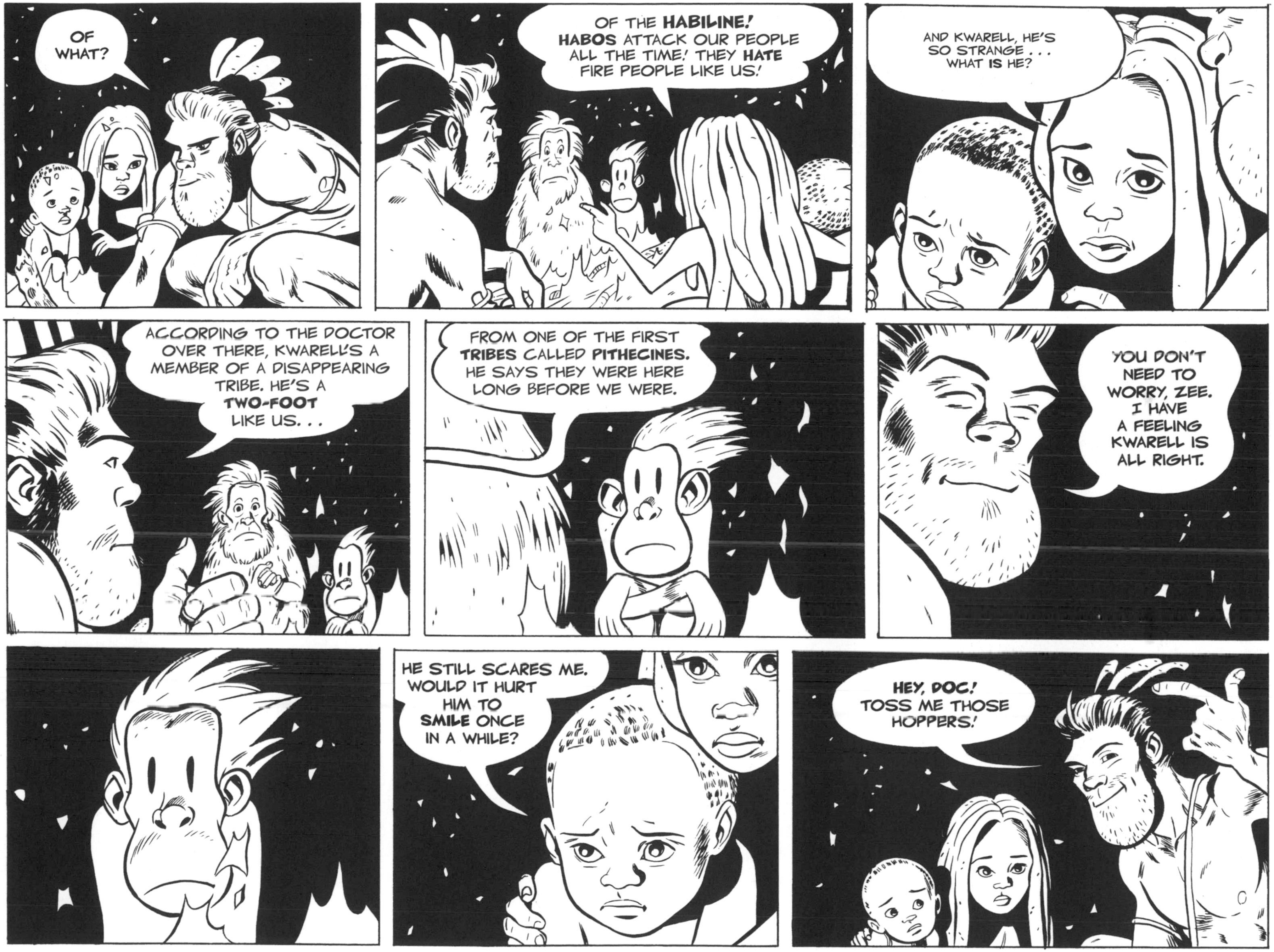
OF WHAT?
OF THE HABILINE! HABOS ATTACK OUR PEOPLE ALL THE TIME! THEY HATE FIRE PEOPLE LIKE US!
AND KWARELL, HE'S SO STRANGE . . . WHAT IS HE?
ACCORDING TO THE DOCTOR OVER THERE, KWARELL'S A MEMBER OF A DISAPPEARING TRIBE. HE'S A TWO-FOOT LIKE US. . .
FROM ONE OF THE FIRST TRIBES CALLED PITHECINES. HE SAYS THEY WERE HERE LONG BEFORE WE WERE.
YOU DON'T NEED TO WORRY, ZEE. I HAVE A FEELING KWARELL IS ALL RIGHT.
HE STILL SCARES ME. WOULD IT HURT HIM TO SMILE ONCE IN A WHILE?
HEY, DOC! TOSS ME THOSE HOPPERS!

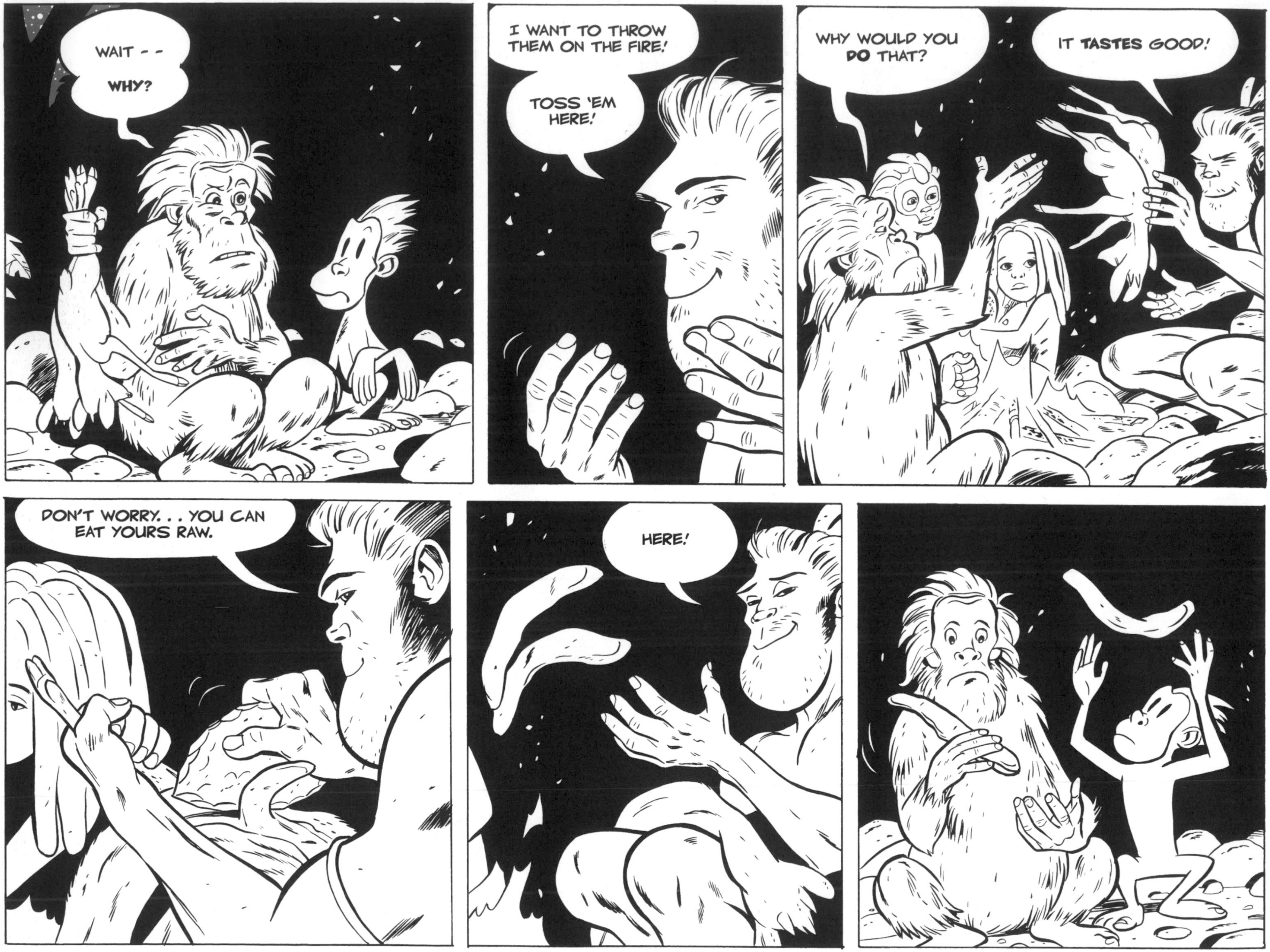
WAIT - - WHY?
I WANT TO THROW THEM ON THE FIRE!
TOSS 'EM HERE!
WHY WOULD YOU DO THAT?
IT TASTES GOOD!
DON'T WORRY. . . YOU CAN EAT YOURS RAW.
HERE!

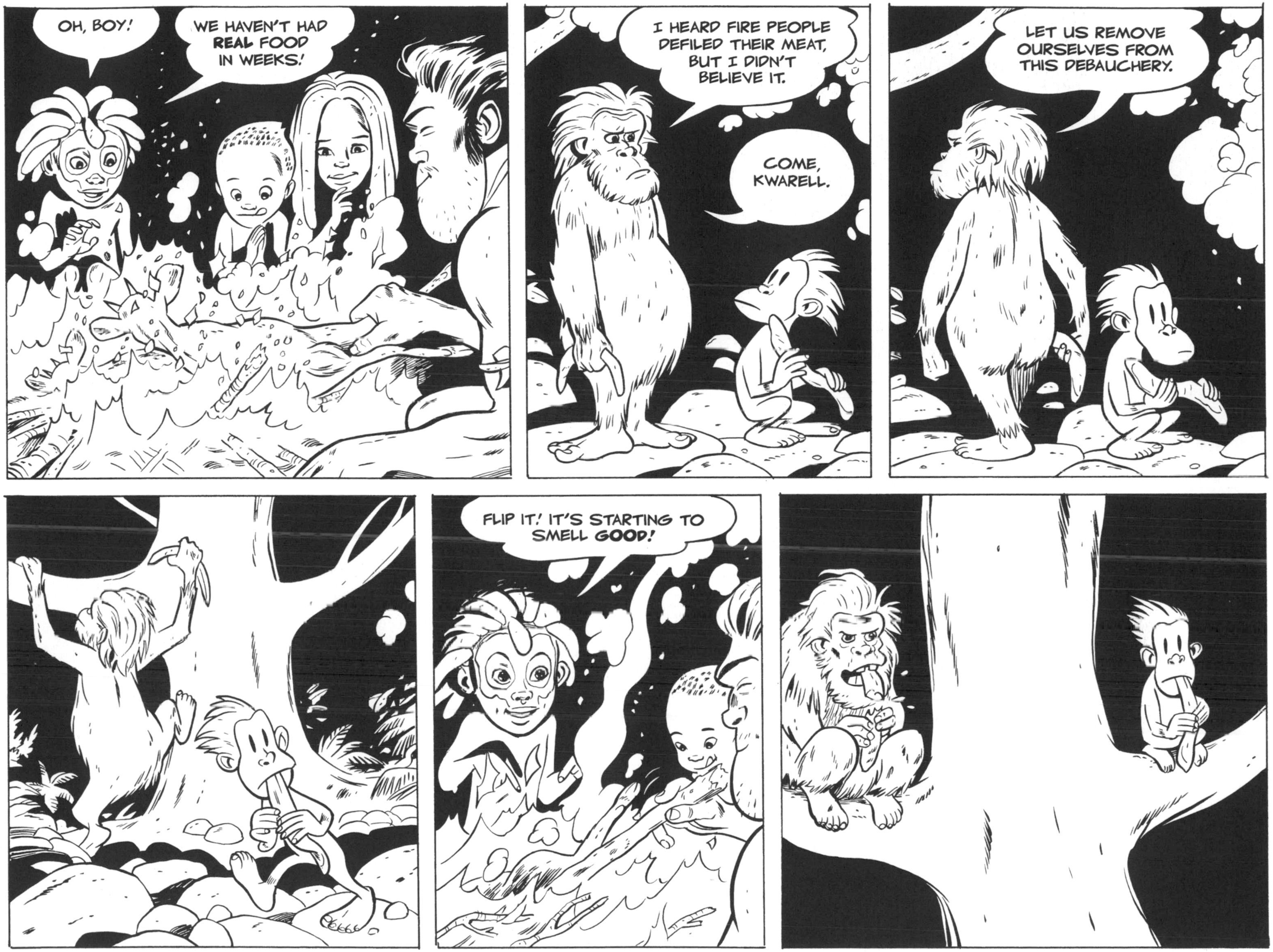
OH, BOY!
WE HAVEN'T HAD **REAL** FOOD IN WEEKS!
I HEARD FIRE PEOPLE DEFILED THEIR MEAT, BUT I DIDN'T BELIEVE IT.
COME, KWARELL.
LET US REMOVE OURSELVES FROM THIS DEBAUCHERY.
FLIP IT! IT'S STARTING TO SMELL **GOOD**!

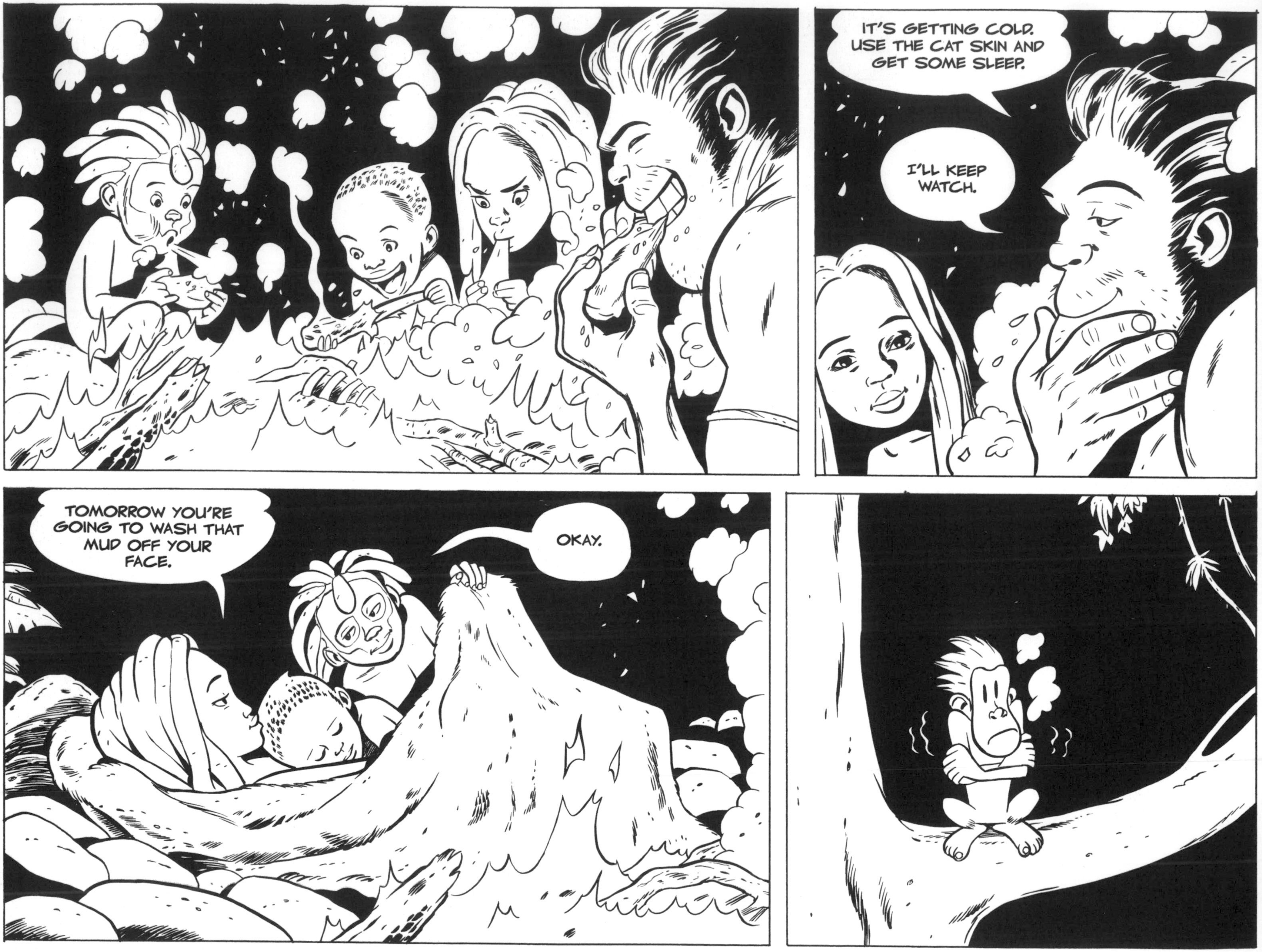
IT'S GETTING COLD. USE THE CAT SKIN AND GET SOME SLEEP.
I'LL KEEP WATCH.
TOMORROW YOU'RE GOING TO WASH THAT MUD OFF YOUR FACE.
OKAY.

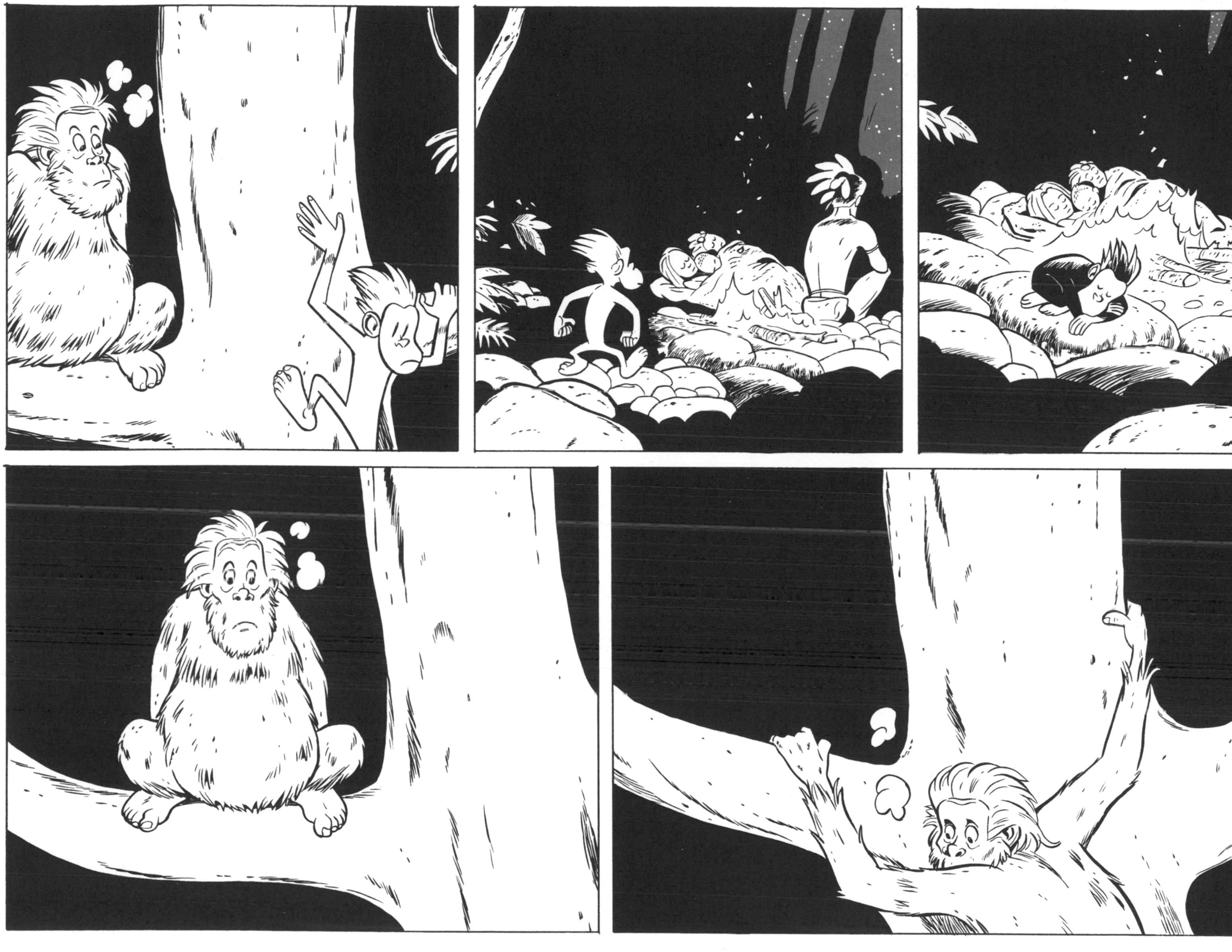

Six

The Gift

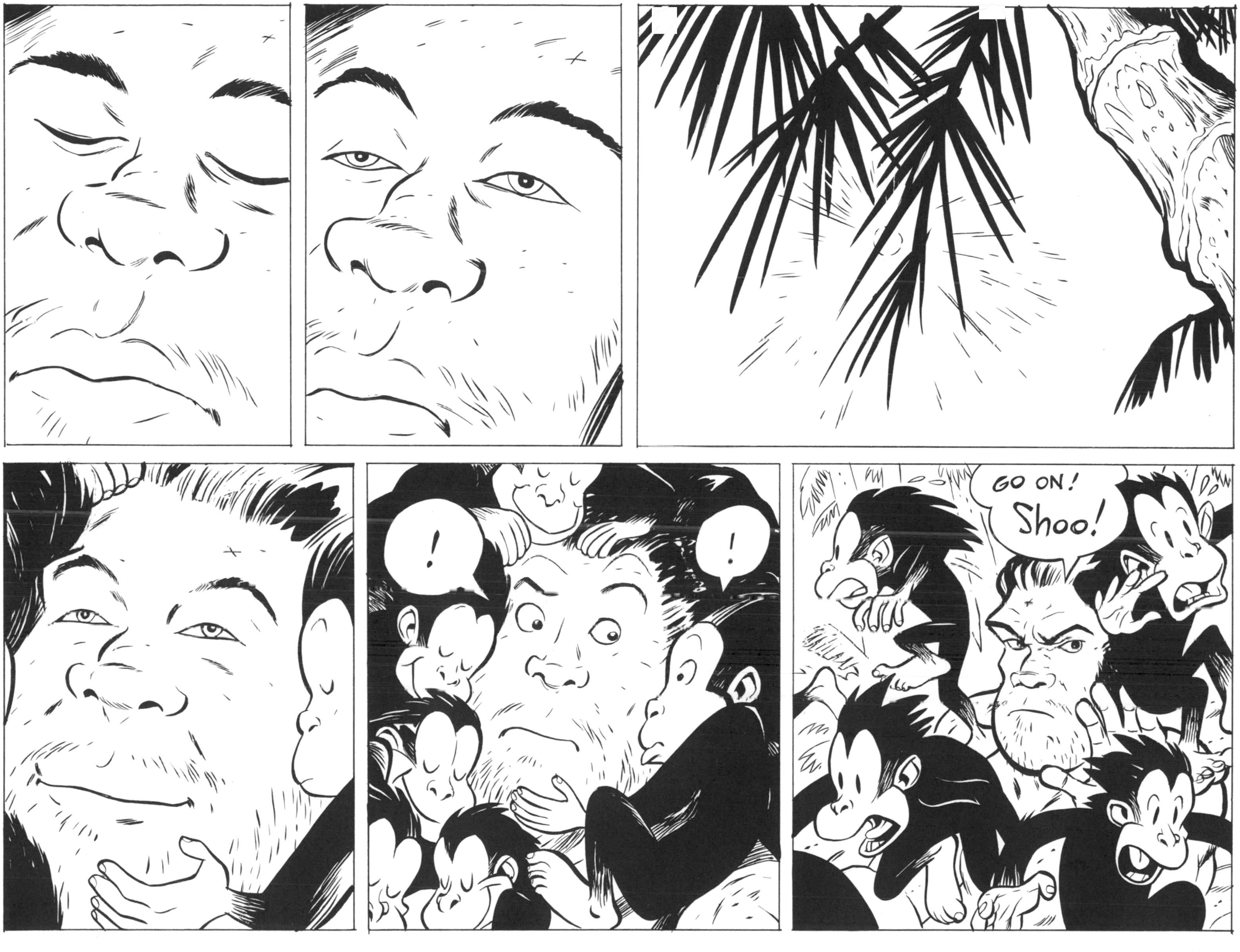
!
!
GO ON!
Shoo!

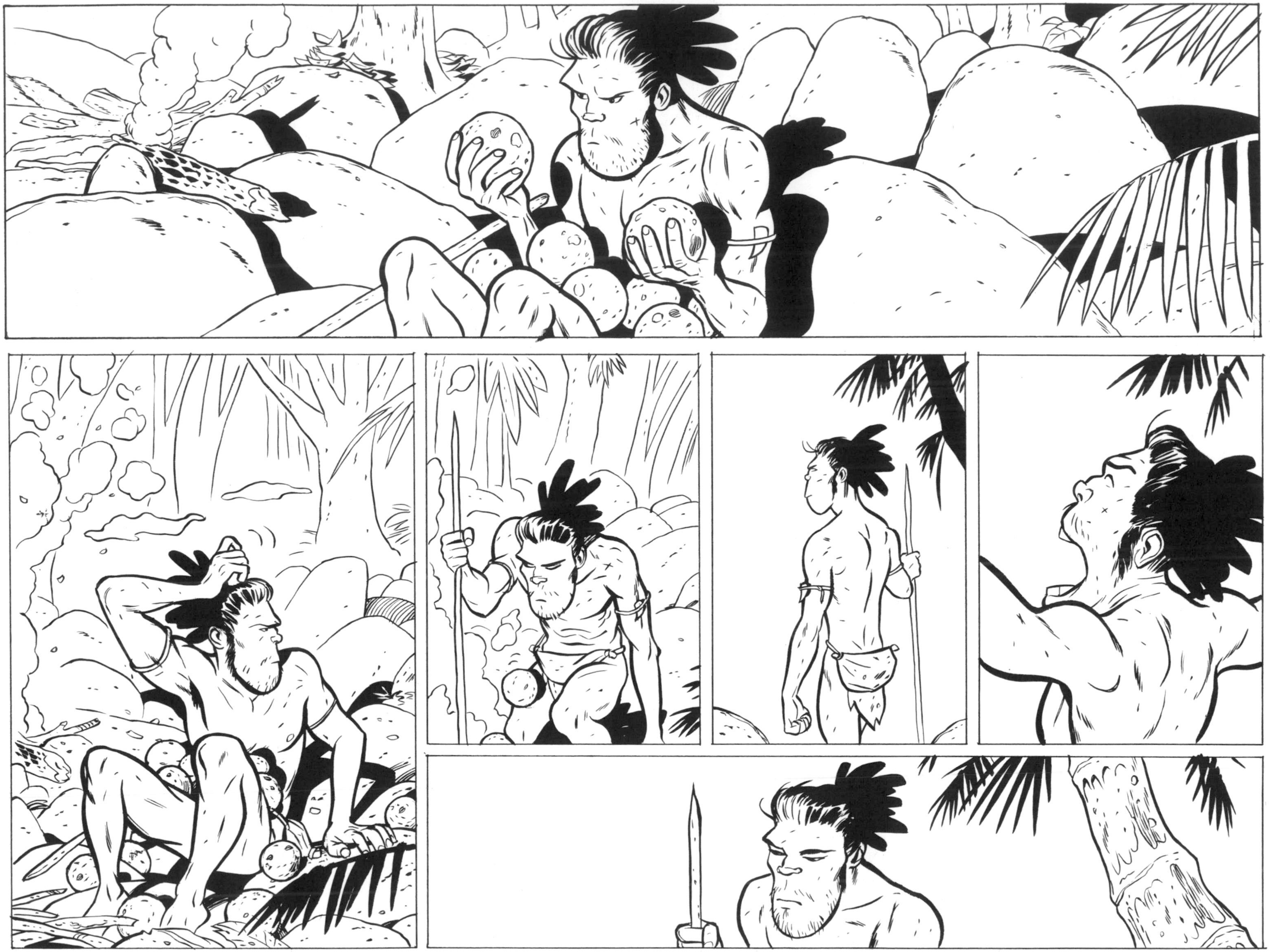

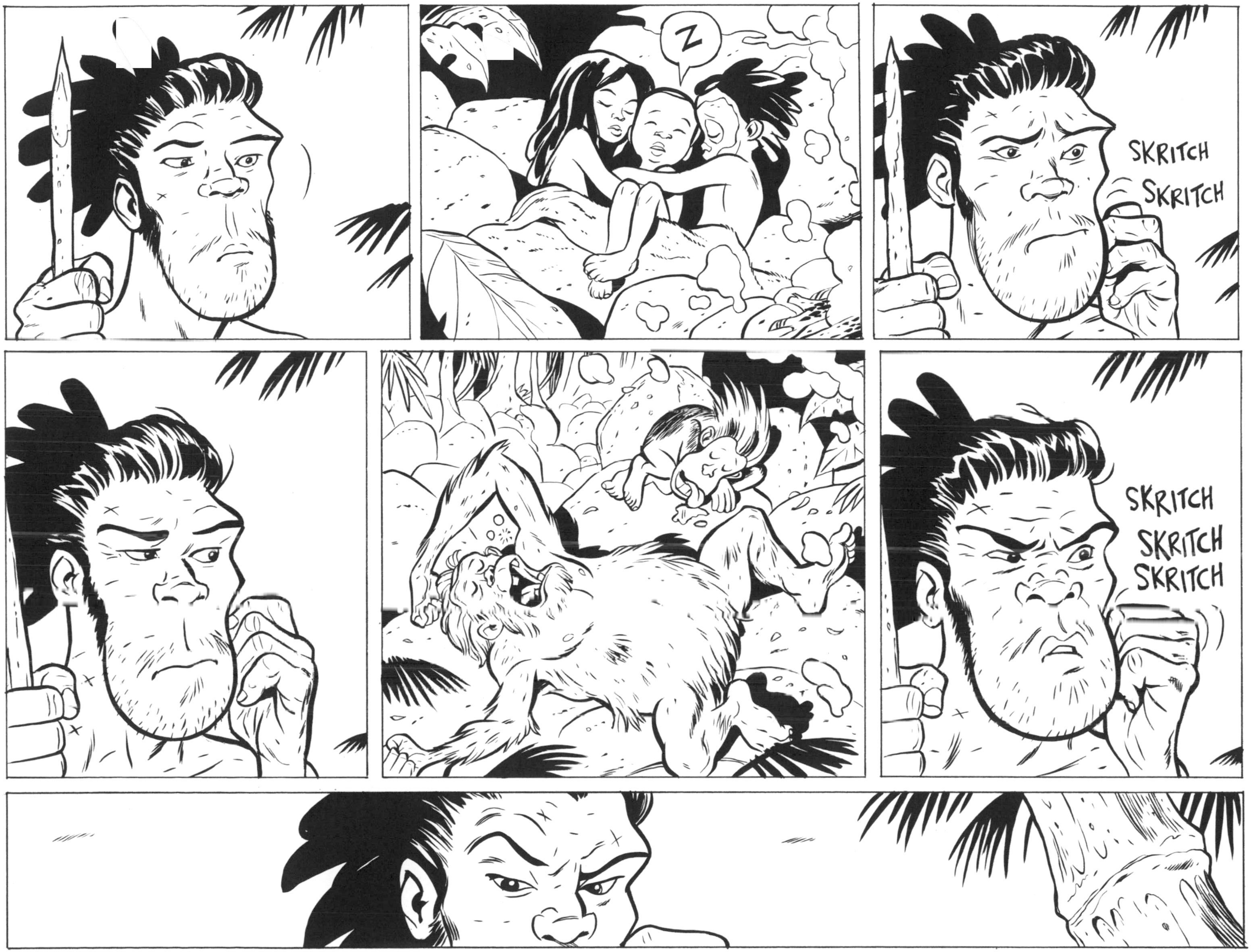
Z
SKRITCH
SKRITCH
SKRITCH
SKRITCH
SKRITCH

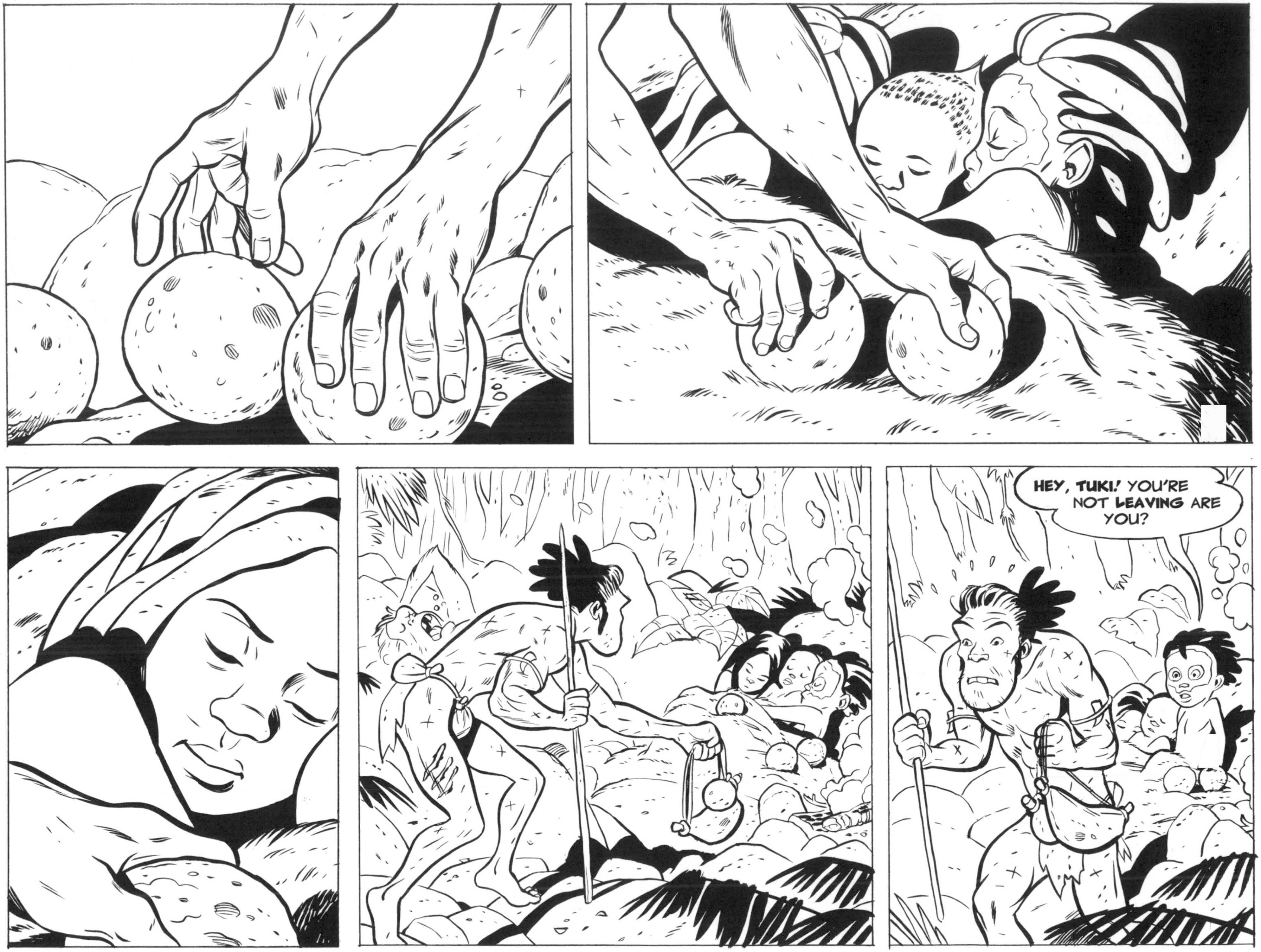
HEY, TUKI! YOU'RE NOT LEAVING ARE YOU?

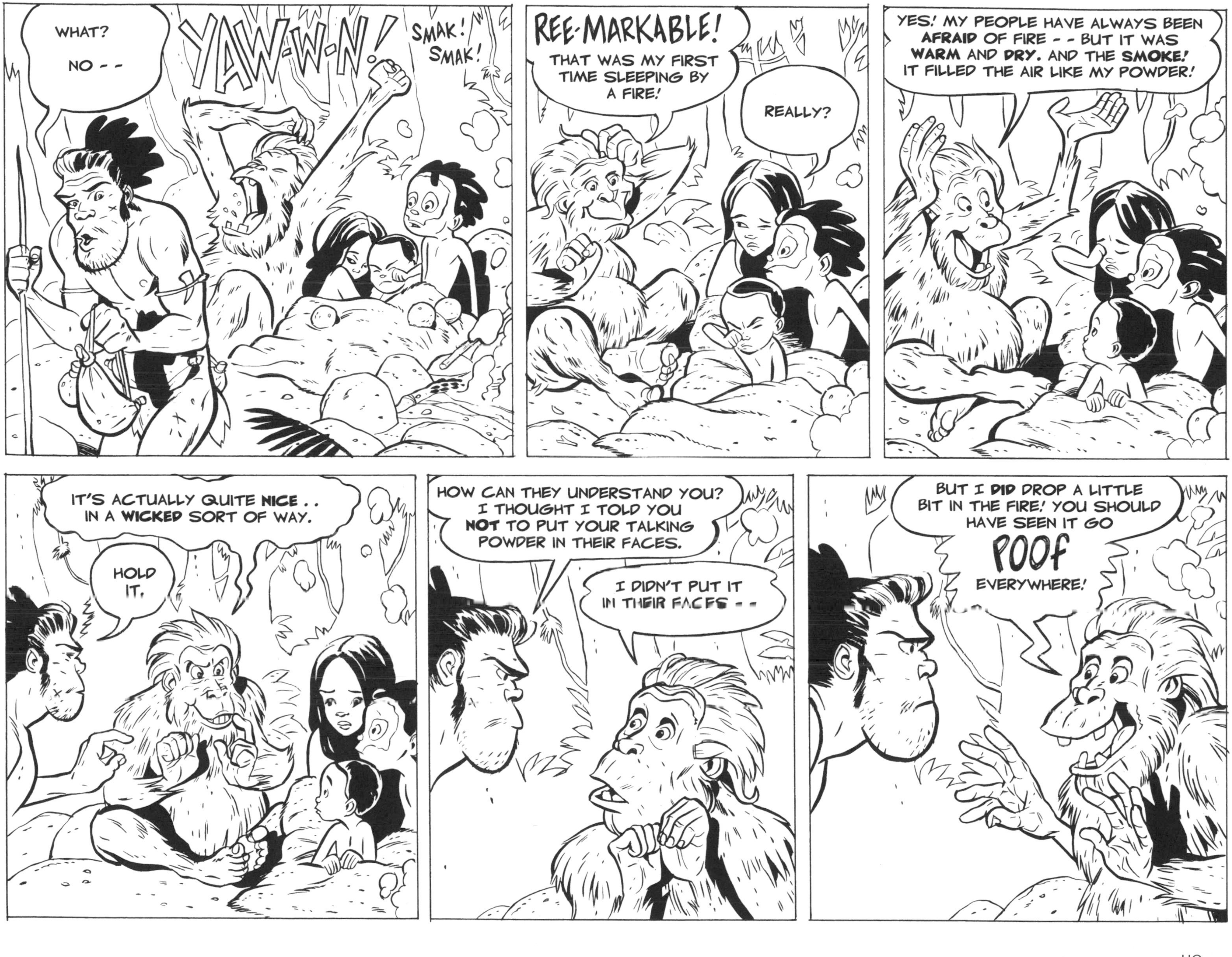
WHAT?
NO - -
YAW-W-N!
SMAK! SMAK!
REE-MARKABLE!
THAT WAS MY FIRST TIME SLEEPING BY A FIRE!
REALLY?
YES! MY PEOPLE HAVE ALWAYS BEEN **AFRAID** OF FIRE - - BUT IT WAS **WARM** AND **DRY**. AND THE **SMOKE!** IT FILLED THE AIR LIKE MY POWDER!
IT'S ACTUALLY QUITE **NICE** . . IN A **WICKED** SORT OF WAY.
HOLD IT.
HOW CAN THEY UNDERSTAND YOU? I THOUGHT I TOLD YOU **NOT** TO PUT YOUR TALKING POWDER IN THEIR FACES.
I DIDN'T PUT IT IN THEIR FACES - -
BUT I **DID** DROP A LITTLE BIT IN THE FIRE! YOU SHOULD HAVE SEEN IT GO
POOF
EVERYWHERE!

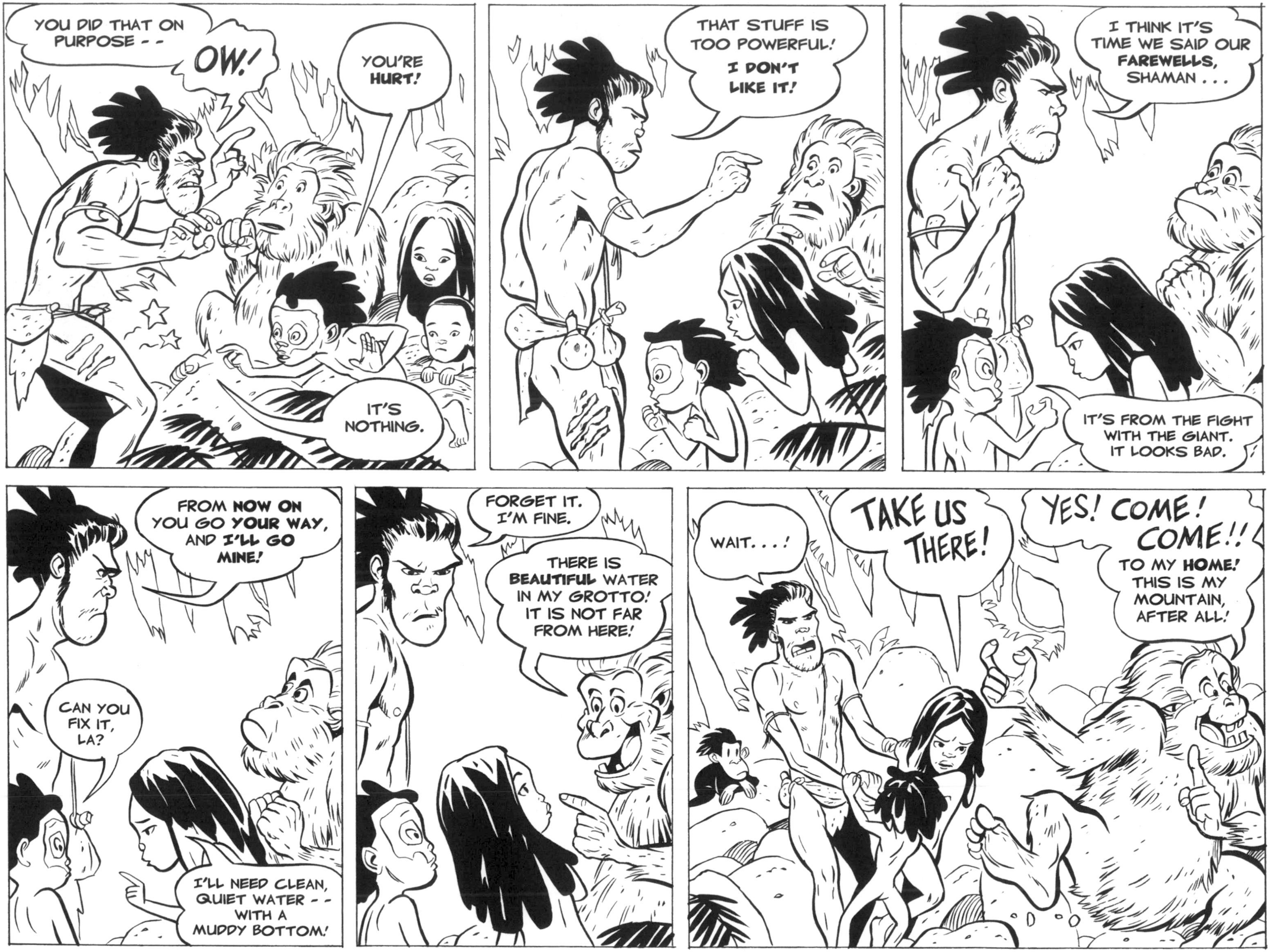
YOU DID THAT ON PURPOSE - -
OW!
YOU'RE **HURT!**
IT'S NOTHING.
THAT STUFF IS TOO POWERFUL! **I DON'T LIKE IT!**
I THINK IT'S TIME WE SAID OUR **FAREWELLS,** SHAMAN . . .
IT'S FROM THE FIGHT WITH THE GIANT. IT LOOKS BAD.
FROM **NOW ON** YOU GO **YOUR** WAY, AND **I'LL GO MINE!**
CAN YOU FIX IT, LA?
I'LL NEED CLEAN, QUIET WATER - - WITH A MUDDY BOTTOM!
FORGET IT. I'M FINE.
THERE IS **BEAUTIFUL** WATER IN MY GROTTO! IT IS NOT FAR FROM HERE!
WAIT. . . !
TAKE US THERE!
YES! COME! COME!!
TO MY **HOME!** THIS IS MY MOUNTAIN, AFTER ALL!

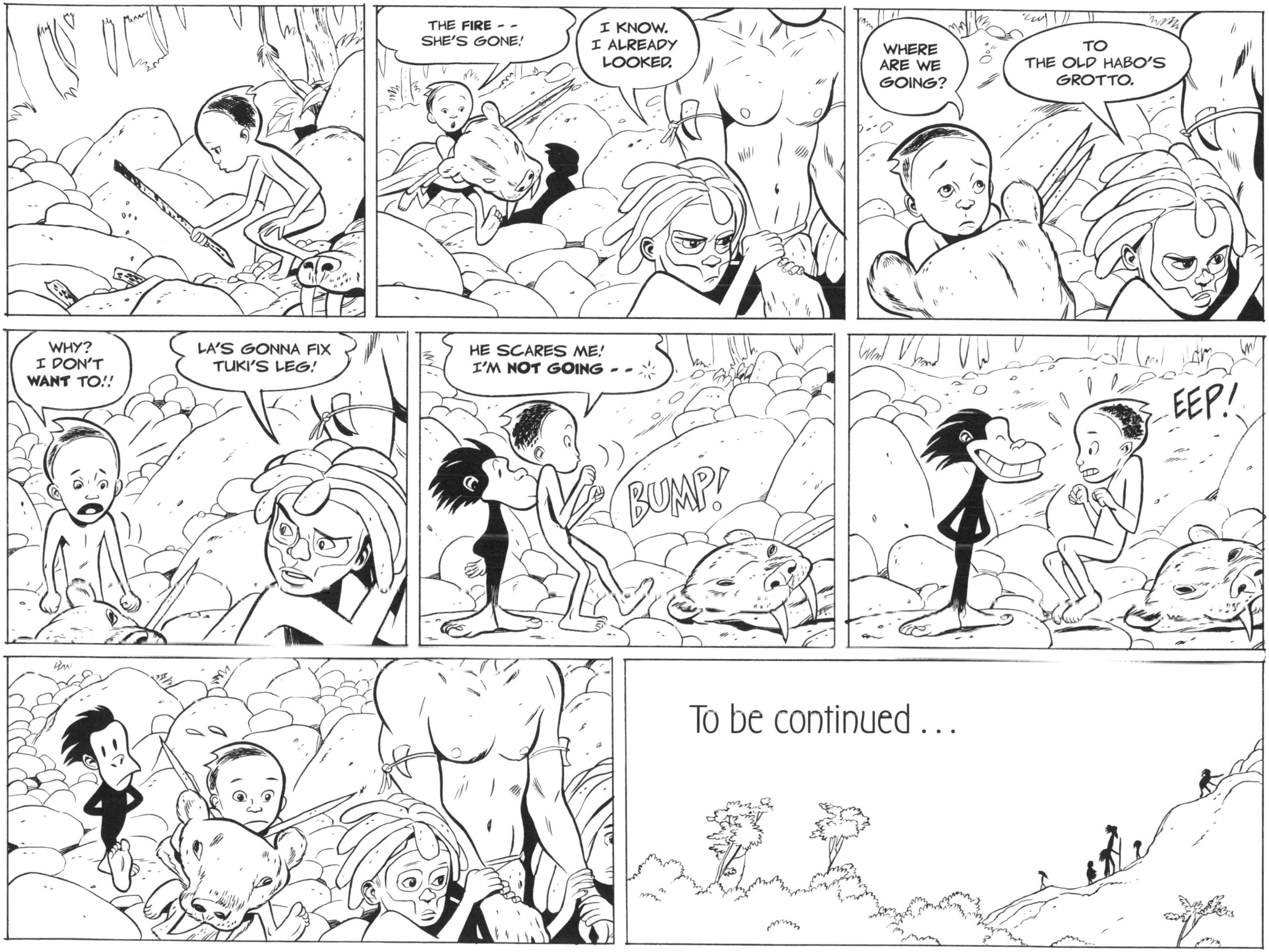
THE **FIRE** - - SHE'S GONE!
I KNOW. I ALREADY LOOKED.
WHERE ARE WE GOING?
TO THE OLD HABO'S GROTTO.
WHY? I DON'T **WANT** TO!!
LA'S GONNA FIX TUKI'S LEG!
HE SCARES ME! I'M **NOT GOING** - -
BUMP!
EEP!
To be continued . . .

JEFF SMITH

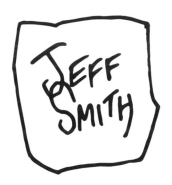

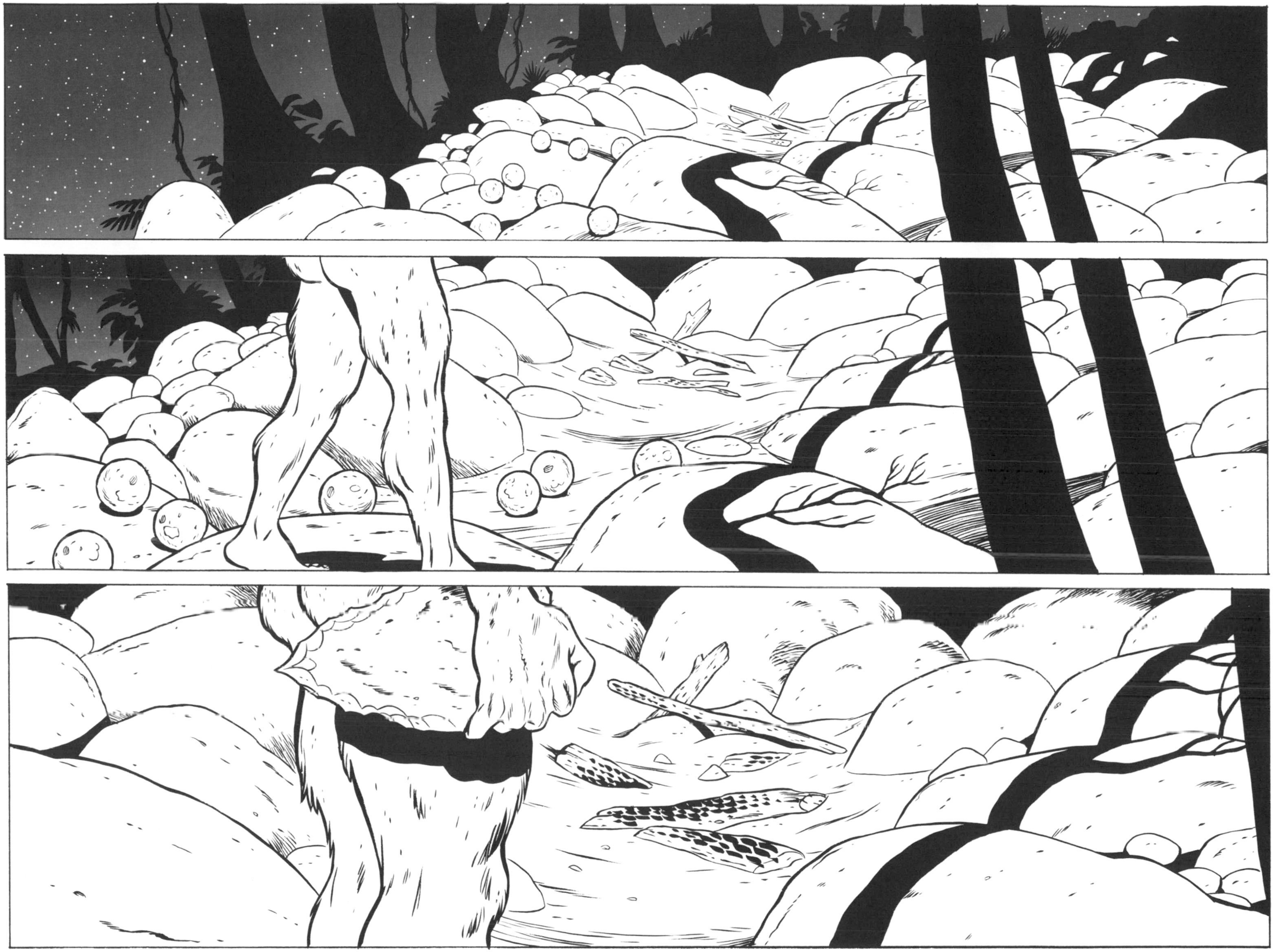

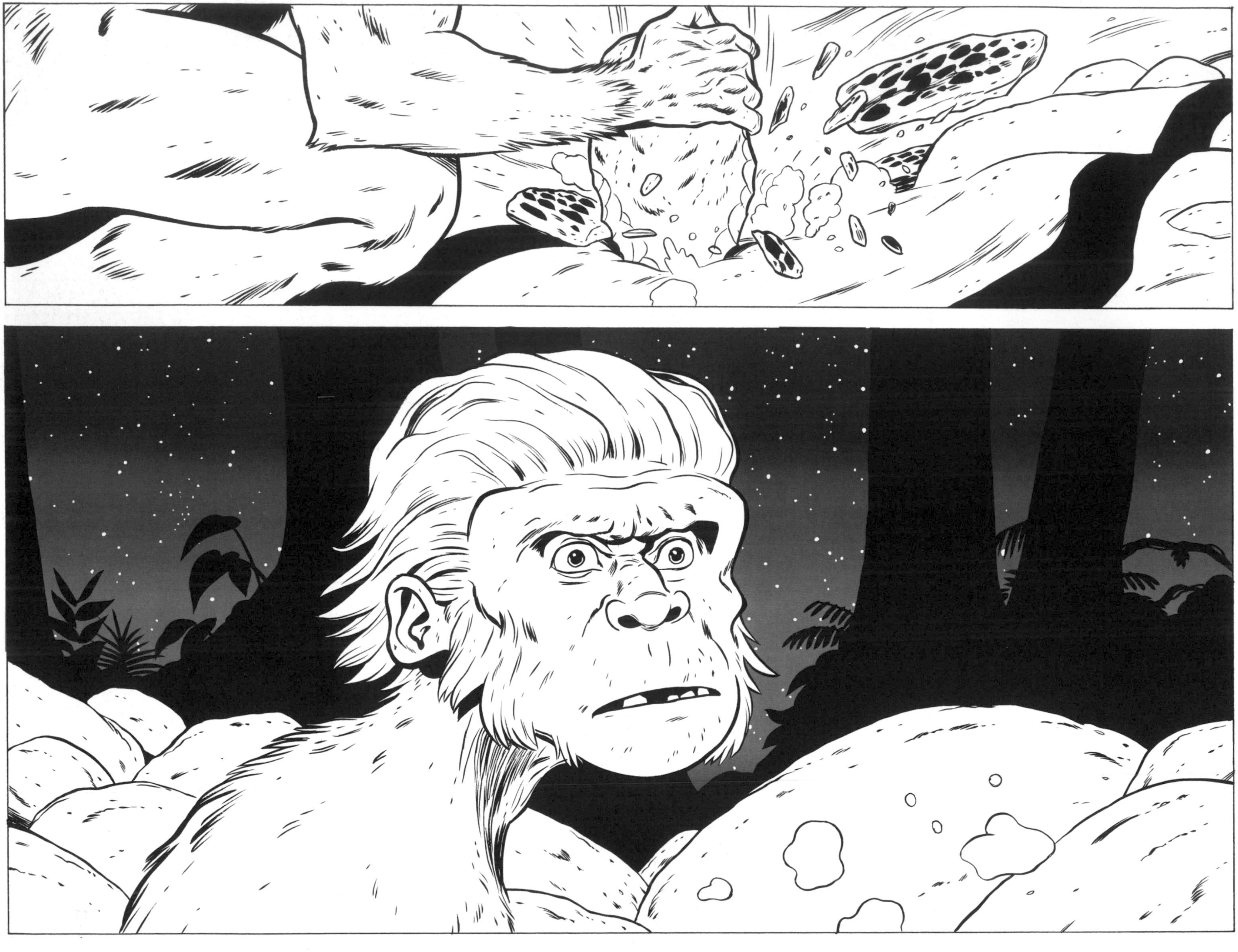

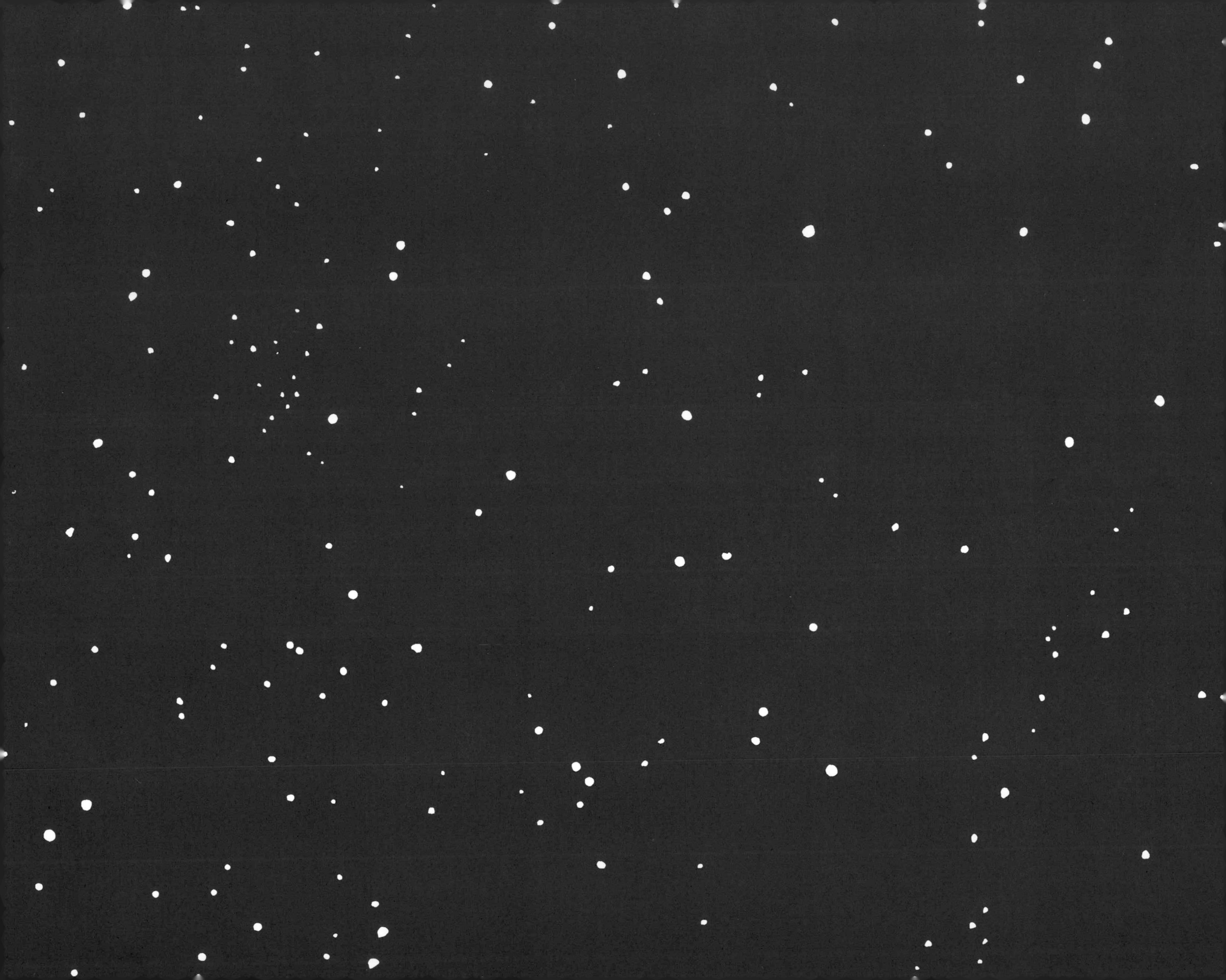

Cartoon Books is

Jeff Smith   Writer and Artist

Vijaya Iyer   Publisher

Kathleen Glosan   Production Manager

Tom Gaadt   Colorist / Pre Press / Design

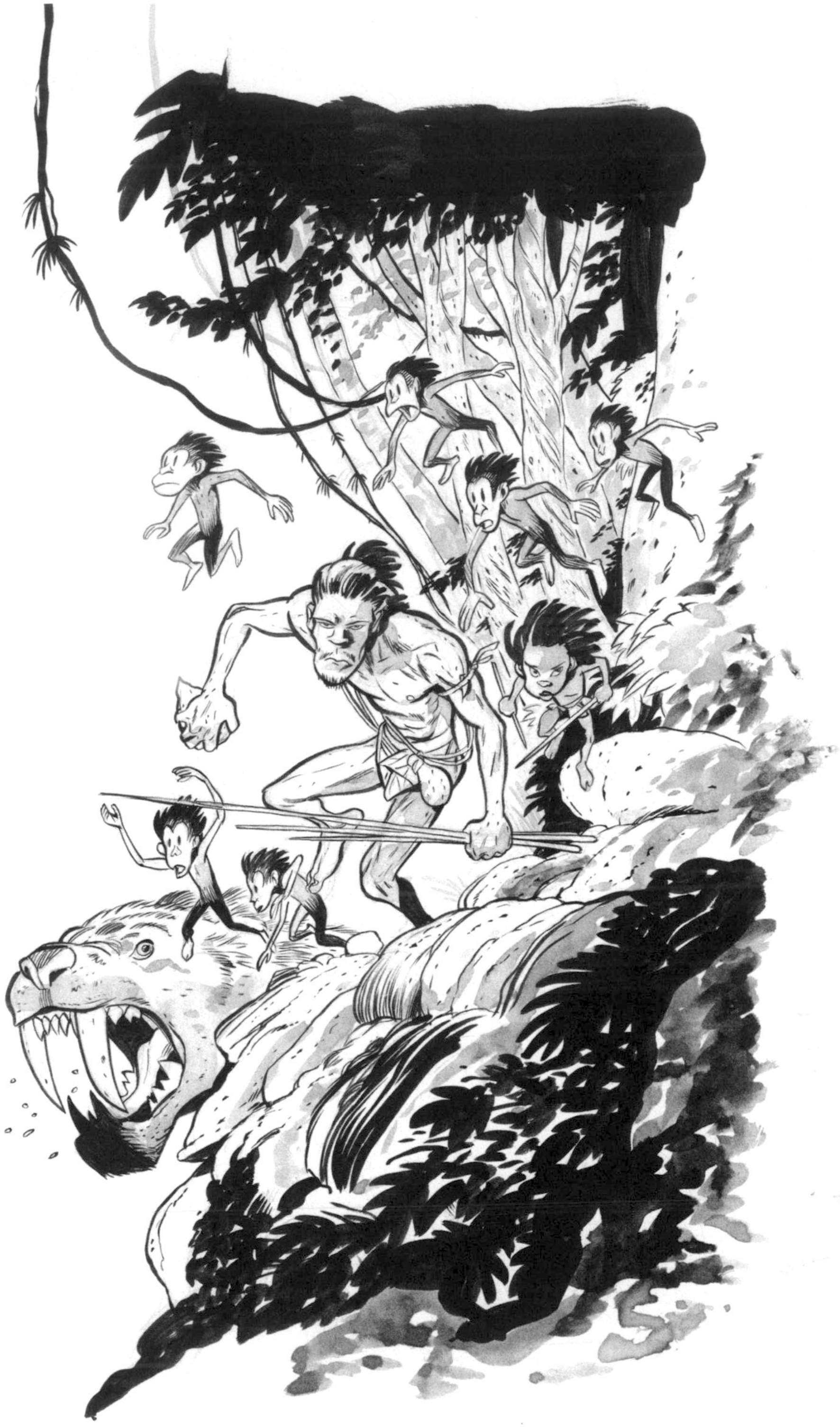

A Note from the Author

TUKI started as a weekly comicstrip on the web and ran for about two years before I set it aside to work on other matters. One of the reasons for the hiatus was to restructure the story and reset the tone between Tuki and the kids. I kept most of the main events, like the meeting with the old Habiline seer and the battle with the Ape god, but everything around them has been expanded, tweaked and the differences in their world views better articulated. I am mostly satisfied, and in retrospect I now view the webcomic as an online pilot for the graphic novel you hold in your hands.

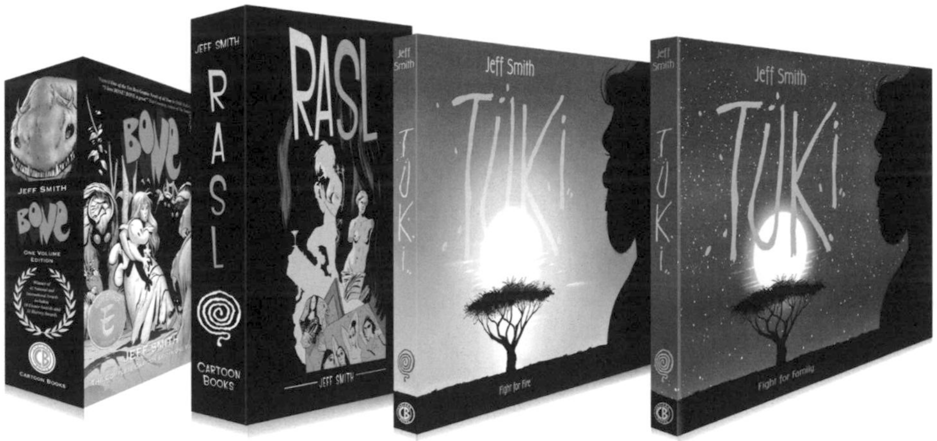
JEFF SMITH
BONE
ONE VOLUME EDITION
CARTOON BOOKS
JEFF SMITH
RASL
RASL
CARTOON BOOKS
JEFF SMITH
Jeff Smith
TUKI
Jeff Smith
TUKI
Fight for Fire
Jeff Smith
TUKI
Jeff Smith
TUKI
Fight for Family

This is my third creator owned, self-published comics work after BONE and RASL, and I hope TUKI: Fight For Fire and TUKI: Fight For Family will be the beginning of a new adventure - for the characters, for readers, and for me!

As with BONE and RASL, the former inspired by a love of adventure stories, comicstrips and epics, the latter by science fiction, physics and noir, TUKI follows that pattern of personal passions. In this case, my love of the fantastic heroes of pulp fiction, mythical lost realms and human evolution.

My fascination with evolution predates the webcomic, going back to my school days, watching nature specials and documentaries about ancient fossils on TV.

In the 90's I visited Olduvai Gorge in Tanzania, the famous archaeological site occupied by many early humans over time. Standing down among the rocks and dirt, looking up at the swaying trees above the gorge, I had a vision of multiple human species walking around and interacting with each other. It was almost like seeing an echo of something that really happened. There was a moment, two million years ago when that actually could have happened; when more than one species of human existed at the same time.

In the early days of the Pleistocene epoch, many different kinds of humans were roaming upright on two legs across East Africa. You met some of them in this story. Australopithecus (the Pithecines), were the species that the famous Lucy was from, part hominid, half human from the waist down. The Habiline people, still shaggy, but with a bigger brain who developed the stone chopper, a crucial tool that gave them protection, food and power.

The world near the dawn of the human race was a dangerous and difficult place. Climate events wrought prolonged drought and massive changes in the landscape. Vast tropical jungles gave way to dry, open grasslands. All living creatures struggled to survive.

Many hominids went extinct. Then came the greatest upheaval yet - a new human, tall and strong, with the biggest brain of all, enters the scene bearing a power never before seen. . . the ability to control Fire.

Here begin the terrors, Here begin the marvels.

The rest of the book is a look at the process of putting TUKI together. This is a gift from the many folks who supported the book on Kickstarter, a dedicated and enthusiastic bunch who helped usher this adventure into being. Thank you to them, and thank you, dear reader.

- Jeff Smith
Key West, May 2021

A Brief Bibliography

Born in Africa: The Quest for the Origins of Human Life by Martin Meredith

Catching Fire: How Cooking Made Us Human by Richard Wrangham

Lone Survivors: How We Came To Be The Only Humans On Earth by Chris Stringer

Prehistoric Life Murals by William Stout

Evolution: The Human Story by Dr. Alice Roberts

Films

NOVA: Becoming Human

National Geographic: The Human Family Tree

Quest for Fire Directed by Jean-Jacques Annaud 1981

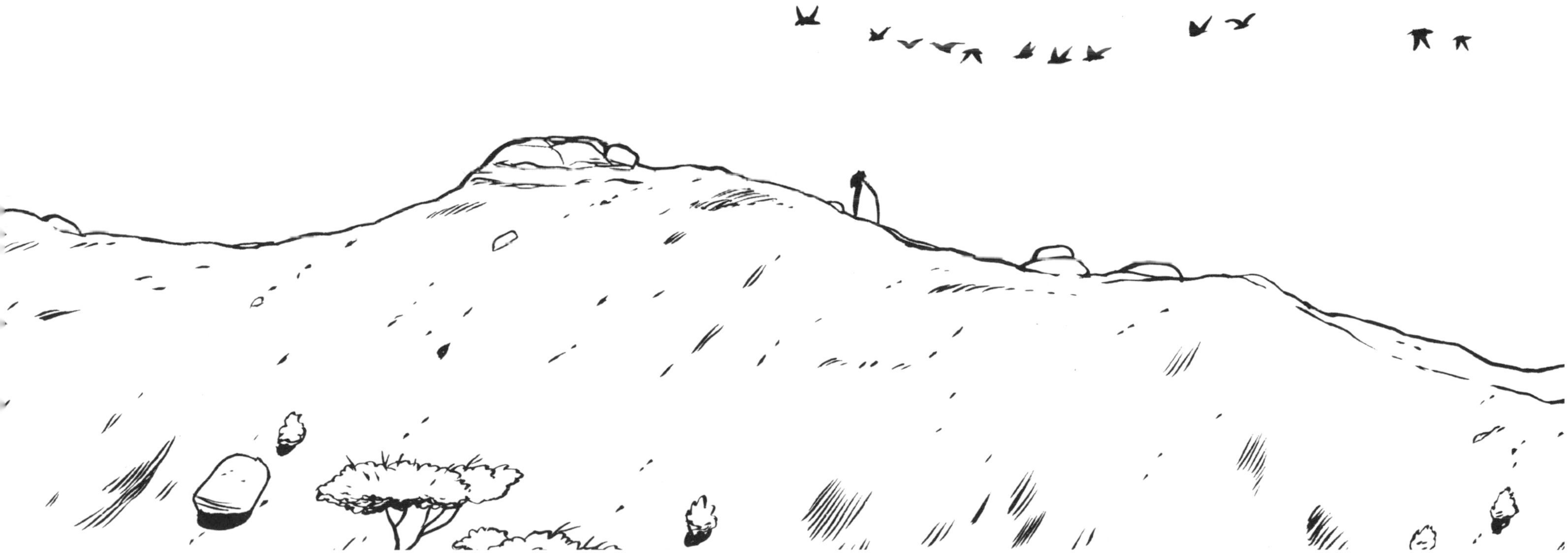

SPECIAL THANKS

Lucy Shelton Caswell, C. Spike Trotman, Eric Reynolds, Terry Moore and Tim Fielder

Asking someone to read a developing work is a big ask. Expecting them to react, respond and advise is even bigger. This is my short list of very busy people who did just that - some multiple times - and I would like to express my gratitude for their encouragement, energy and counsel.

Francisca Pulido & Brian Pulido and Deborah Tucci & Billy Tucci

For insisting Vijaya and I open our eyes to Kickstarter!

Tom Spurgeon

Who was always interested in what I was doing, and who left us too soon.

MORE THANKS

Larry Marder • Cory Marder • Skottie Young • Fabio Moon • Kyle Baker

Charles Vess • Oriana Leckert • David Hyde • Karl Kessel • Gib Bickel

Rich Wagner • Jared Petersen • Patrick Jodoin • Sarah Rosenberg

Brian Santin • Crystal Santin • Team Worldwide

and all of our supporters on Kickstarter

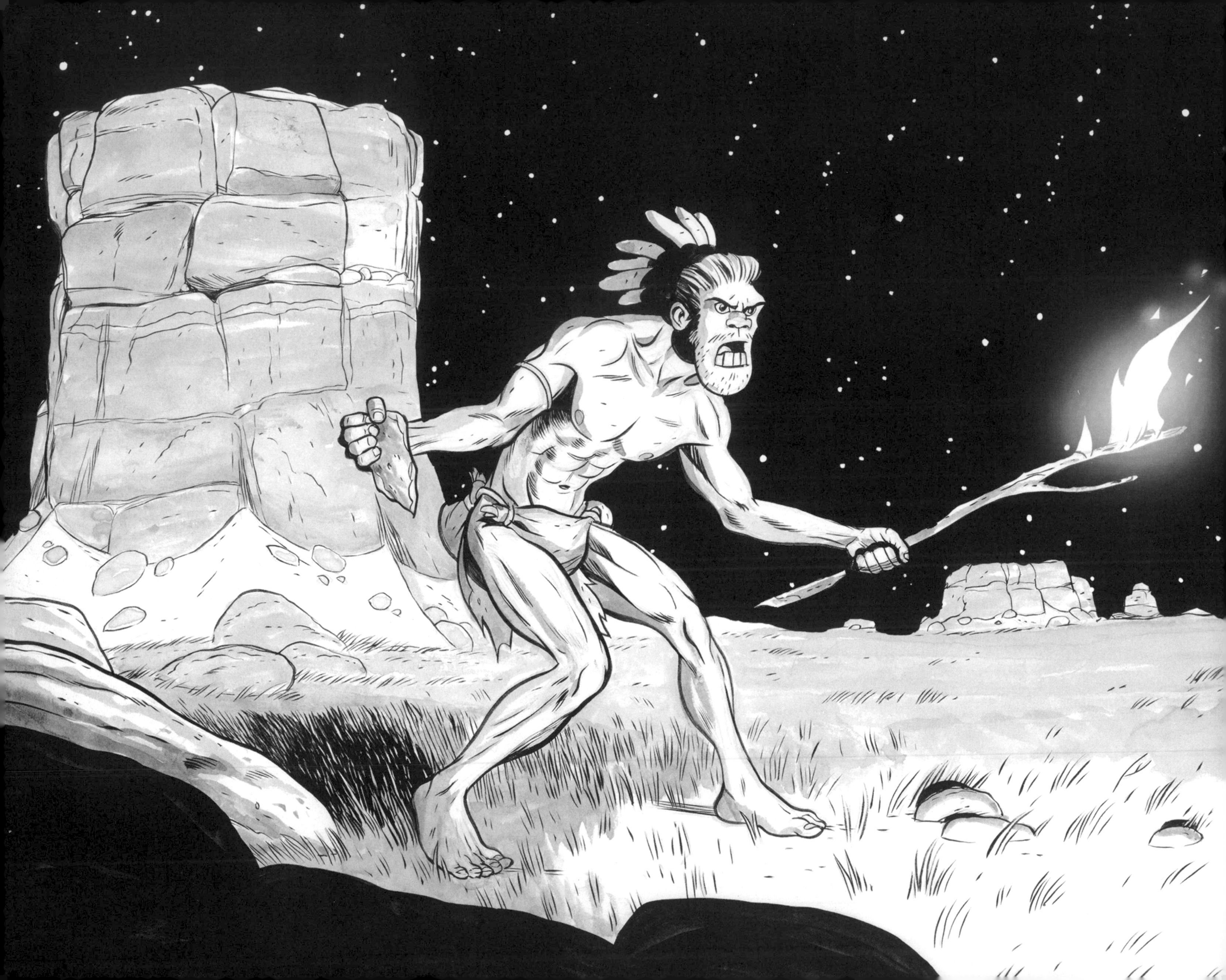

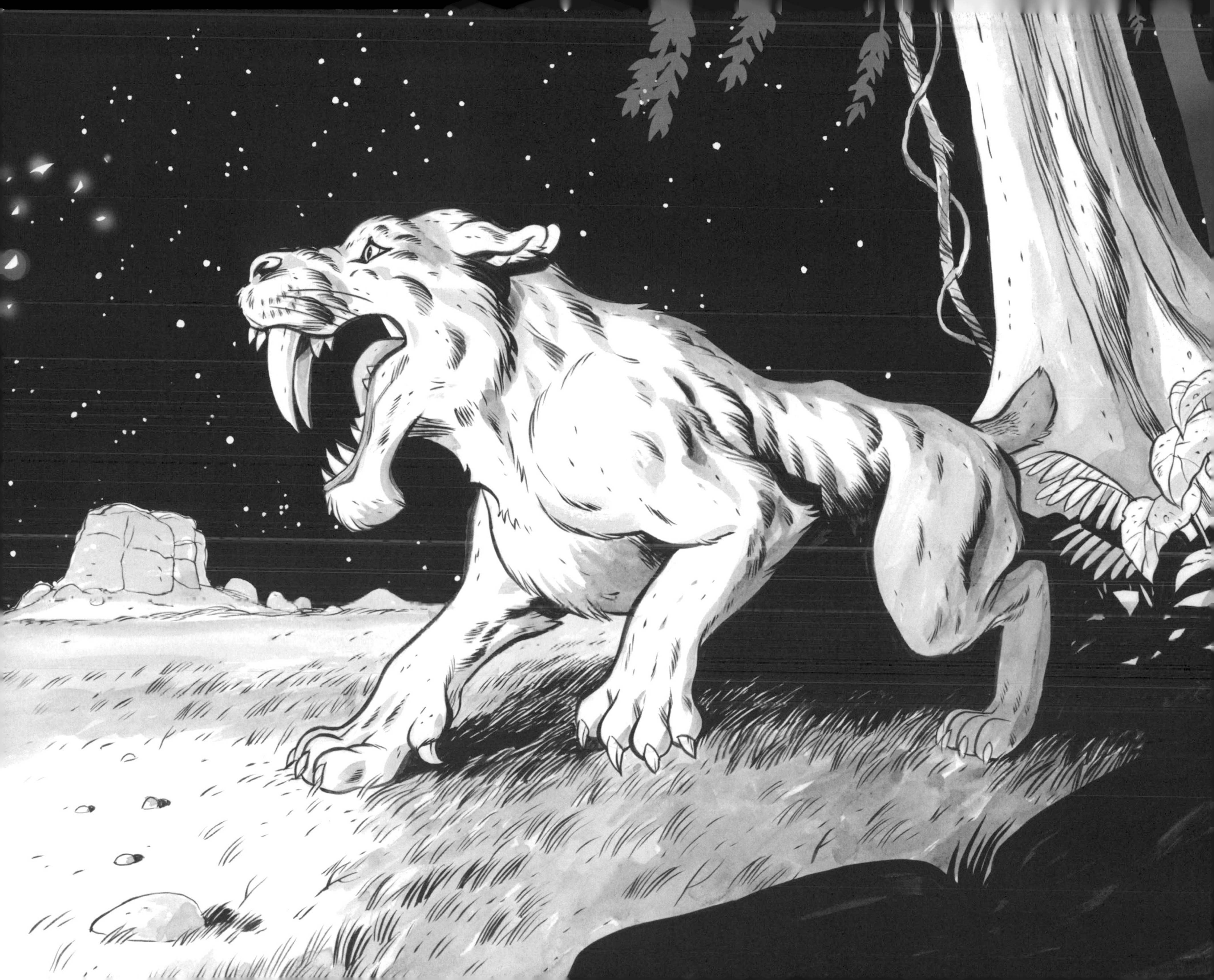

APPENDIX A
Story Notes

* Page 21: One of my favorite things about making comics is doing the research. There is always so much to discover. The fruit Tuki is holding is a Monkey Orange. An ancient fruit (strychnine spinosa) that still exists today in Eastern Africa. It is fragrant with a delicious sweet/sour flavor. The Monkey Orange has never been crossbred or cultivated and so remains much as it would have been in Tuki's day.

* Page 27: We know early humans carried stone hand weapons with razor sharp edges for stripping meat quickly off of bones. You don't want to hang around a kill too long; speed is necessary when you aren't the only hungry animal out there...

* Page 28: This Saber-toothed cat is most likely a Megantereon. Saber-tooths were big, but this one is big even by their standards.

* Page 30: Baobab trees store water in natural hollows between branches. A source of water for passing animals and humans.

* Page 29: Evidence suggests that all early humans would carry things great distances. Even the tiny Australopithecines carried not only small rock chip tools, but the heavy core stone that they preferred for making new tools. Even though there is nothing in the fossil record showing how they accomplished this, I used it as an excuse to give Tuki some crude slings as a means to haul his goods around. And as a handy way to preserve his modesty, since it's pretty unlikely that anyone wore clothes back then.

* Page 31: As mentioned, the current thought on evolution is not a straight line. At the time of our story, different groups all separated by distance and environment have adapted and evolved on their own over thousands or millions of years, creating a world where multiple species of humans overlapped. The fellow who just entered the scene is Habiline, also known as Homo habilis.

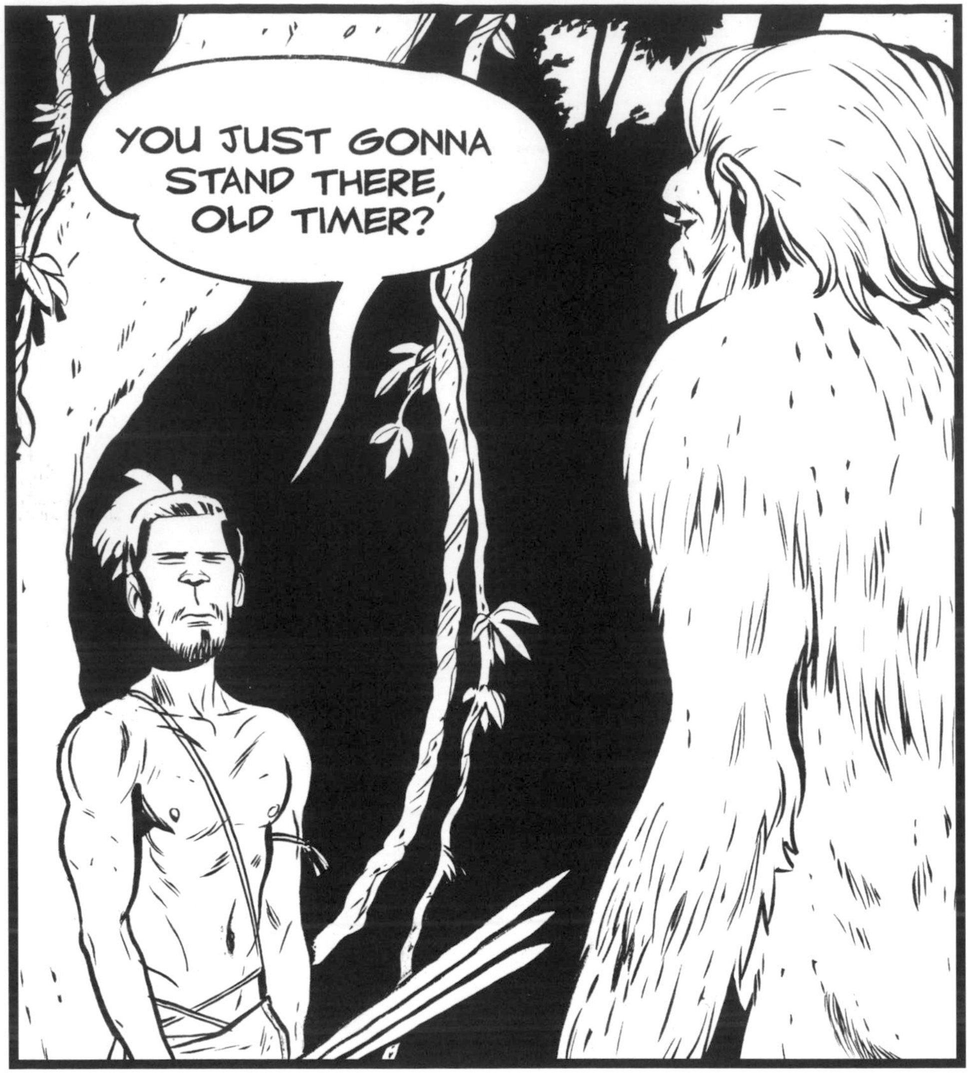
YOU JUST GONNA STAND THERE, OLD TIMER?

* Page 32: Could Tuki talk? When we look at our ancestors' fossils from that time, experts see on the base of the skull a voice box long enough to modulate sound. Impressions from inside the skull show they had a Broca's area; which is a major speech center of the brain. We don't know if two million years ago these ancestors could actually speak in a way that we would recognize, but they were the first ones to have the equipment!

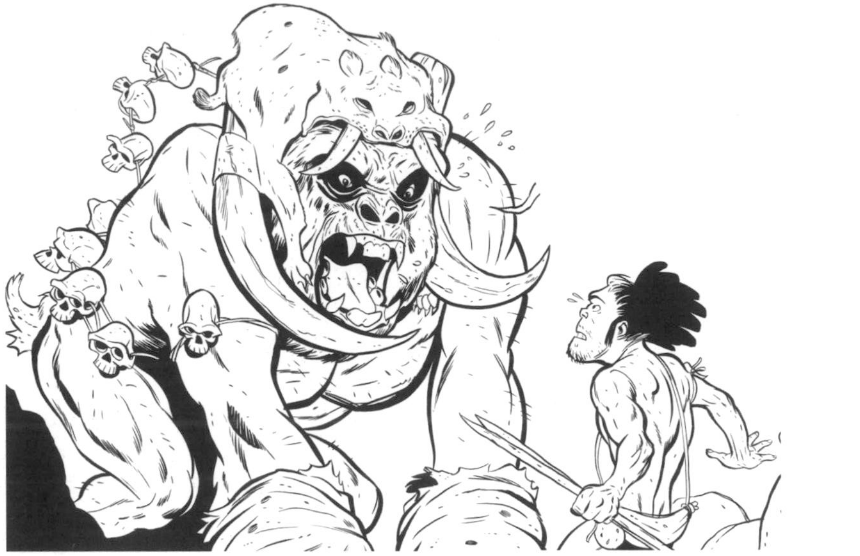

* Page 71: This creature is a demon, or a malignant force from the Hidden World. It has chosen to manifest itself as a Gigantopithecus, a 12 ft. tall relative of the orangutans in Asia. This giant lived at the time of this tale, but no fossils of Gigantopithecus have ever been found in Africa. Still, demons gonna do what demons gonna do.

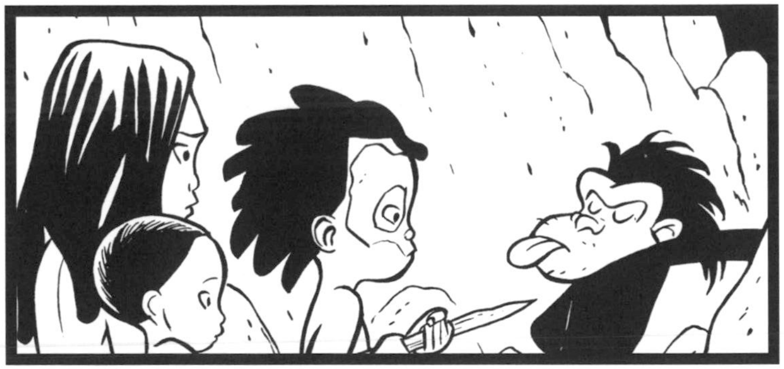

* Page 95: Our first look at a Pithie. The Australopithecines were the first hominids to walk upright on two legs. The famous Lucy was an Australopithicus afarensis. Kwarell is more likely a slightly younger version, Australopithicus africanus.

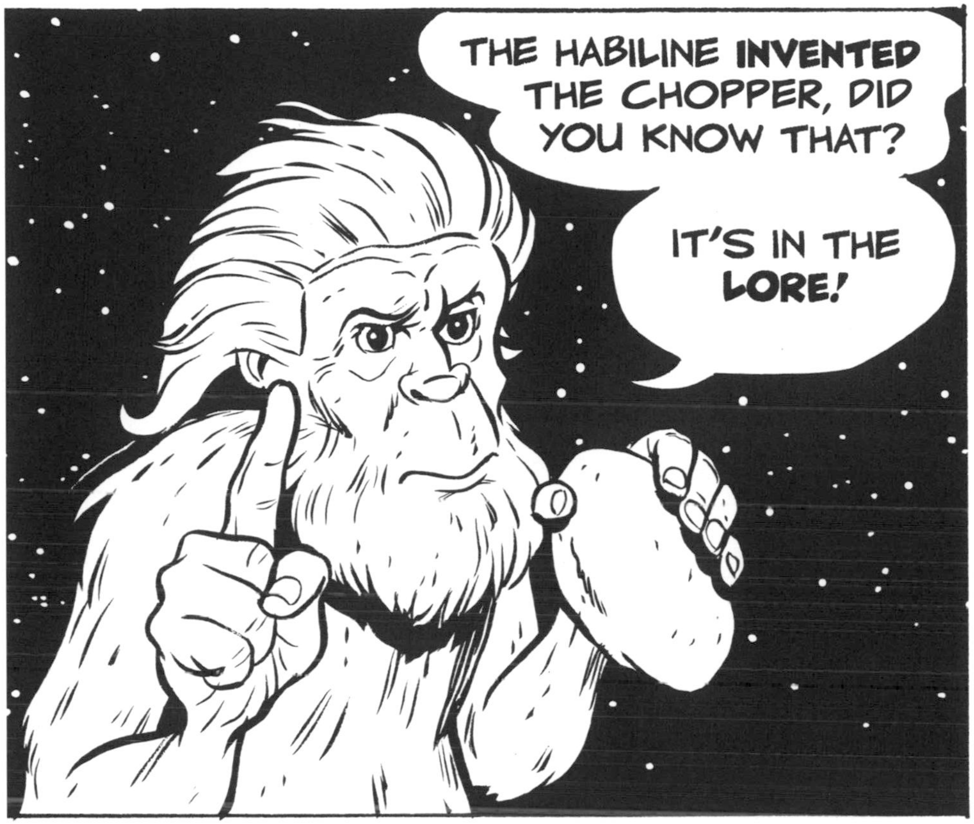
THE HABILINE INVENTED THE CHOPPER, DID YOU KNOW THAT?
IT'S IN THE LORE!

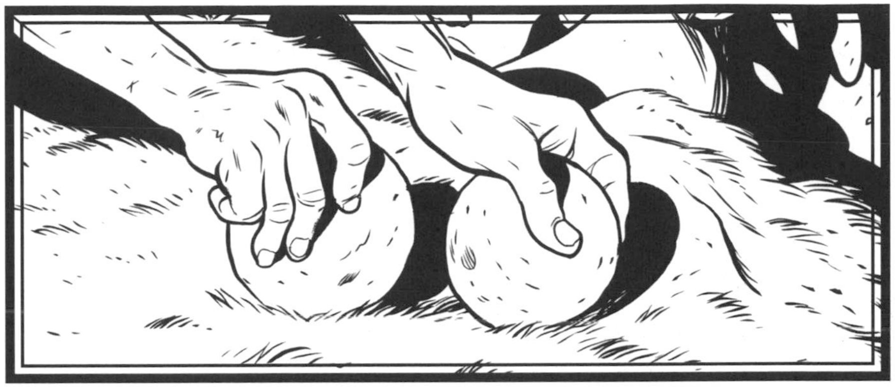

* Page 118: The Monkey Oranges are back. I like Monkey Oranges. We start the book with Monkey Oranges and we end with Monkey Oranges.

* Page 105: The Habiline did indeed invent the stone chopper allowing them to broaden their feeding strategies, like crushing bones to reach the marrow, providing more protein to fuel a larger brain. The name Homo habilis means Able Man or Handy Man.

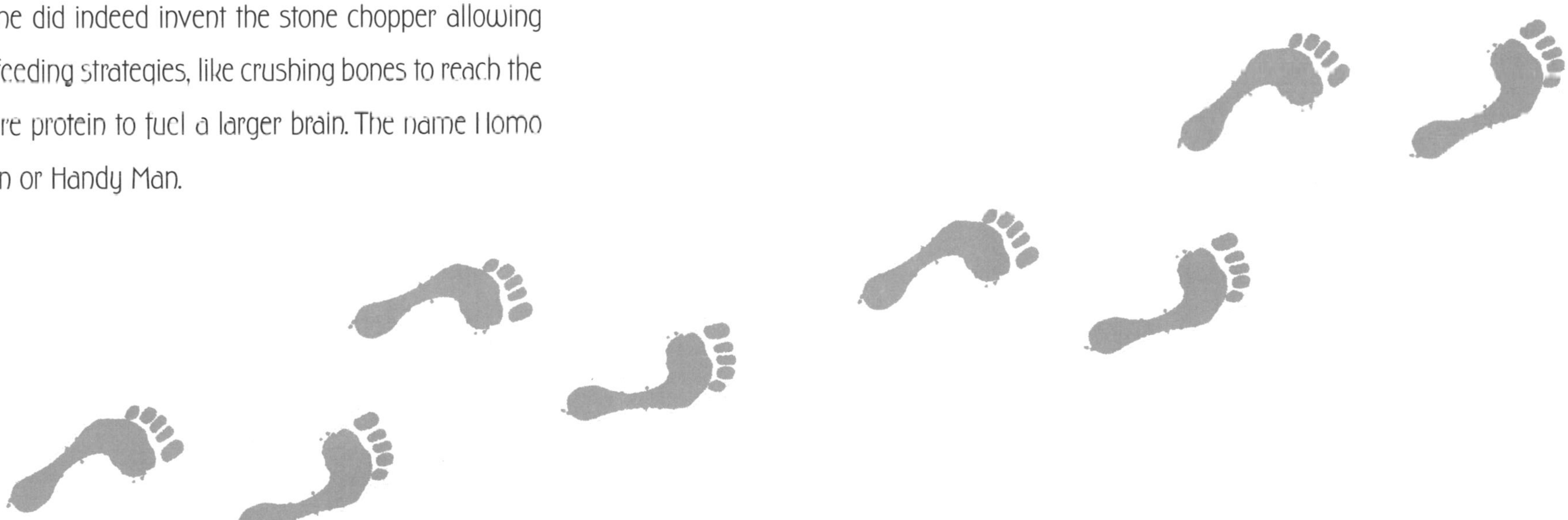

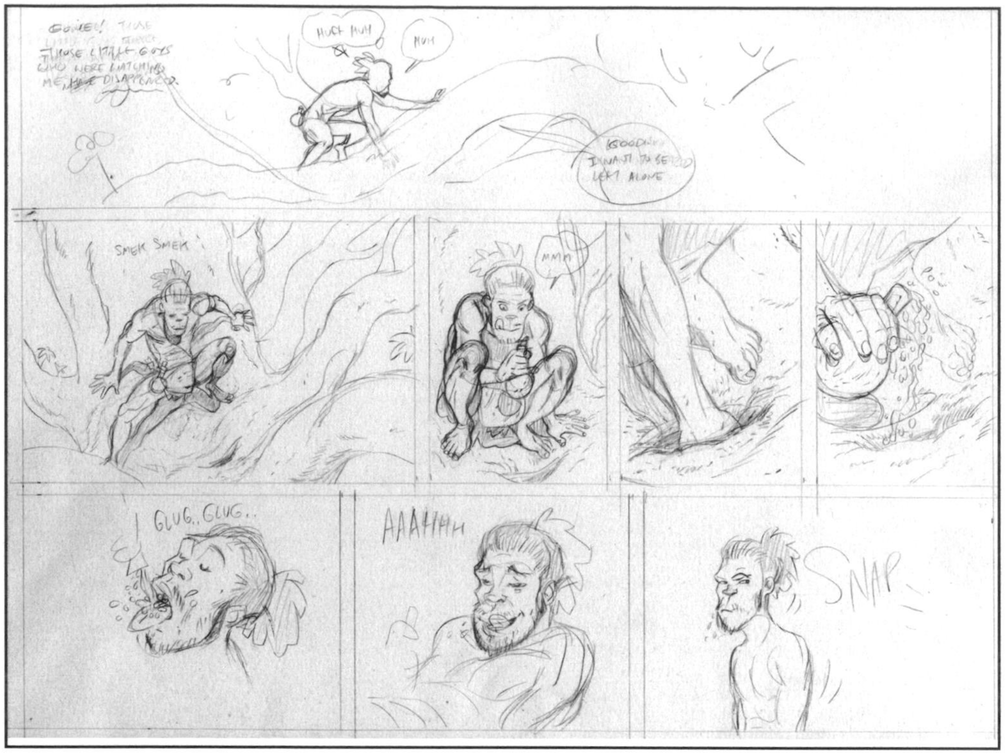
HUH HUH
HUH
SMEK SMEK
MMM
GLUG, GLUG..
AAAHHH
SNAP

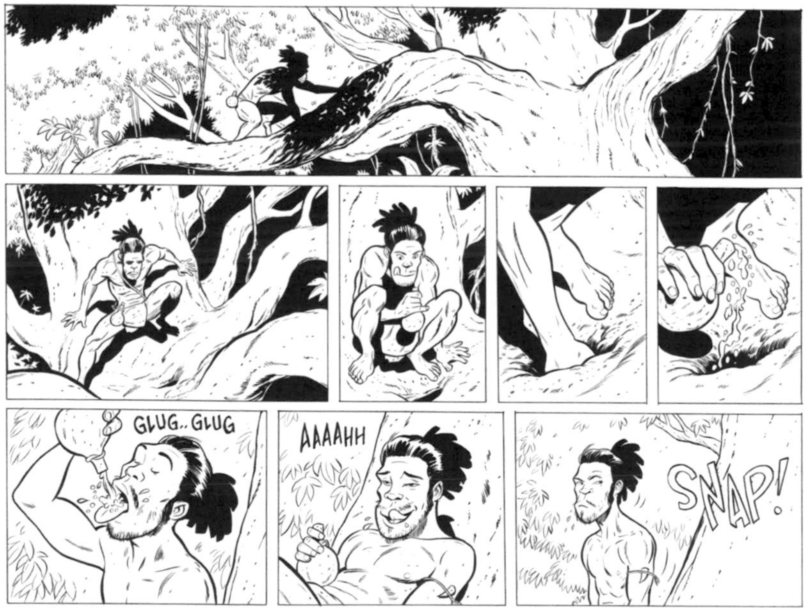
GLUG.. GLUG
AAAAHH
SNAP!

Above: Penciled page and finished inks from the original webcomic

APPENDIX B
The Making of TUKI: Fight for Fire

The first thing to do was sit down and re-examine my unfinished project TUKI: Save the Humans (T:StH). There were 70+ pages of pretty good art, interesting characters, an intriguing lost world to explore. But there was something missing.

I had set the webcomic aside in early 2016, but I continued to think about it. The first serious attempt to return to the story was in 2018, and then again in 2019. During all these efforts I used the reprint comic books to keep notes in. Dozens and dozens, even hundreds of post-it notes tracking characters and events in relation to future plot lines filled their pages. It was in March of 2020, that a lightbulb really turned on and I saw the way forward. I could see the characters, the story, the stakes, all

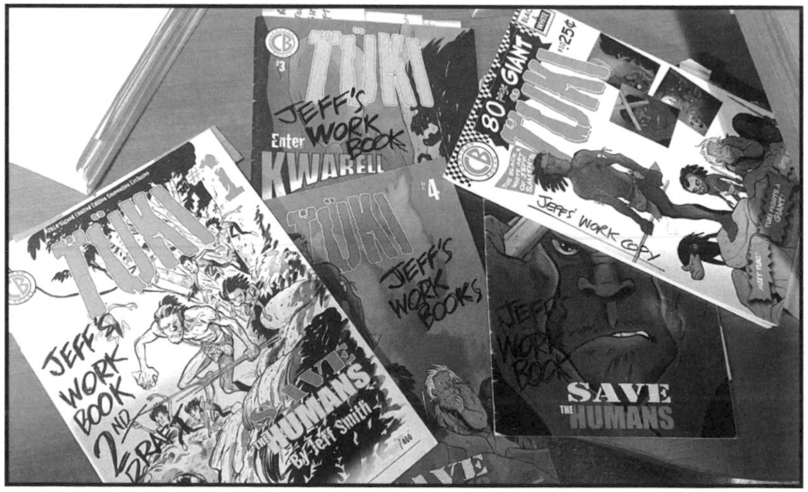
TUKI
JEFF'S WORK BOOK
Enter KWARELL
80 PAGE GIANT
TUKI
JEFF'S WORK COPY
TUKI
JEFF'S WORK BOOK 2ND DRAFT
HUMANS
By Jeff Smith
TUKI
JEFF'S WORK BOOKS
JEFF'S WORK BOOK
SAVE THE HUMANS

of it, and began scaling everything up for a proper epic series of graphic novels in the vein of BONE and RASL. I hoped to save the good art, but adjustments and new story ideas would be needed to seamlessly integrate everything into a new whole.

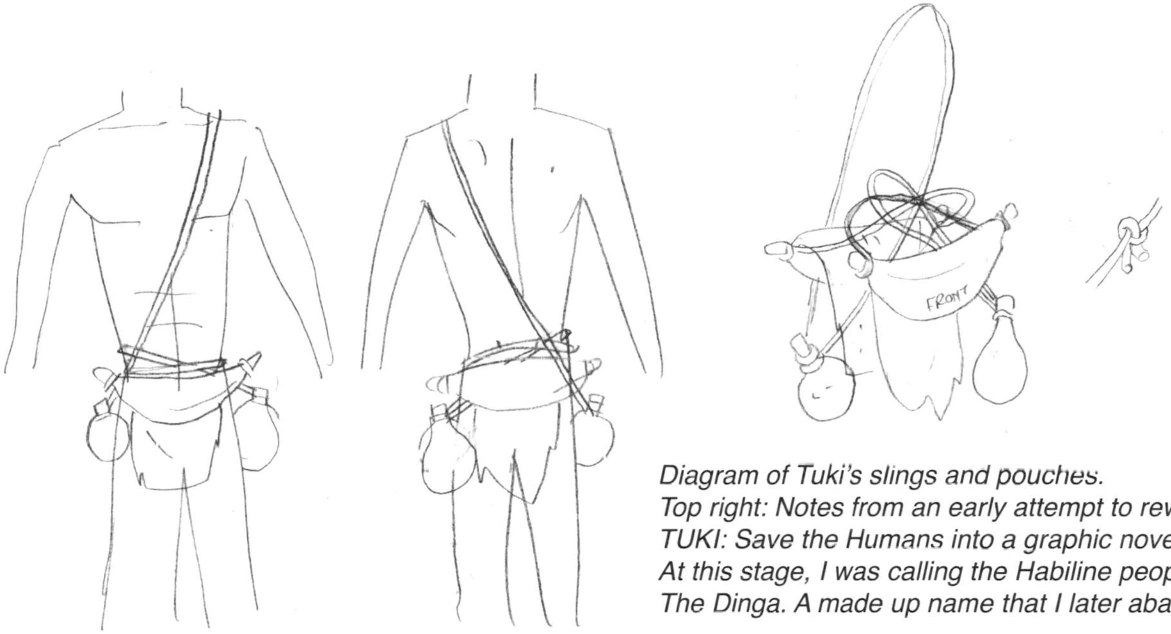
FRONT

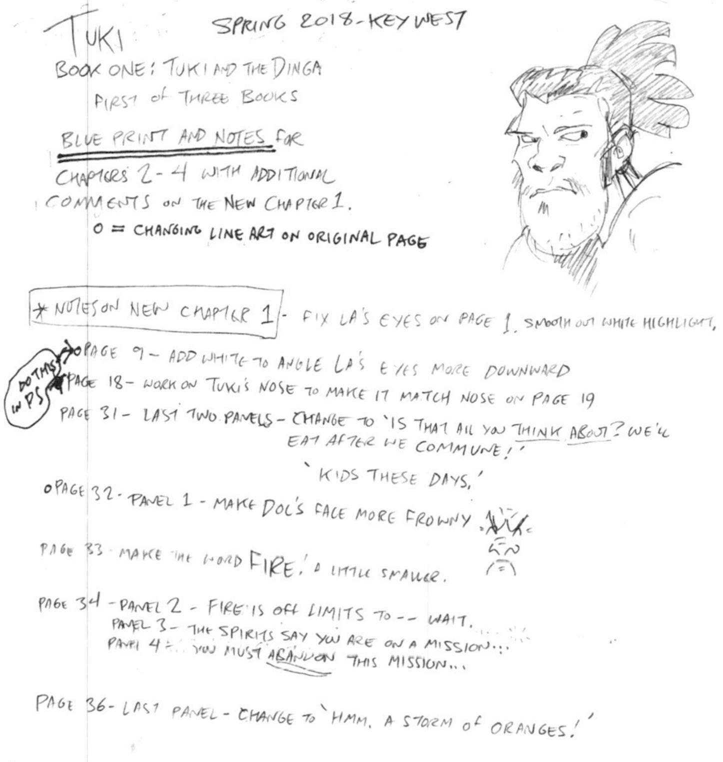
TUKI
SPRING 2018-KEY WEST
BOOK ONE: TUKI AND THE DINGA
FIRST OF THREE BOOKS
BLUE PRINT AND NOTES FOR
CHAPTERS 2-4 WITH ADDITIONAL
COMMENTS ON THE NEW CHAPTER 1.
O = CHANGING LINE ART ON ORIGINAL PAGE
* NOTES ON NEW CHAPTER 1 - FIX LA'S EYES ON PAGE 1. SMOOTH OUT WHITE HIGHLIGHT,
DO THIS IN PS
O PAGE 9 - ADD WHITE TO ANGLE LA'S EYES MORE DOWNWARD
PAGE 18 - WORK ON TUKI'S NOSE TO MAKE IT MATCH NOSE ON PAGE 19
PAGE 31 - LAST TWO PANELS - CHANGE TO 'IS THAT ALL YOU THINK ABOUT? WE'LL EAT AFTER WE COMMUNE!'
'KIDS THESE DAYS.'
O PAGE 32 - PANEL 1 - MAKE DOL'S FACE MORE FROWNY
PAGE 33 - MAKE THE WORD FIRE! A LITTLE SMALLER.
PAGE 34 - PANEL 2 - FIRE IS OFF LIMITS TO -- WAIT.
PANEL 3 - THE SPIRITS SAY YOU ARE ON A MISSION...
PANEL 4 - YOU MUST ABANDON THIS MISSION...
PAGE 36 - LAST PANEL - CHANGE TO 'HMM. A STORM OF ORANGES!'

Diagram of Tuki's slings and pouches.
Top right: Notes from an early attempt to rework TUKI: Save the Humans into a graphic novel. At this stage, I was calling the Habiline people The Dinga. A made up name that I later abandoned.

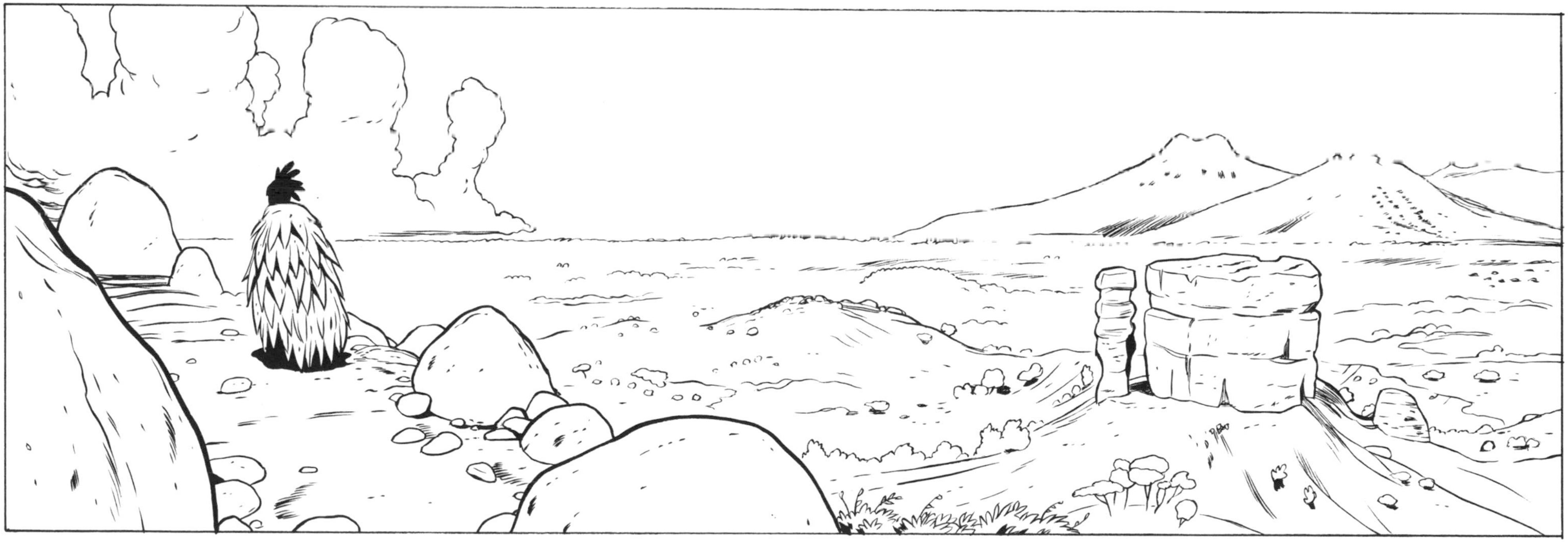

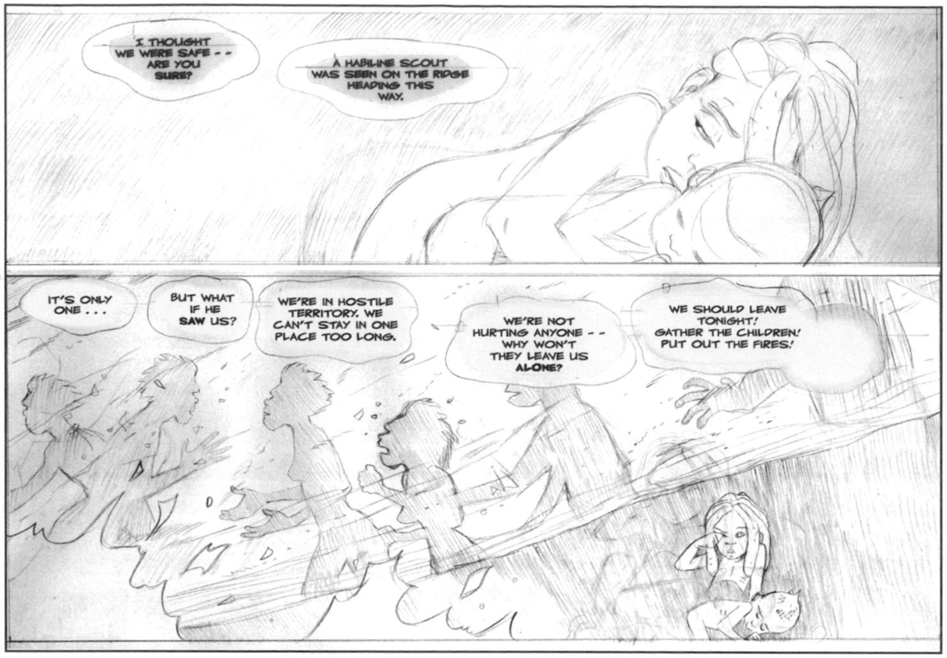
I THOUGHT WE WERE SAFE - - ARE YOU SURE?
A HABILINE SCOUT WAS SEEN ON THE RIDGE HEADING THIS WAY.
IT'S ONLY ONE . . .
BUT WHAT IF HE SAW US?
WE'RE IN HOSTILE TERRITORY. WE CAN'T STAY IN ONE PLACE TOO LONG.
WE'RE NOT HURTING ANYONE - - WHY WON'T THEY LEAVE US ALONE?
WE SHOULD LEAVE TONIGHT! GATHER THE CHILDREN! PUT OUT THE FIRES!

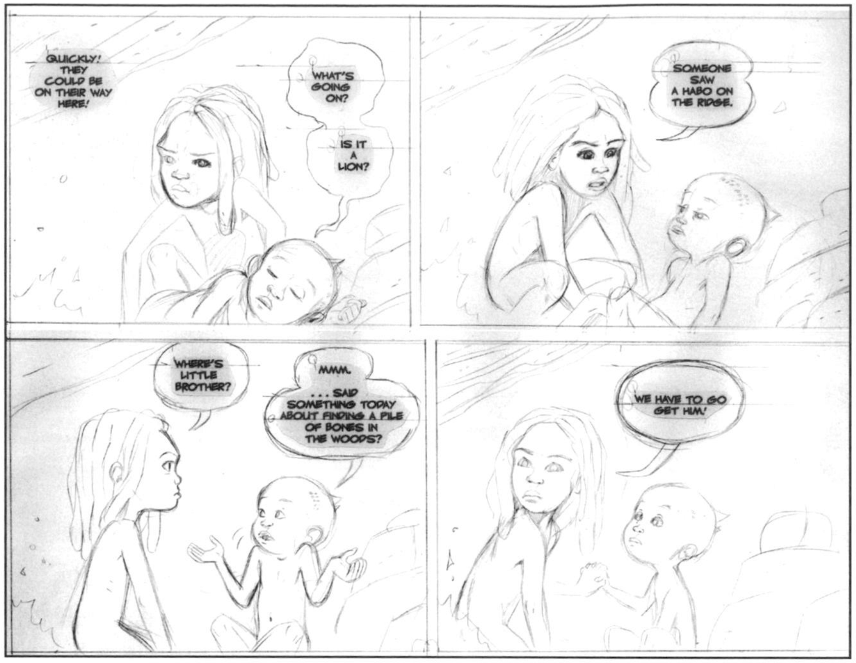
QUICKLY! THEY COULD BE ON THEIR WAY HERE!
WHAT'S GOING ON?
IS IT A LION?
SOMEONE SAW A HABO ON THE RIDGE.
WHERE'S LITTLE BROTHER?
MMM.
. . . SAID SOMETHING TODAY ABOUT FINDING A PILE OF BONES IN THE WOODS?
WE HAVE TO GO GET HIM!

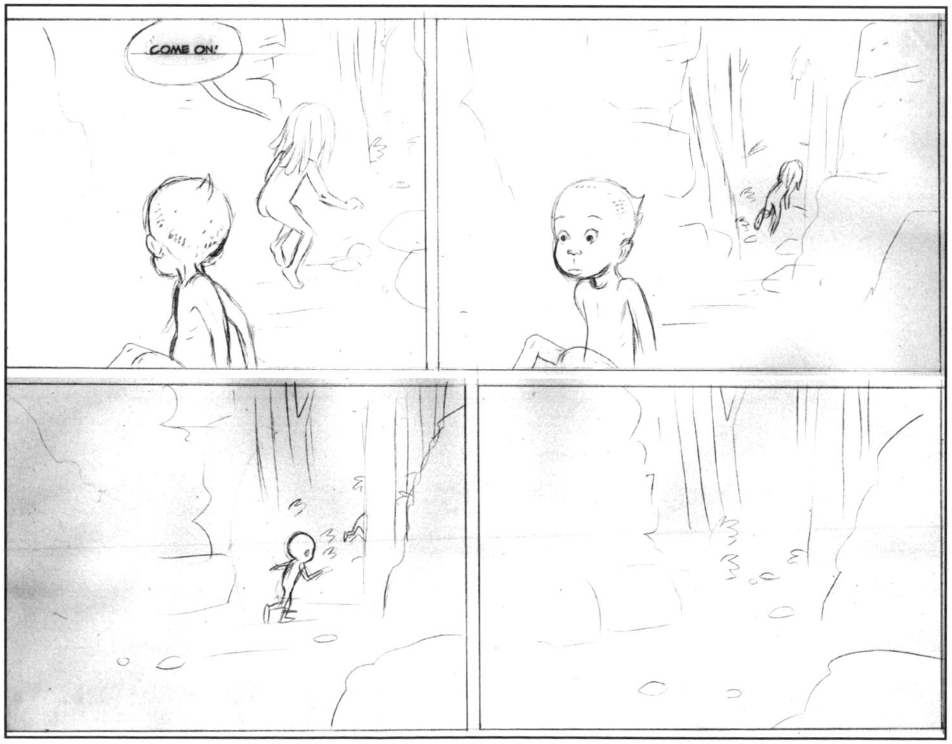
COME ON!

Building Bridges: Making the Webcomic into a Graphic Novel

To expand and improve the flow of the story from the webcomic material, very often it was necessary to add pages or even whole scenes to smooth out the narrative. In many instances, panels were shifted, altered and fused together with new ones.

Example of a completely new scene.
The book now opens with the children La & Zee. from pages 15,16,17

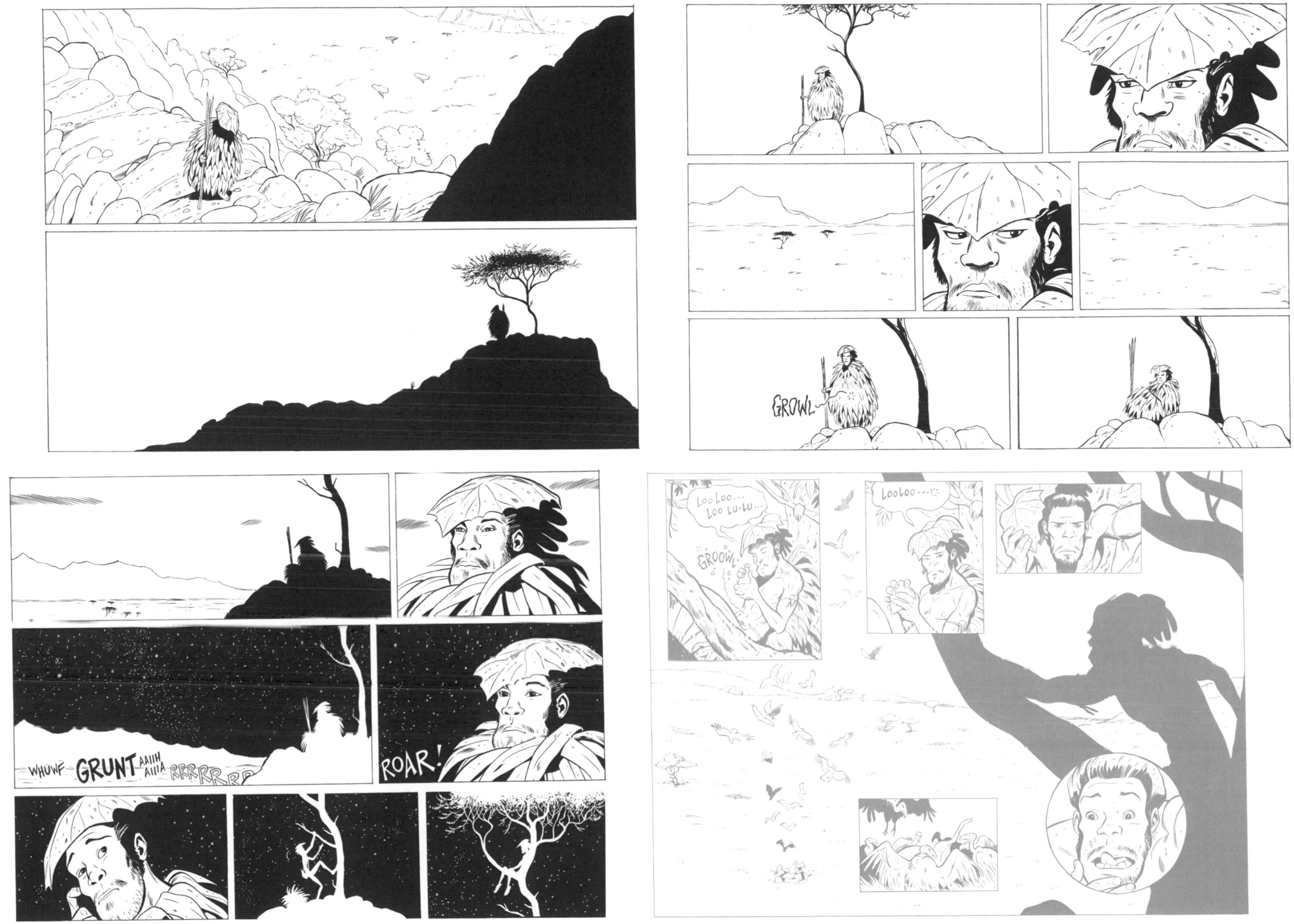
GROWL
WHUWF
GRUNT
ROAR!
Loo Loo...
Loo Lu-Lu...
GROOW
Looloo

Example of extending a scene. The three pages in black are new, the page in the lower right corner, in light gray, is from the webcomic TUKI: Save the Humans (T:StH)

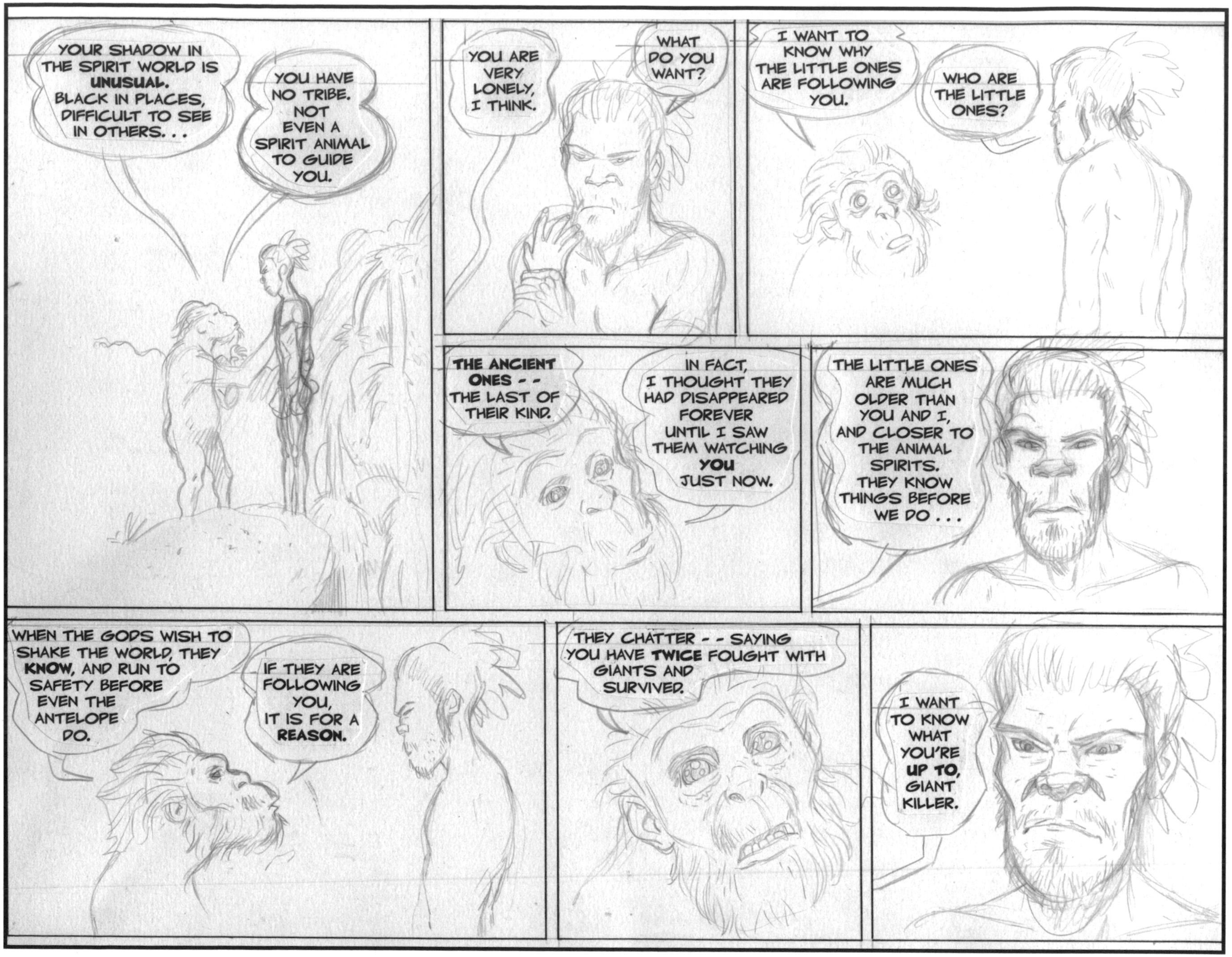
YOUR SHADOW IN THE SPIRIT WORLD IS UNUSUAL. BLACK IN PLACES, DIFFICULT TO SEE IN OTHERS. . .
YOU HAVE NO TRIBE. NOT EVEN A SPIRIT ANIMAL TO GUIDE YOU.
YOU ARE VERY LONELY, I THINK.
WHAT DO YOU WANT?
I WANT TO KNOW WHY THE LITTLE ONES ARE FOLLOWING YOU.
WHO ARE THE LITTLE ONES?
THE ANCIENT ONES - - THE LAST OF THEIR KIND.
IN FACT, I THOUGHT THEY HAD DISAPPEARED FOREVER UNTIL I SAW THEM WATCHING YOU JUST NOW.
THE LITTLE ONES ARE MUCH OLDER THAN YOU AND I, AND CLOSER TO THE ANIMAL SPIRITS. THEY KNOW THINGS BEFORE WE DO . . .
WHEN THE GODS WISH TO SHAKE THE WORLD, THEY KNOW, AND RUN TO SAFETY BEFORE EVEN THE ANTELOPE DO.
IF THEY ARE FOLLOWING YOU, IT IS FOR A REASON.
THEY CHATTER - - SAYING YOU HAVE TWICE FOUGHT WITH GIANTS AND SURVIVED.
I WANT TO KNOW WHAT YOU'RE UP TO, GIANT KILLER.

A Crucial Scene: Tuki Meets Doc. The core of this scene, starting when Doc confronts Tuki (shown above in pencil from T:StH) to the moment when Tuki snaps out of the old Habiline's spell, was originally only four pages. Compare to the current graphic novel you hold in your hands where it is over a dozen pages long.

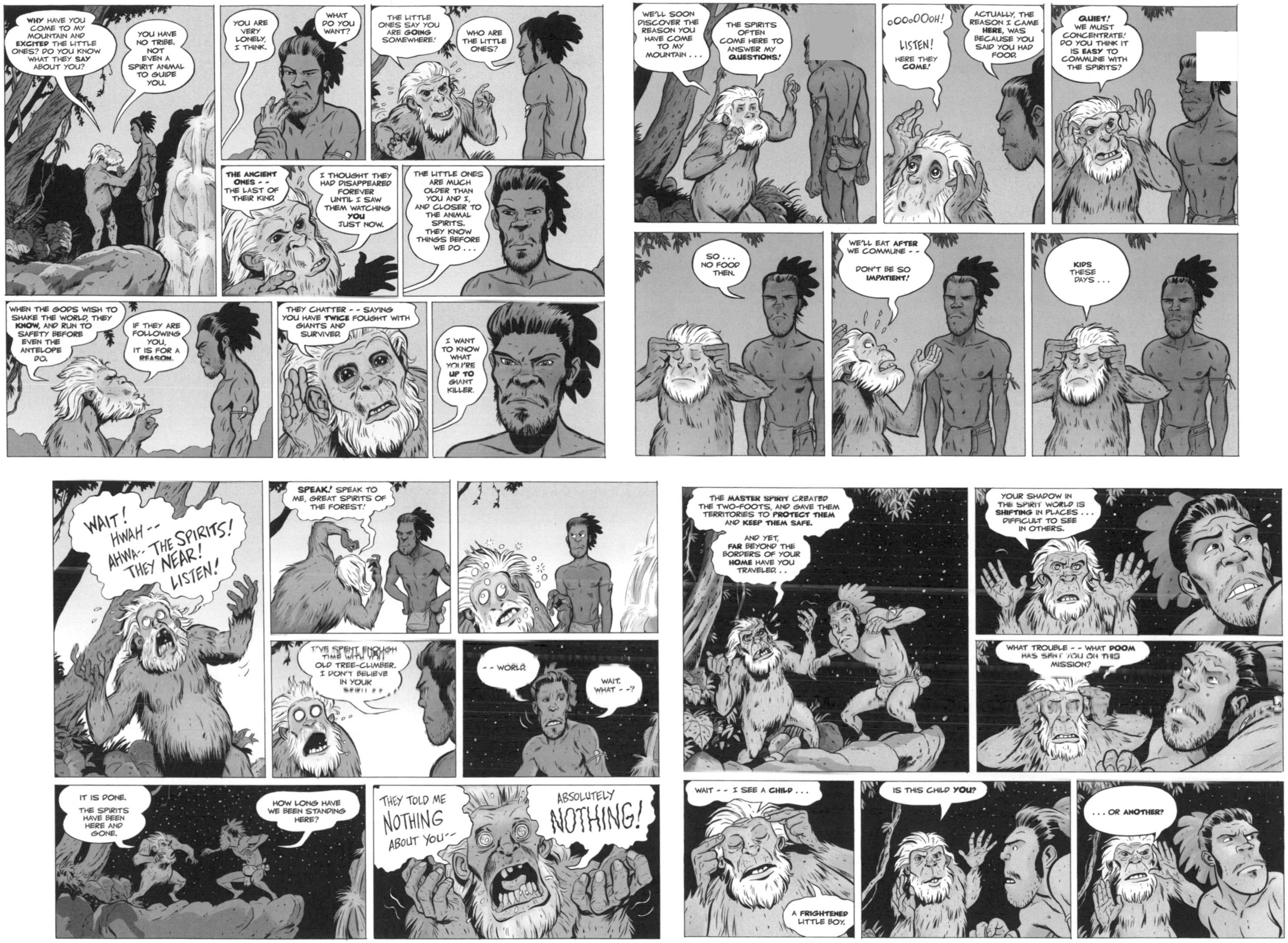
WHY HAVE YOU COME TO MY MOUNTAIN AND EXCITED THE LITTLE ONES? DO YOU KNOW WHAT THEY SAY ABOUT YOU?
YOU HAVE NO TRIBE. NOT EVEN A SPIRIT ANIMAL TO GUIDE YOU.
WHAT DO YOU WANT?
YOU ARE VERY LONELY, I THINK.
THE LITTLE ONES SAY YOU ARE GOING SOMEWHERE!
WHO ARE THE LITTLE ONES?
THE ANCIENT ONES - - THE LAST OF THEIR KIND.
I THOUGHT THEY HAD DISAPPEARED FOREVER UNTIL I SAW THEM WATCHING YOU JUST NOW.
THE LITTLE ONES ARE MUCH OLDER THAN YOU AND I, AND CLOSER TO THE ANIMAL SPIRITS. THEY KNOW THINGS BEFORE WE DO . . .
WHEN THE GODS WISH TO SHAKE THE WORLD, THEY KNOW, AND RUN TO SAFETY BEFORE EVEN THE ANTELOPE DO.
IF THEY ARE FOLLOWING YOU, IT IS FOR A REASON.
THEY CHATTER - - SAYING YOU HAVE TWICE FOUGHT WITH GIANTS AND SURVIVED.
I WANT TO KNOW WHAT YOU'RE UP TO GIANT KILLER.
WE'LL SOON DISCOVER THE REASON YOU HAVE COME TO MY MOUNTAIN . . .
THE SPIRITS OFTEN COME HERE TO ANSWER MY QUESTIONS!
oOOoOOoH! LISTEN! HERE THEY COME!
ACTUALLY, THE REASON I CAME HERE, WAS BECAUSE YOU SAID YOU HAD FOOD.
QUIET! WE MUST CONCENTRATE! DO YOU THINK IT IS EASY TO COMMUNE WITH THE SPIRITS?
SO . . . NO FOOD THEN.
WE'LL EAT AFTER WE COMMUNE - - DON'T BE SO IMPATIENT!
KIDS THESE DAYS . . .
WAIT! HWAH - - AHWA - - THE SPIRITS! THEY NEAR! LISTEN!
SPEAK! SPEAK TO ME, GREAT SPIRITS OF THE FOREST!
I'VE SPENT ENOUGH OLD TREE-CLIMBER. I DON'T BELIEVE IN YOUR
- - WORLD.
WAIT. WHAT - -?
IT IS DONE. THE SPIRITS HAVE BEEN HERE AND GONE.
HOW LONG HAVE WE BEEN STANDING HERE?
THEY TOLD ME NOTHING ABOUT YOU - -
ABSOLUTELY NOTHING!
THE MASTER SPIRIT CREATED THE TWO-FOOTS, AND GAVE THEM TERRITORIES TO PROTECT THEM AND KEEP THEM SAFE.
AND YET, FAR BEYOND THE BORDERS OF YOUR HOME HAVE YOU TRAVELED . . .
YOUR SHADOW IN THE SPIRIT WORLD IS SHIFTING IN PLACES . . . DIFFICULT TO SEE IN OTHERS.
WHAT TROUBLE - - WHAT DOOM HAS SENT YOU ON THIS MISSION?
WAIT - - I SEE A CHILD . . .
A FRIGHTENED LITTLE BOY.
IS THIS CHILD YOU?
. . . OR ANOTHER?

The original four page version of TUKI MEETS DOC from TUKI: Save the Humans webcomic.

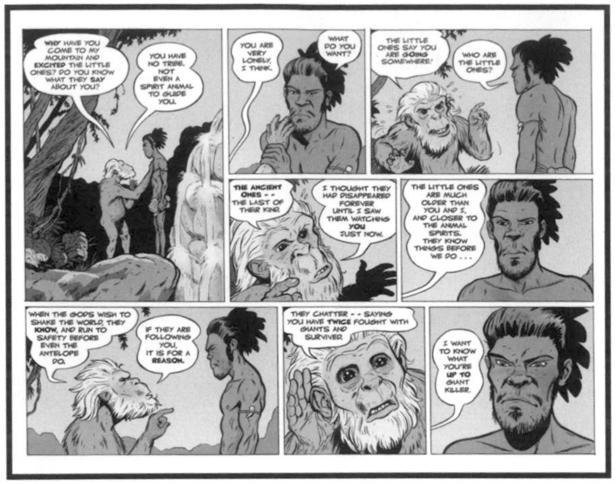

WHY HAVE YOU COME TO MY MOUNTAIN AND EXCITED THE LITTLE ONES? DO YOU KNOW WHAT THEY SAY ABOUT YOU?
YOU HAVE NO TRIBE. NOT EVEN A SPIRIT ANIMAL TO GUIDE YOU.
YOU ARE VERY LONELY, I THINK.
WHAT DO YOU WANT?
THE LITTLE ONES SAY YOU ARE GOING SOMEWHERE!
WHO ARE THE LITTLE ONES?
THE ANCIENT ONES - - THE LAST OF THEIR KIND.
I THOUGHT THEY HAD DISAPPEARED FOREVER UNTIL I SAW THEM WATCHING YOU JUST NOW.
THE LITTLE ONES ARE MUCH OLDER THAN YOU AND I, AND CLOSER TO THE ANIMAL SPIRITS. THEY KNOW THINGS BEFORE WE DO . . .
WHEN THE GODS WISH TO SHAKE THE WORLD, THEY KNOW, AND RUN TO SAFETY BEFORE EVEN THE ANTELOPE DO.
IF THEY ARE FOLLOWING YOU, IT IS FOR A REASON.
THEY CHATTER - - SAYING YOU HAVE TWICE FOUGHT WITH GIANTS AND SURVIVED.
I WANT TO KNOW WHAT YOU'RE UP TO GIANT KILLER.

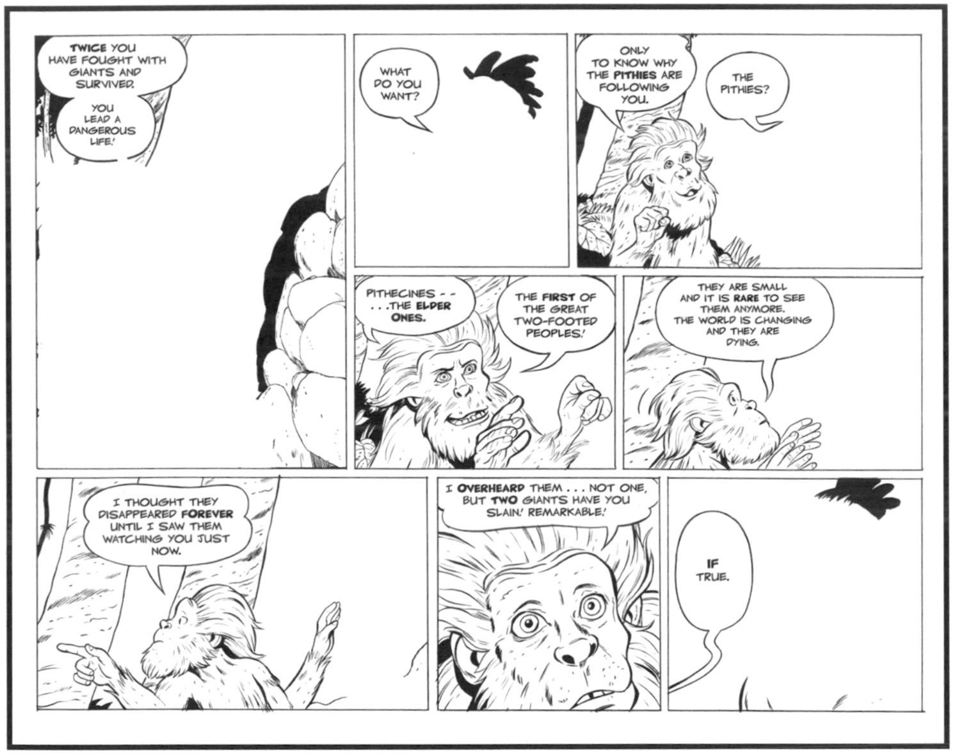

TWICE YOU HAVE FOUGHT WITH GIANTS AND SURVIVED.
YOU LEAD A DANGEROUS LIFE!
WHAT DO YOU WANT?
ONLY TO KNOW WHY THE PITHIES ARE FOLLOWING YOU.
THE PITHIES?
PITHECINES - - . . . THE ELDER ONES.
THE FIRST OF THE GREAT TWO-FOOTED PEOPLES!
THEY ARE SMALL AND IT IS RARE TO SEE THEM ANYMORE. THE WORLD IS CHANGING AND THEY ARE DYING.
I THOUGHT THEY DISAPPEARED FOREVER UNTIL I SAW THEM WATCHING YOU JUST NOW.
I OVERHEARD THEM . . . NOT ONE, BUT TWO GIANTS HAVE YOU SLAIN! REMARKABLE!
IF TRUE.

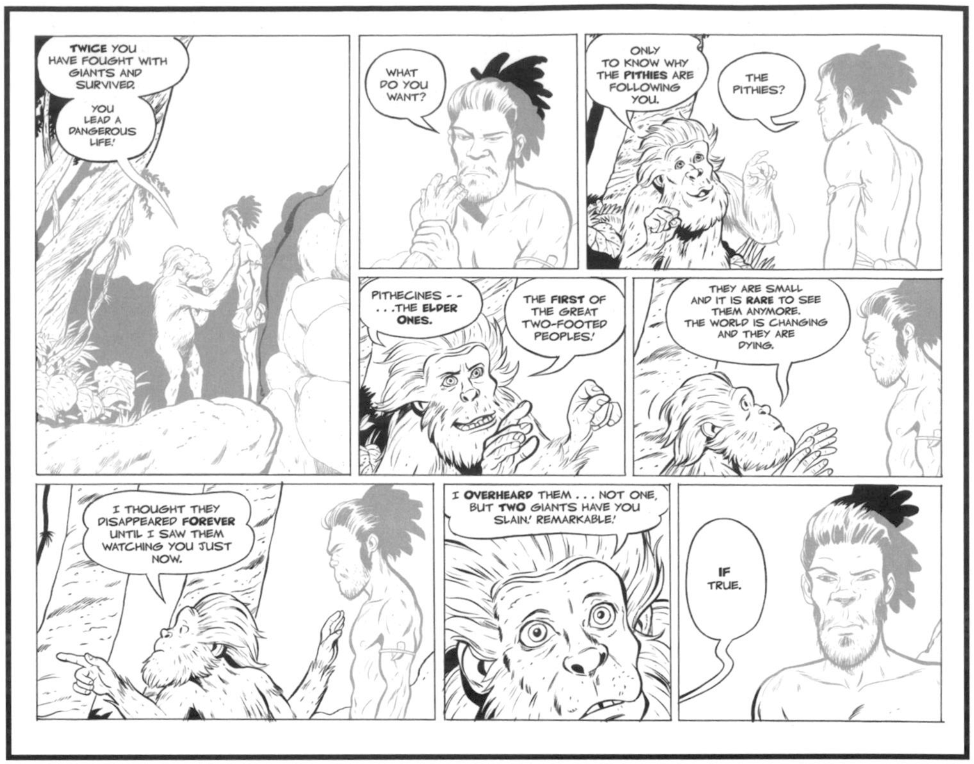

TWICE YOU HAVE FOUGHT WITH GIANTS AND SURVIVED.
YOU LEAD A DANGEROUS LIFE!
WHAT DO YOU WANT?
ONLY TO KNOW WHY THE PITHIES ARE FOLLOWING YOU.
THE PITHIES?
PITHECINES - - . . . THE ELDER ONES.
THE FIRST OF THE GREAT TWO-FOOTED PEOPLES!
THEY ARE SMALL AND IT IS RARE TO SEE THEM ANYMORE. THE WORLD IS CHANGING AND THEY ARE DYING.
I THOUGHT THEY DISAPPEARED FOREVER UNTIL I SAW THEM WATCHING YOU JUST NOW.
I OVERHEARD THEM . . . NOT ONE, BUT TWO GIANTS HAVE YOU SLAIN! REMARKABLE!
IF TRUE.

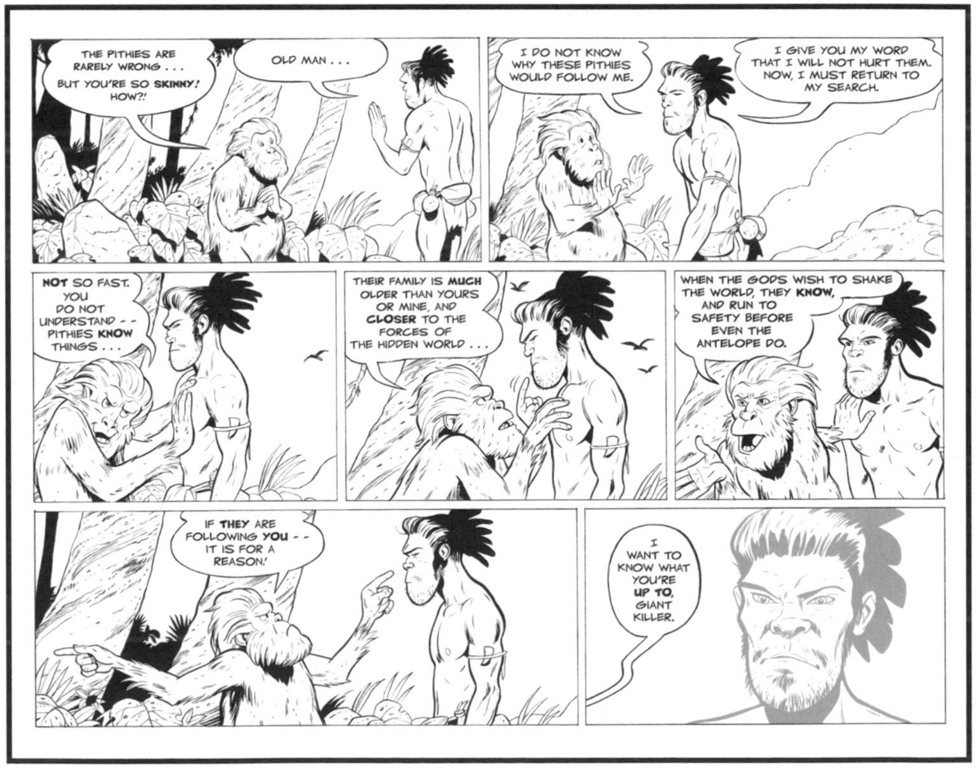

THE PITHIES ARE RARELY WRONG . . . BUT YOU'RE SO SKINNY! HOW?!
OLD MAN . . .
I DO NOT KNOW WHY THESE PITHIES WOULD FOLLOW ME.
I GIVE YOU MY WORD THAT I WILL NOT HURT THEM. NOW, I MUST RETURN TO MY SEARCH.
NOT SO FAST. YOU DO NOT UNDERSTAND - - PITHIES KNOW THINGS . . .
THEIR FAMILY IS MUCH OLDER THAN YOURS OR MINE, AND CLOSER TO THE FORCES OF THE HIDDEN WORLD . . .
WHEN THE GODS WISH TO SHAKE THE WORLD, THEY KNOW, AND RUN TO SAFETY BEFORE EVEN THE ANTELOPE DO.
IF THEY ARE FOLLOWING YOU - - IT IS FOR A REASON!
I WANT TO KNOW WHAT YOU'RE UP TO, GIANT KILLER.

Top left: Page from T:StH.
Bottom left: New art.
Top right: New art with existing art dropped in (light gray).
Bottom right: New art with existing art shown in light gray.

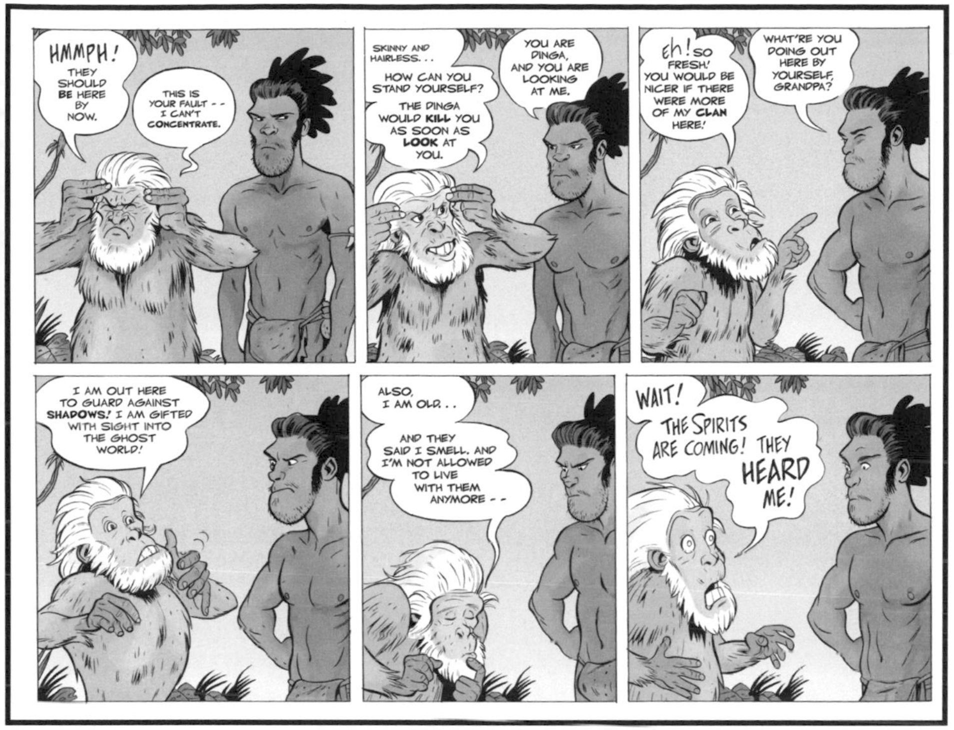
HMMPH! THEY SHOULD BE HERE BY NOW.
THIS IS YOUR FAULT - - I CAN'T CONCENTRATE.
SKINNY AND HAIRLESS . . .
HOW CAN YOU STAND YOURSELF?
THE DINGA WOULD KILL YOU AS SOON AS LOOK AT YOU.
YOU ARE DINGA, AND YOU ARE LOOKING AT ME.
Eh! SO FRESH! YOU WOULD BE NICER IF THERE WERE MORE OF MY CLAN HERE!
WHAT'RE YOU DOING OUT HERE BY YOURSELF, GRANDPA?
I AM OUT HERE TO GUARD AGAINST SHADOWS! I AM GIFTED WITH SIGHT INTO THE GHOST WORLD!
ALSO, I AM OLD . . .
AND THEY SAID I SMELL, AND I'M NOT ALLOWED TO LIVE WITH THEM ANYMORE - -
WAIT!
THE SPIRITS ARE COMING! THEY HEARD ME!

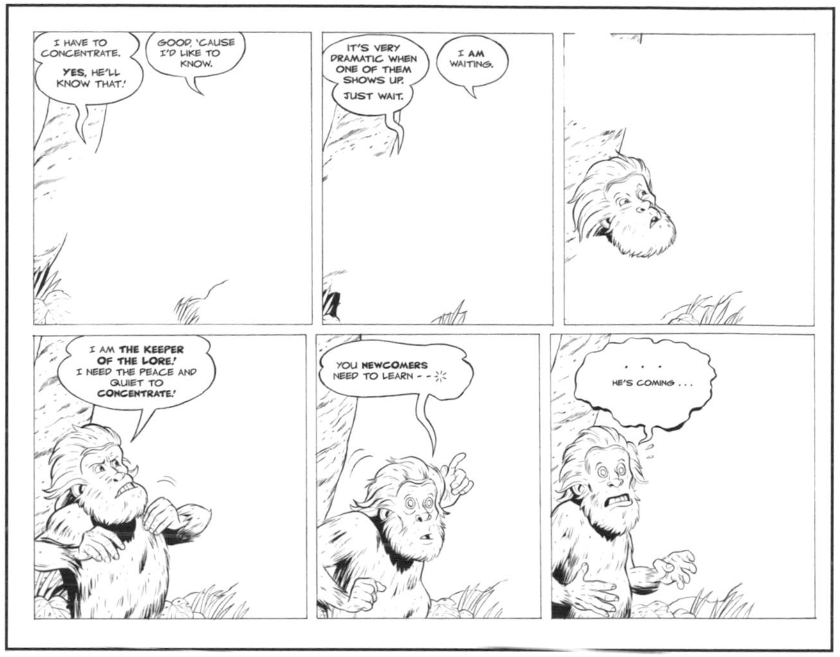
I HAVE TO CONCENTRATE.
YES, HE'LL KNOW THAT!
GOOD, 'CAUSE I'D LIKE TO KNOW.
IT'S VERY DRAMATIC WHEN ONE OF THEM SHOWS UP.
JUST WAIT.
I AM WAITING.
I AM THE KEEPER OF THE LORE! I NEED THE PEACE AND QUIET TO CONCENTRATE!
YOU NEWCOMERS NEED TO LEARN - -
. . . HE'S COMING . . .

An example of repurposed art. I loved this joke, and I loved Tuki's expressions on this page, but the forward momentum of the story needed something different. Don't worry, the smelly joke resurfaces in TUKI: Fight for Family.

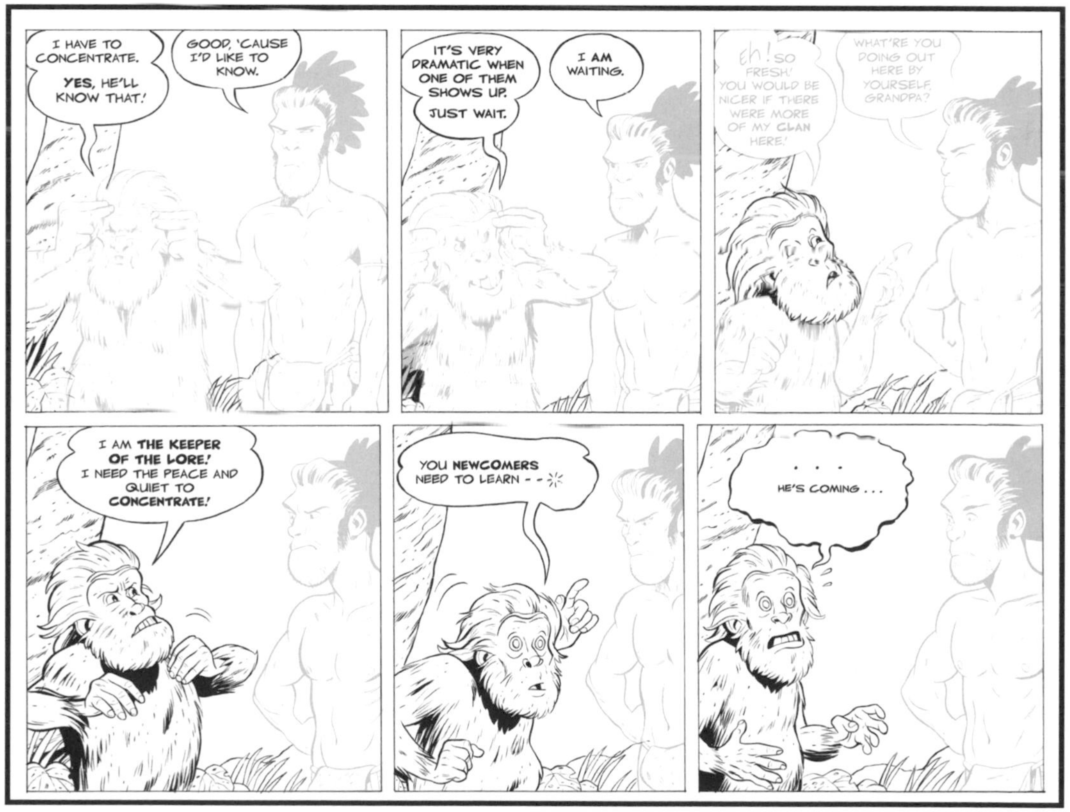
I HAVE TO CONCENTRATE.
YES, HE'LL KNOW THAT!
GOOD, 'CAUSE I'D LIKE TO KNOW.
IT'S VERY DRAMATIC WHEN ONE OF THEM SHOWS UP.
JUST WAIT.
I AM WAITING.
Eh! SO FRESH! YOU WOULD BE NICER IF THERE WERE MORE OF MY CLAN HERE!
WHAT'RE YOU DOING OUT HERE BY YOURSELF, GRANDPA?
I AM THE KEEPER OF THE LORE! I NEED THE PEACE AND QUIET TO CONCENTRATE!
YOU NEWCOMERS NEED TO LEARN - -
. . . HE'S COMING . . .

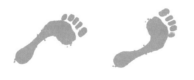

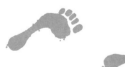

Above: page from T:StH.
Top right: New art.
Bottom: Existing art in light gray.

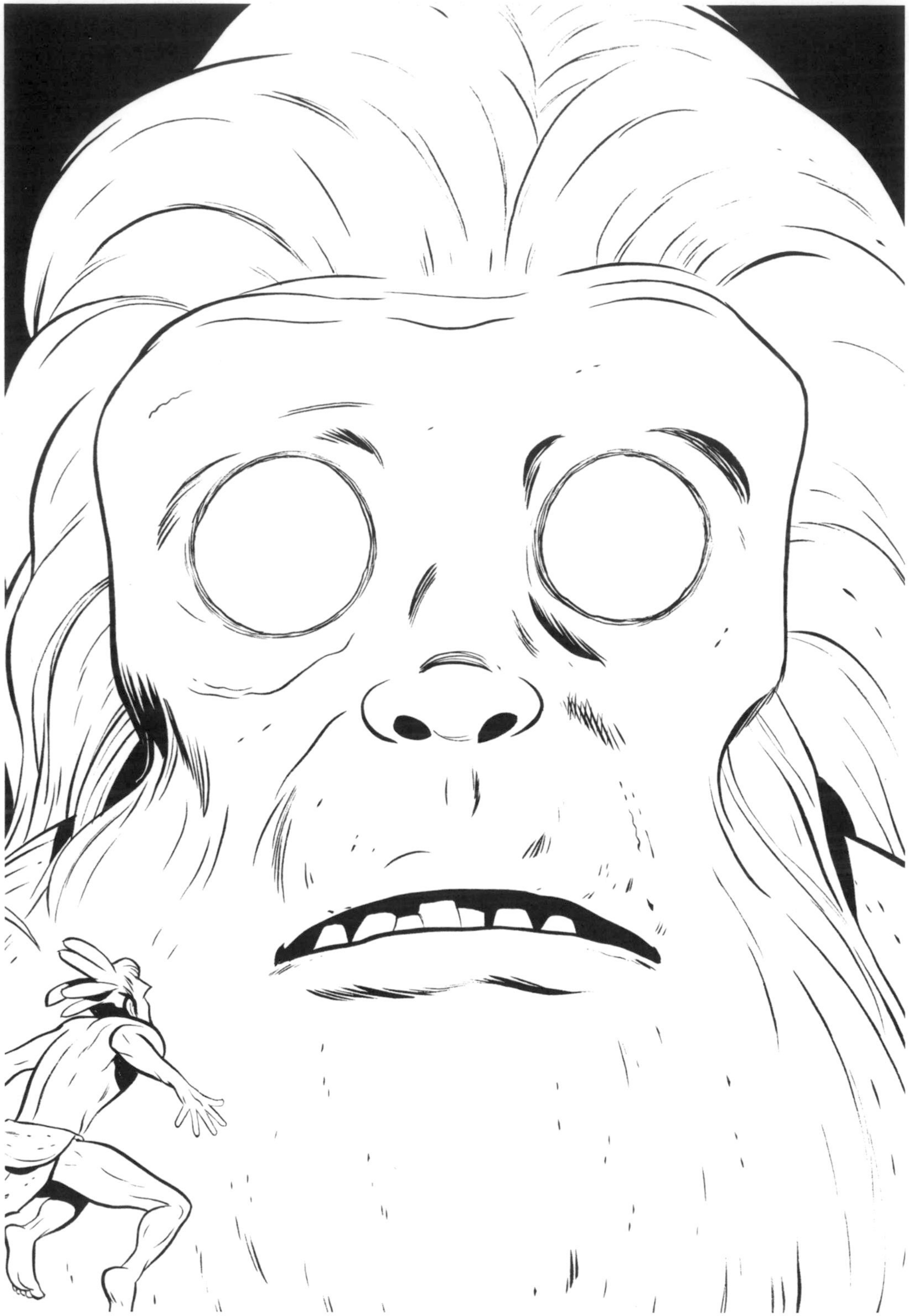

The Hidden World

The new thing that excited me in this scene was the apparition of the force power. Up until now, other than the turning of day into night, there was only Doc's warning to assuage Tuki. Now Tuki has something to think about!

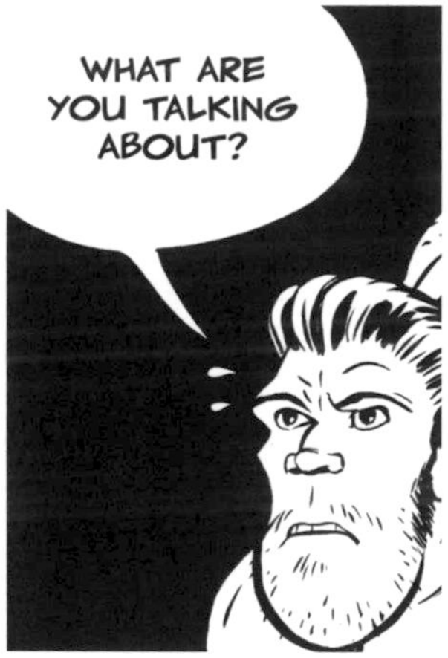
WHAT ARE YOU TALKING ABOUT?

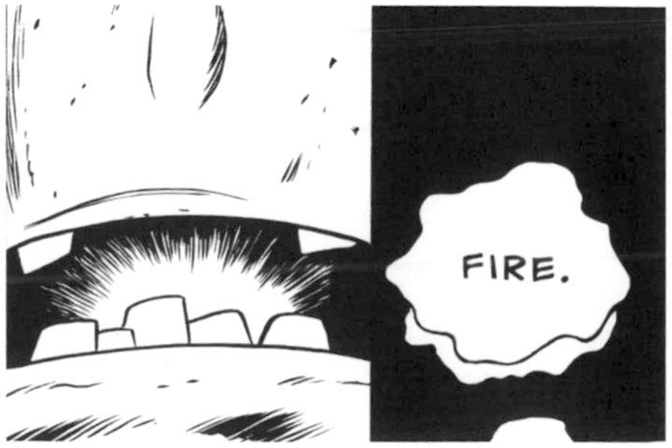
FIRE.

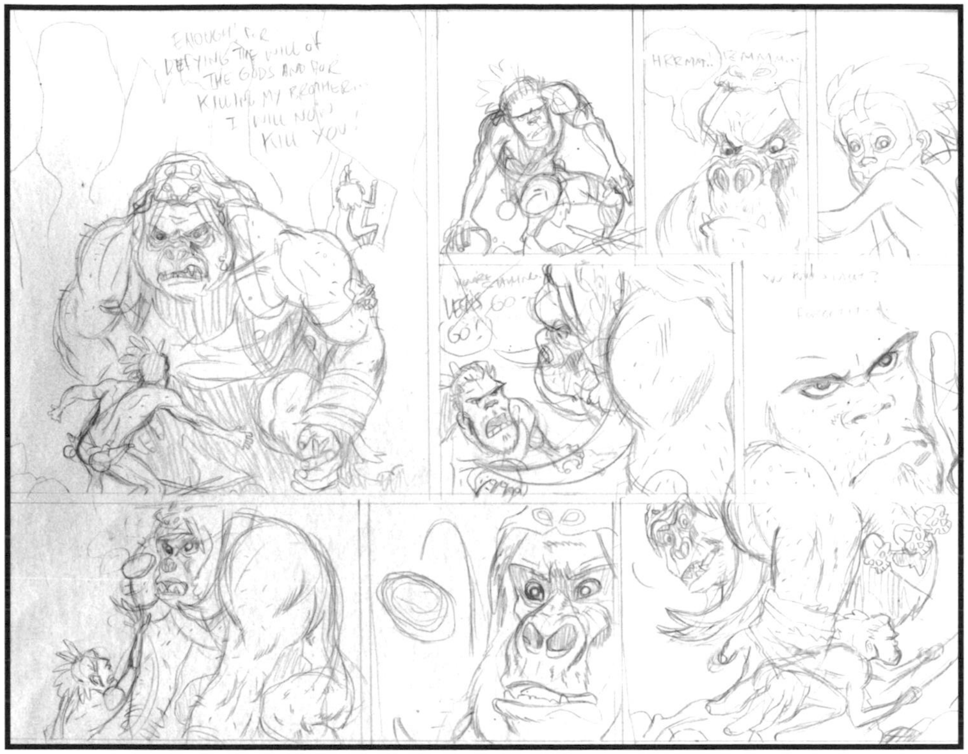

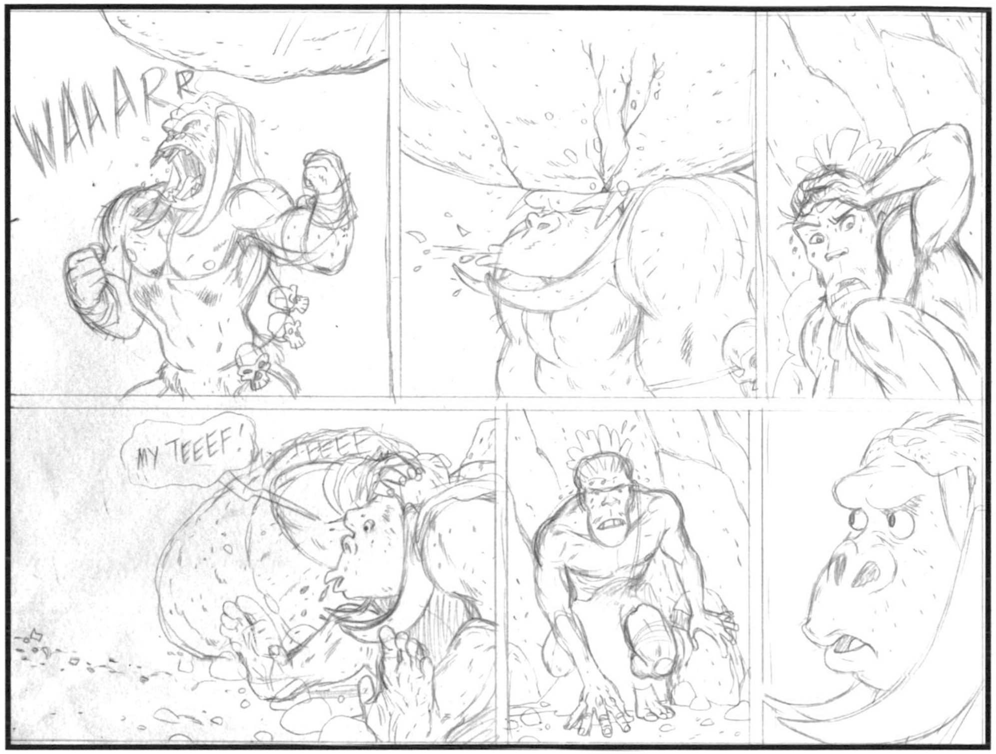
WAAARR
MY TEEEF!

Tuki's second encounter with the Hidden World in our story comes from beyond the Three Waterfalls at the hands of an angry giant. This is virtually the only scene from T:StH that made it through unscathed.

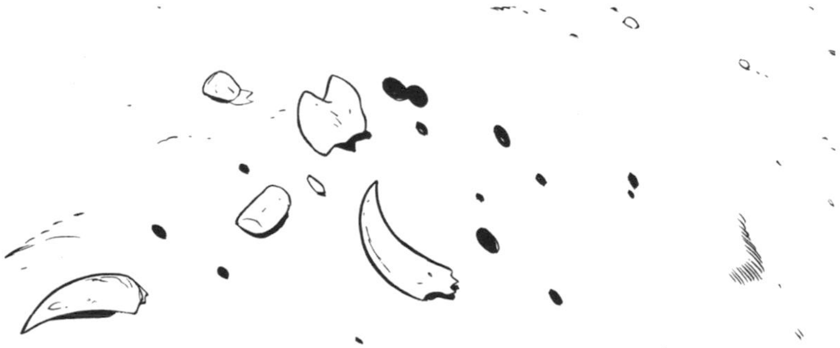

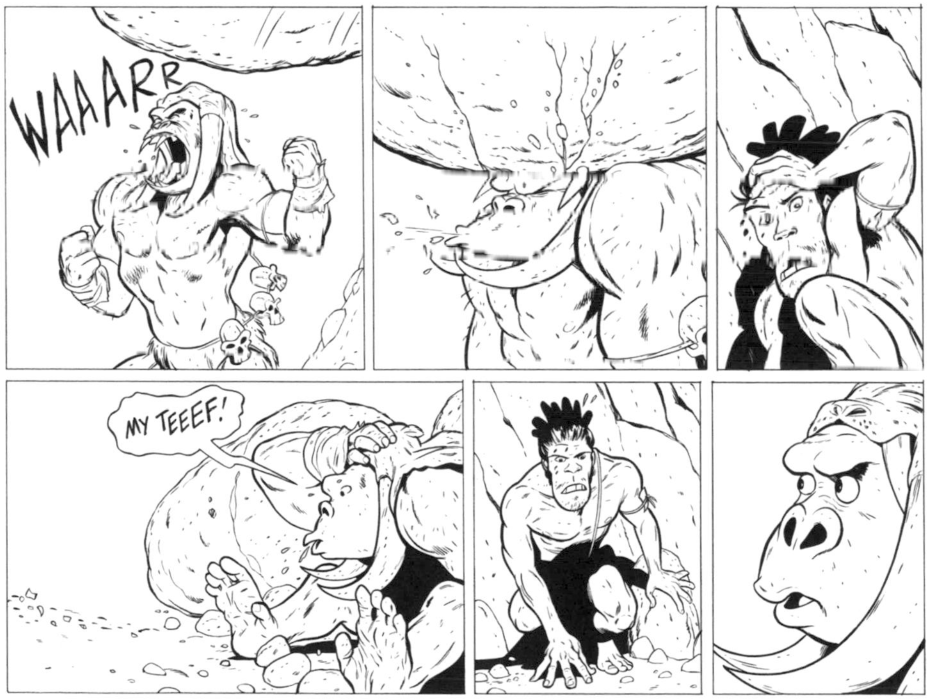
WAAARR
MY TEEEF!

Hey, Pup . . . C'mere

This is a new page created to bridge the giant ape-god battle with the reemergence of our new troop back out of the swamp. Not only is it a final beat of reflection on their ordeal, it sets up questions for later.

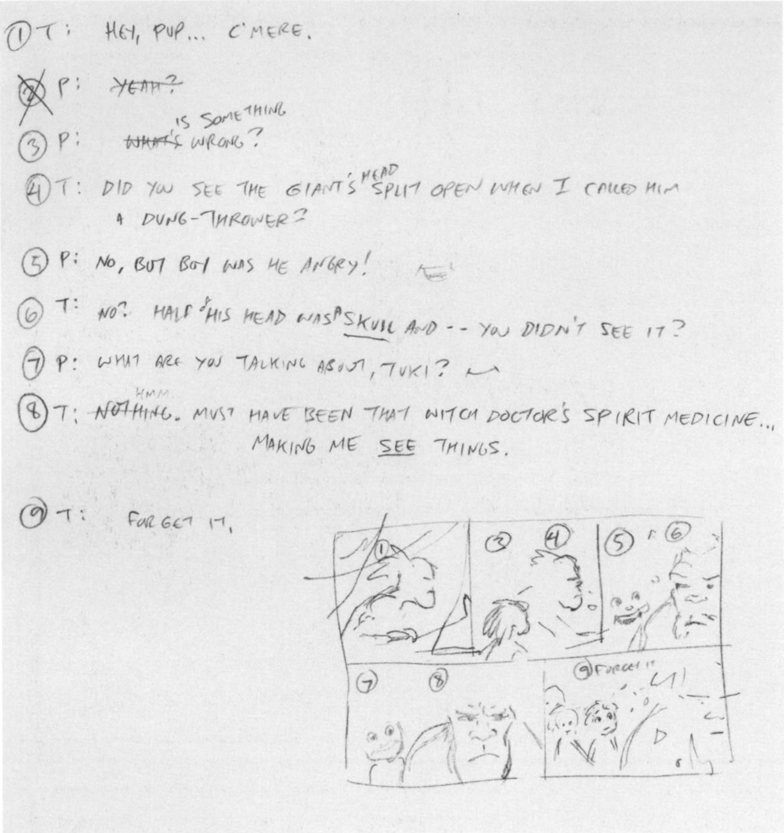
1 T: HEY, PUP... C'MERE.
2 P: YEAH?
3 P: IS SOMETHING WRONG?
4 T: DID YOU SEE THE GIANT'S HEAD SPLIT OPEN WHEN I CALLED HIM A DUNG-THROWER?
5 P: NO, BUT BOY WAS HE ANGRY!
6 T: NO? HALF OF HIS HEAD WAS A SKULL AND -- YOU DIDN'T SEE IT?
7 P: WHAT ARE YOU TALKING ABOUT, TUKI?
8 T: HMM. MUST HAVE BEEN THAT WITCH DOCTOR'S SPIRIT MEDICINE... MAKING ME SEE THINGS.
9 T: FORGET IT.

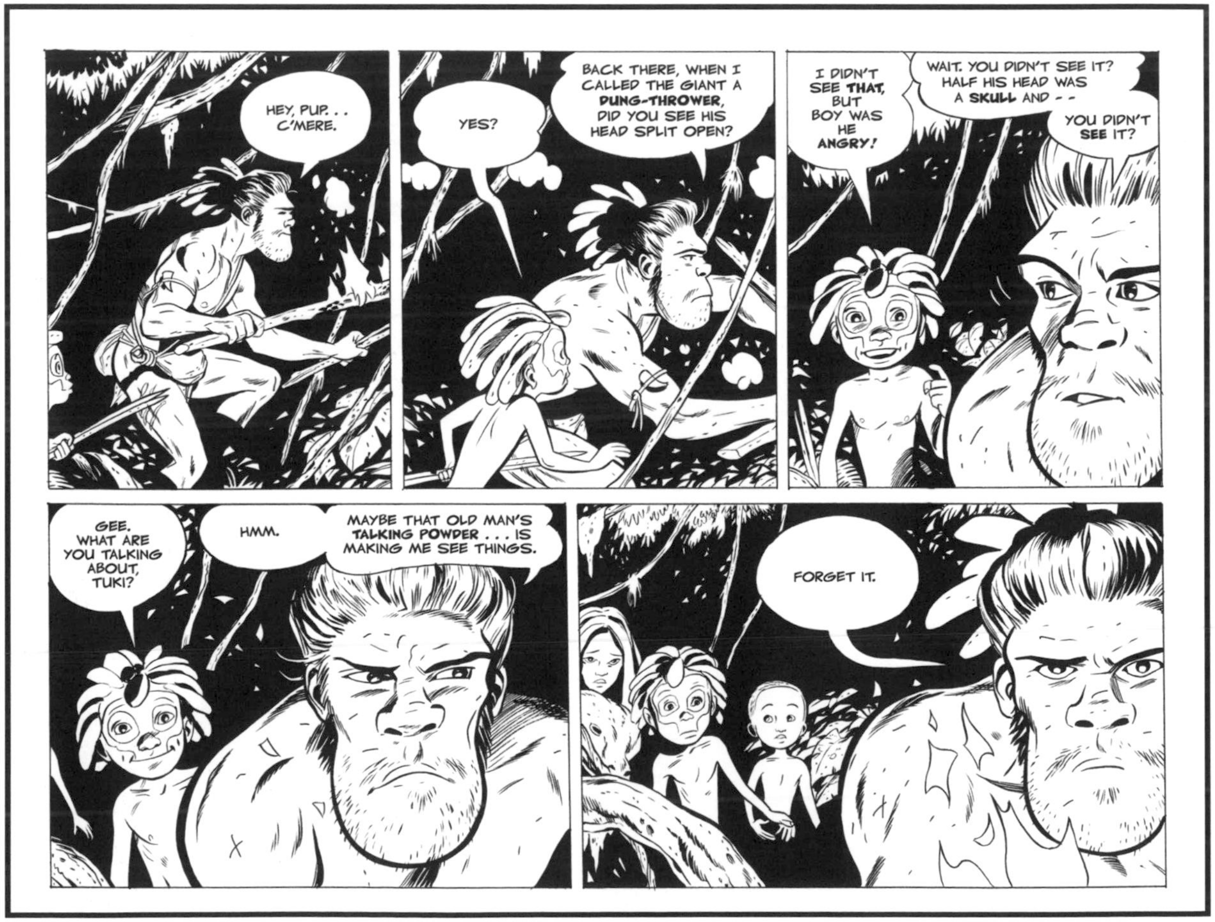
HEY, PUP . . C'MERE.
YES?
BACK THERE, WHEN I CALLED THE GIANT A DUNG-THROWER, DID YOU SEE HIS HEAD SPLIT OPEN?
I DIDN'T SEE THAT, BUT BOY WAS HE ANGRY!
WAIT. YOU DIDN'T SEE IT? HALF HIS HEAD WAS A SKULL AND - -
YOU DIDN'T SEE IT?
GEE. WHAT ARE YOU TALKING ABOUT, TUKI?
HMM.
MAYBE THAT OLD MAN'S TALKING POWDER . . . IS MAKING ME SEE THINGS.
FORGET IT.

On this page:
The script and the finished art.

Much of the first graphic novel contains new or reimagined material, and most of the second is all new. Chapter 5 of Fight for Fire is titled "FIRE". This scene is new. Grab your supper, old timer! Let's go build a fire!

CHAPTER 3 CONTINUED…

TUKI STEALS TWO BURNING LOGS FROM THE GIANTS FIRE AND LEADS THE CHILDREN OUT OF THE SWAMP. UNIVITED, KWARELL FOLLOWS. AT THE EDGE OF THE SWAMP THEY DISCOVER THE SHAMAN HAS BEEN WAITING FOR THEM. WHILE THE KIDS ARE APREHENSIVE OF THE DINGA, THE SHAMAN IS INTRIGUED BY THEM -- WANTING TO KEEP THEM AS PETS. ONCE KWARELL ESTABLISHES THAT THERE WILL BE NO MONKEY BUSINESS (BY GIVING THE SHAMAN A PLAYFUL NIP ON THE NOSE), TUKI LEADS THE RAG TAG GROUP TO SAFE PLACE TO SPEND THE NIGHT AND BUILD A FIRE.

END OF ACT 1

FIRE SCENE STARS DOC, KWARELL AND ZEE. KWARELL GOES AND SITS IN A TREE. ZEE REMARKS "WOULD IT KILL HIM TO SMILE ONCE IN A WHILE?" DOC TALKS ABOUT LITTLE FOLK NOT MONKEYS BUT PEOPLE LIKE US. IT'S STUFF LIKE THAT WHICH GOT HIM BANNED. ALSO OLD & SMELLY.

CHAPTER 4 (NEW - THE FIRE SCENE)

AS NIGHT DESCENDS, TUKI AND THE CHILDREN BUILD A FIRE WHILE THE SHAMAN AND KWARELL WATCH WITH A MIXTURE OF HORROR AND CURIOSITY. THE RAW DIFFERENCES BETWEEN THE OLDER ORDER OF HUMAN TWO-FOOTS AND THE NEW TALLER, SLEEKER VERSION REPRESENTED BY TUKI AND THE CHILDREN IS EXPLORED. THE SHAMAN AND KWARELL ARE FRIGHTENED AND REPELLED, THE CHILDREN SEE THE FIRE AS WARMTH AND PROTECTION. THE DINGA VIEW FIRE AS AN UNCONTROLED DEMEON WITH EVIL INTENTIONS. A BEING ONLY THE GODS CAN CONTROL AND USE.

TUKI EXPLAIN'S THE FIRE IS NOT AN EVIL SPIRIT -- JUST A HUNGRY ONE. IF YOU FEED HER, SHE STAYS CALM AND PROVIDES WARMTH & PROTECTION AGAINST THE GREAT BEASTS WHO HUNT IN THE JUNGLE.

TENSIONS RISE* WITH THE SHAMAN AND KWARELL CLIMBING INTO THE TREES TO SLEEP AND THE CHILDREN LYING BY THE FIRE. BUT AFTER SHIVERING AND LISTENING TO THE SOUNDS IN THE BLACK JUNGLE BEHIND THEM, BOTH THE SHAMAN AND KWARELL SLIP DOWN TO SLEEP BY THE FIRE.

(* THE DINGA FEAR THESE NEW FIRE WORSHIPING TWO-FOOTS)

NOTE * ZEE IS SCARED OF KWARELL -- WOULD IT HURT HIM TO SMILE SOMETIMES? → ALSO, ZEE IS SCARED TO HAVE A FIRE -- PERIOD! IT'S WHAT BROUGHT THE DINGAS IN THE FIRST PLACE.

CHAPTER 5 (PREVIOUSLY ISSUE 4)

TENSIONS ARE PUT ASIDE WHEN TUKI'S WOUND, SUSTAINED WHEN HE FOUGHT THE GIANT, BEGINS TO ACT UP. IT IS DECIDED AS A GROUP TO TAKE TUKI TO THE SHAMAN'S GROTTO WHERE HE CAN BE HEALED.

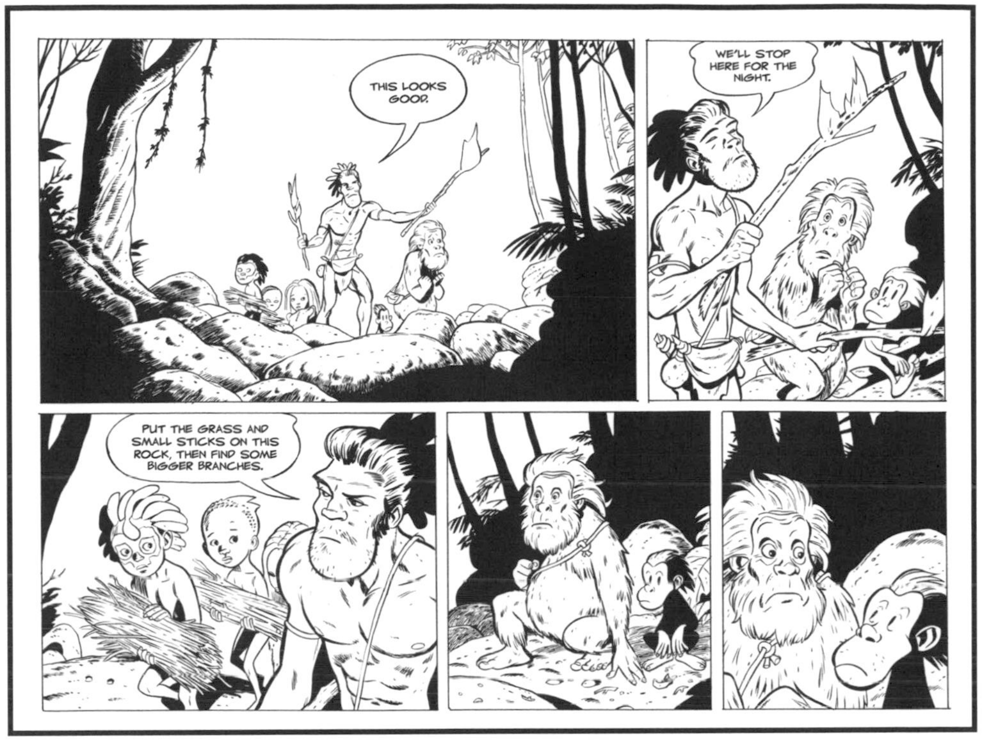
THIS LOOKS GOOD.
WE'LL STOP HERE FOR THE NIGHT.
PUT THE GRASS AND SMALL STICKS ON THIS ROCK, THEN FIND SOME BIGGER BRANCHES.

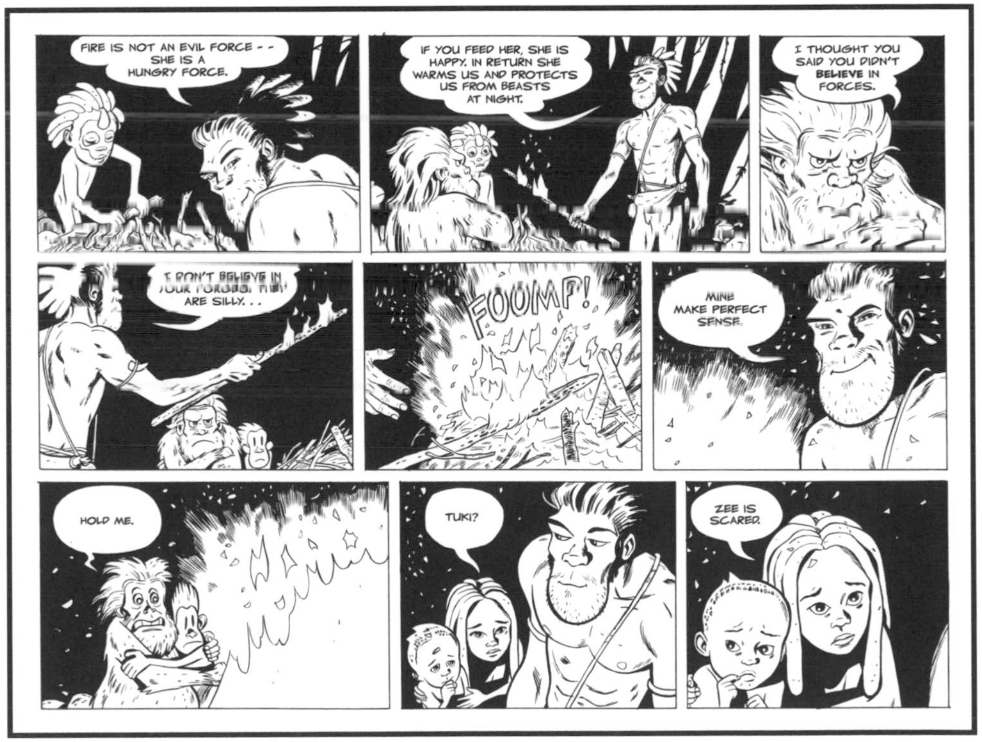
FIRE IS NOT AN EVIL FORCE - - SHE IS A HUNGRY FORCE.
IF YOU FEED HER, SHE IS HAPPY. IN RETURN SHE WARMS US AND PROTECTS US FROM BEASTS AT NIGHT.
I THOUGHT YOU SAID YOU DIDN'T BELIEVE IN FORCES.
I DON'T BELIEVE IN
ARE SILLY. . .
FOOMP!
MINE MAKE PERFECT SENSE.
HOLD ME.
TUKI?
ZEE IS SCARED.

Above: Outline bringing book one to a close.
Right: Two new pages from FIRE. The star field in the night sky was added later.

Making the Cover

When it came time to create a cover, I needed two things, a logo and, hopefully, an iconic image. We had a logo for the webcomic, but I was looking for something different for the graphic novel, something that felt ancient, like a scratching on the side of a rock face. A loose scrawl emerged on a page of lettering and I liked it.

The cover took awhile. Unlike the cover image of a comic book, which can convey the excitement and drama of the immediate moment, this has to sit in people's minds. I was playing with the edge of a face against an orange sunrise. Somehow the silhouette popped in. I liked it and began to play with images of multiple volumes with similar themes - at night, at midday, etc. When I turned over the finished inked piece to my colorist Tom Gaadt, I never imagined how sweet he would make it. The way he lost the logo in the sun - the color of the sky - he nailed it. And did it again for book two, but at night!

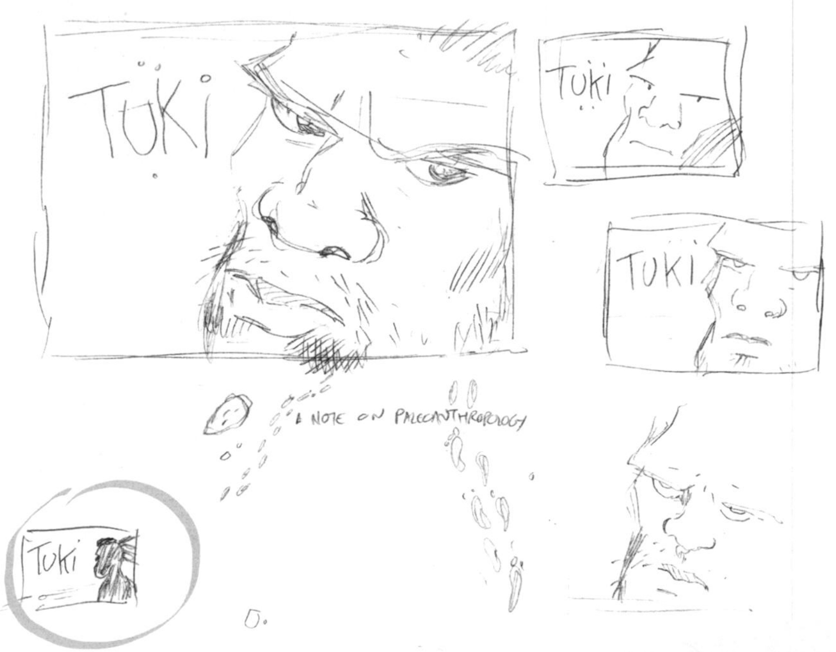
TUKI
TUKI
TUKI
A NOTE ON PALEOANTHROPOLOGY
TUKI

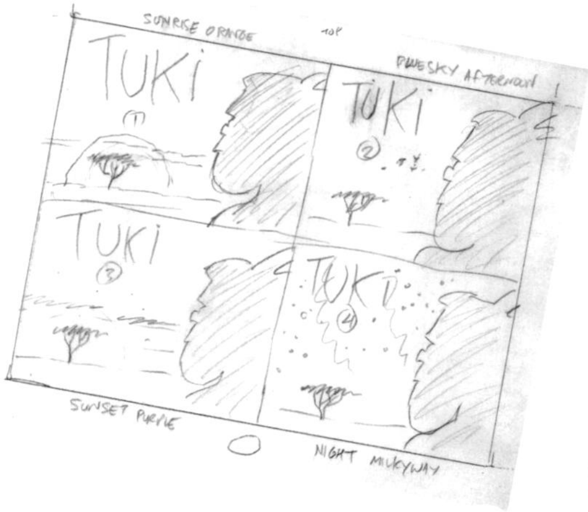
SUNRISE ORANGE
TUKI
TUKI
TUKI
TUKI
SUNSET PURPLE
NIGHT MILKYWAY

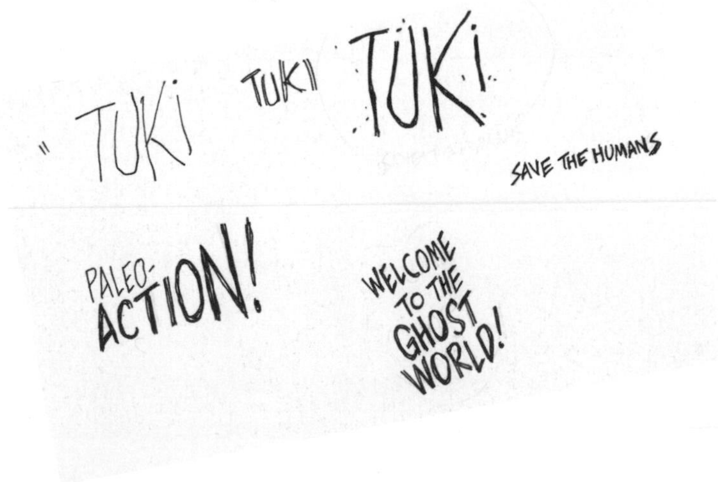
TUKI
TUKI
TUKI
SAVE THE HUMANS
PALEO-ACTION!
WELCOME TO THE GHOST WORLD!

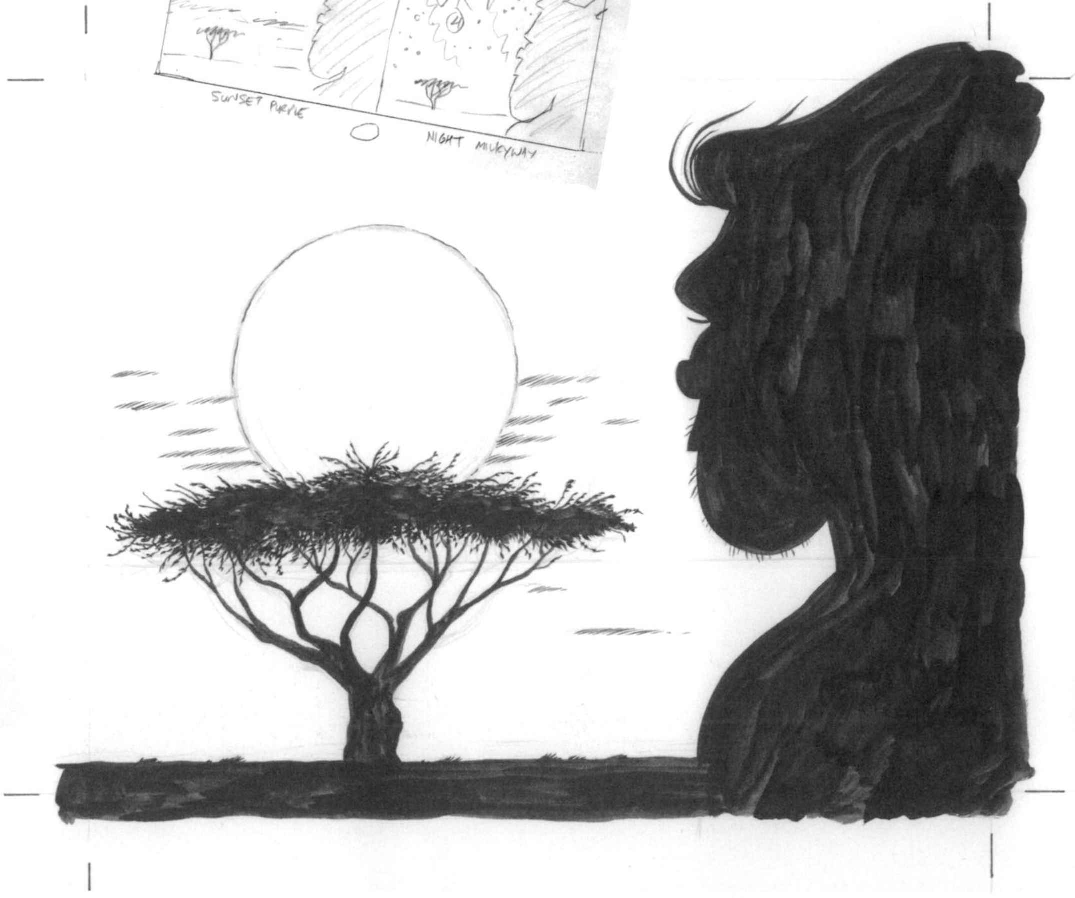

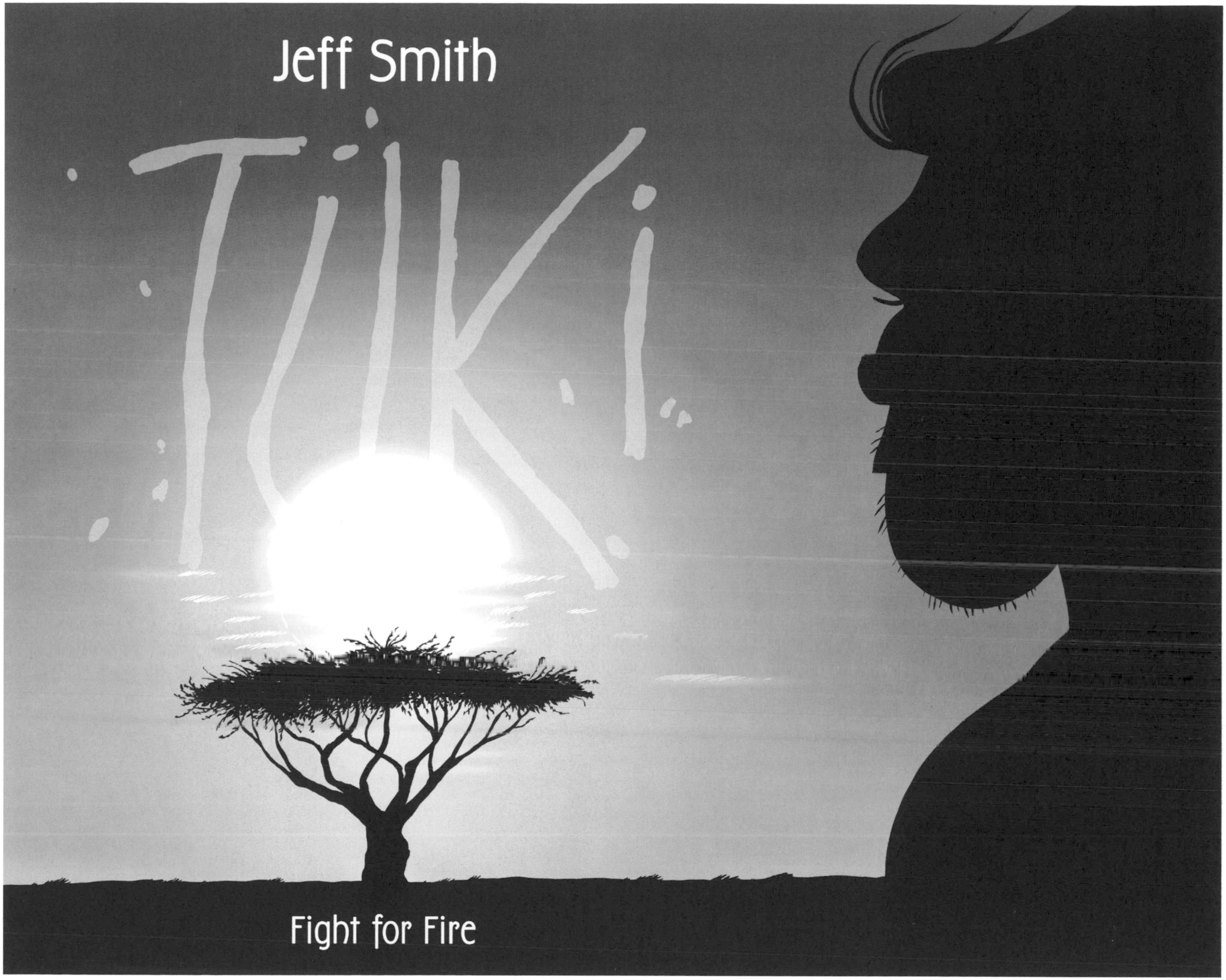
Jeff Smith
TUKI
Fight for Fire

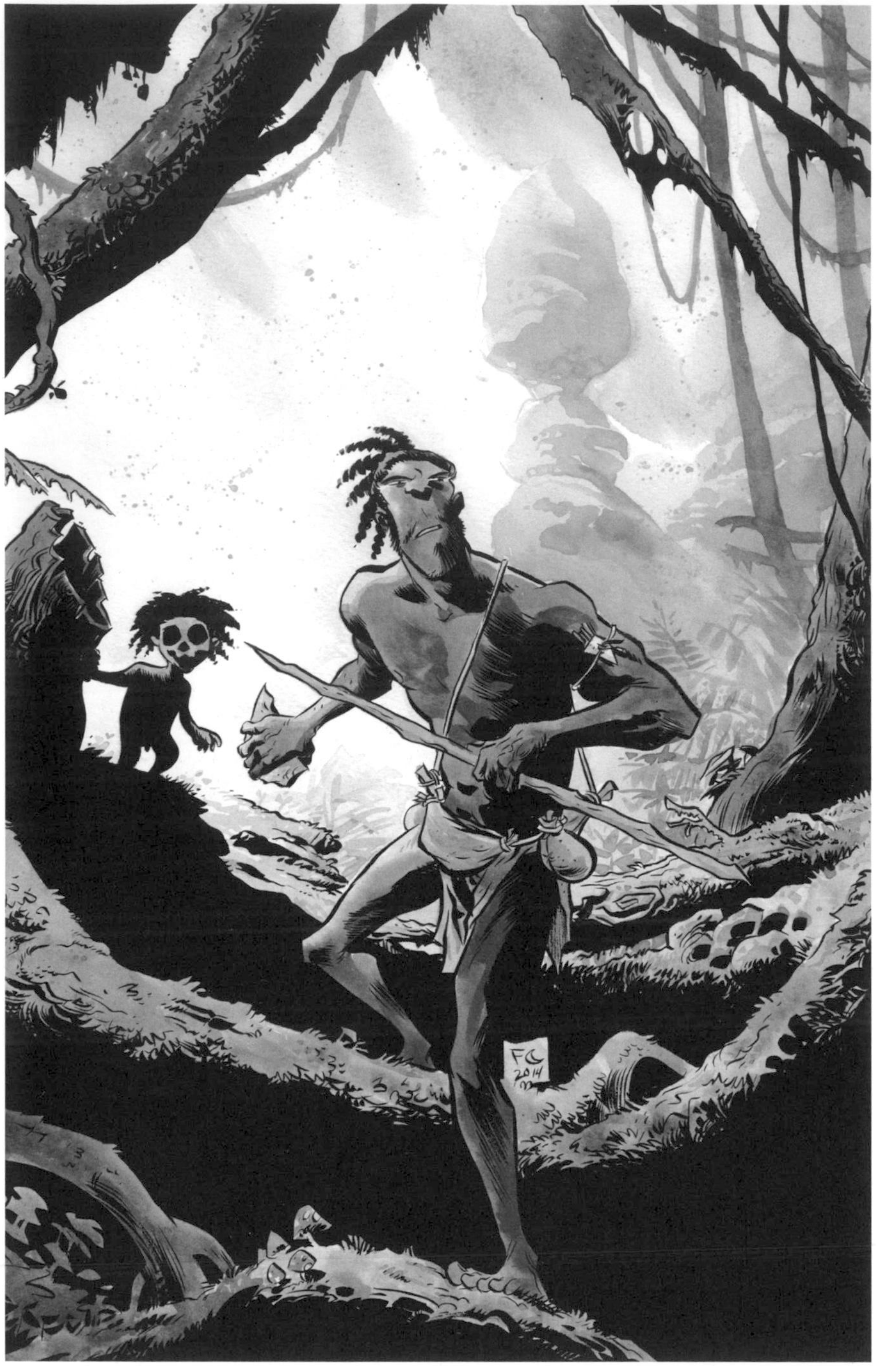

Tuki and Pup in the Giant's Swamp
by Fabio Moon (Casanova, Daytripper)

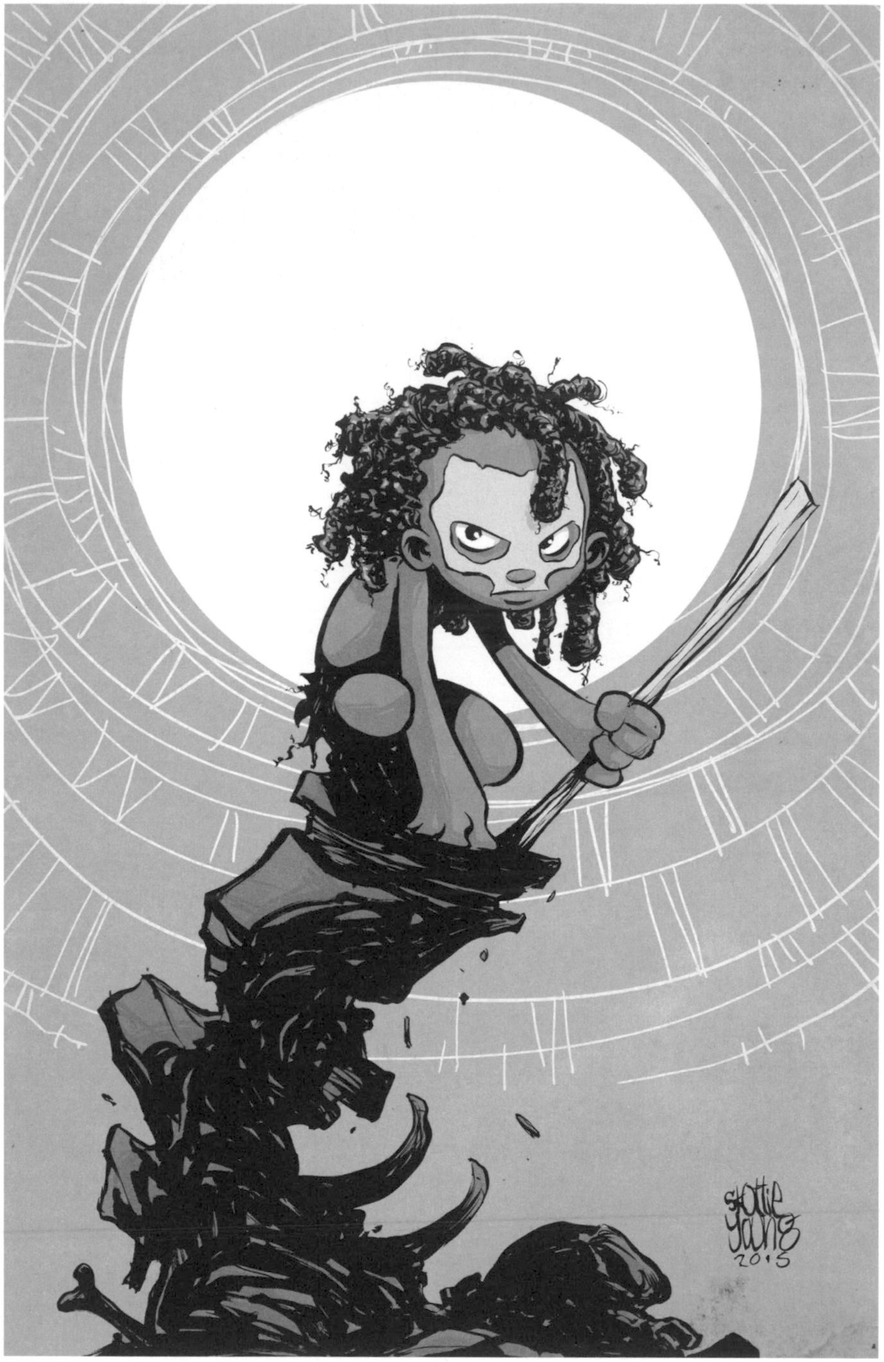

Tuki's Right Hand Man
by Skottie Young (I Hate Fairyland, Middlewest, Strange Academy)

The Pin-up Prints

As part of the marketing for TUKI, we asked some friends to make some pin-ups.

I call them pin-up prints because I love the Kirby pin-ups from the Fantastic Four comics. These TUKI pieces are beautifully created and professionally printed in full color, done by some of the best artists in the field.

Tuki on the Move
by Jeff Smith, color by Tom Gaadt

Rough sketch by Tim Fielder (INFINITUM)

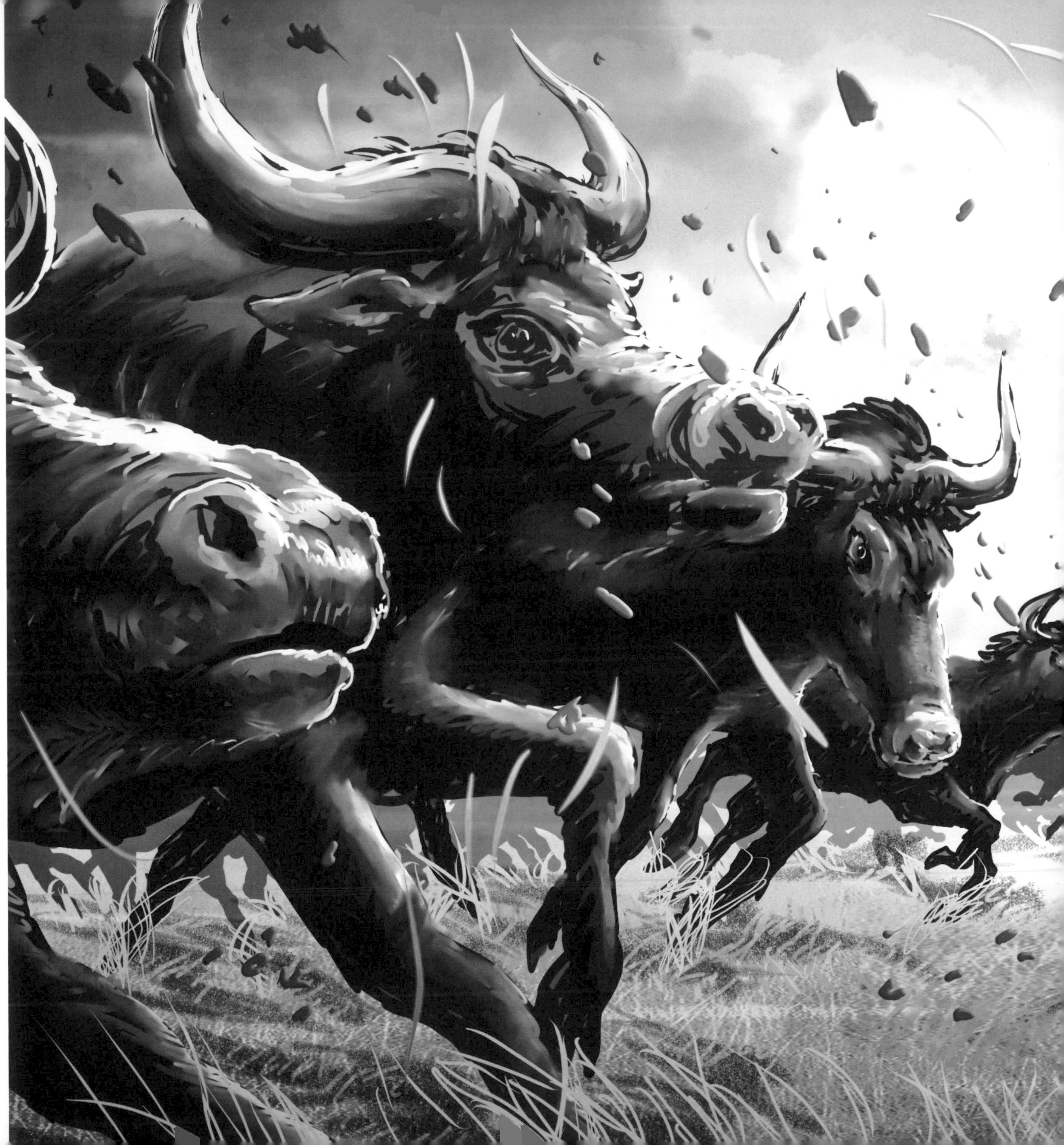

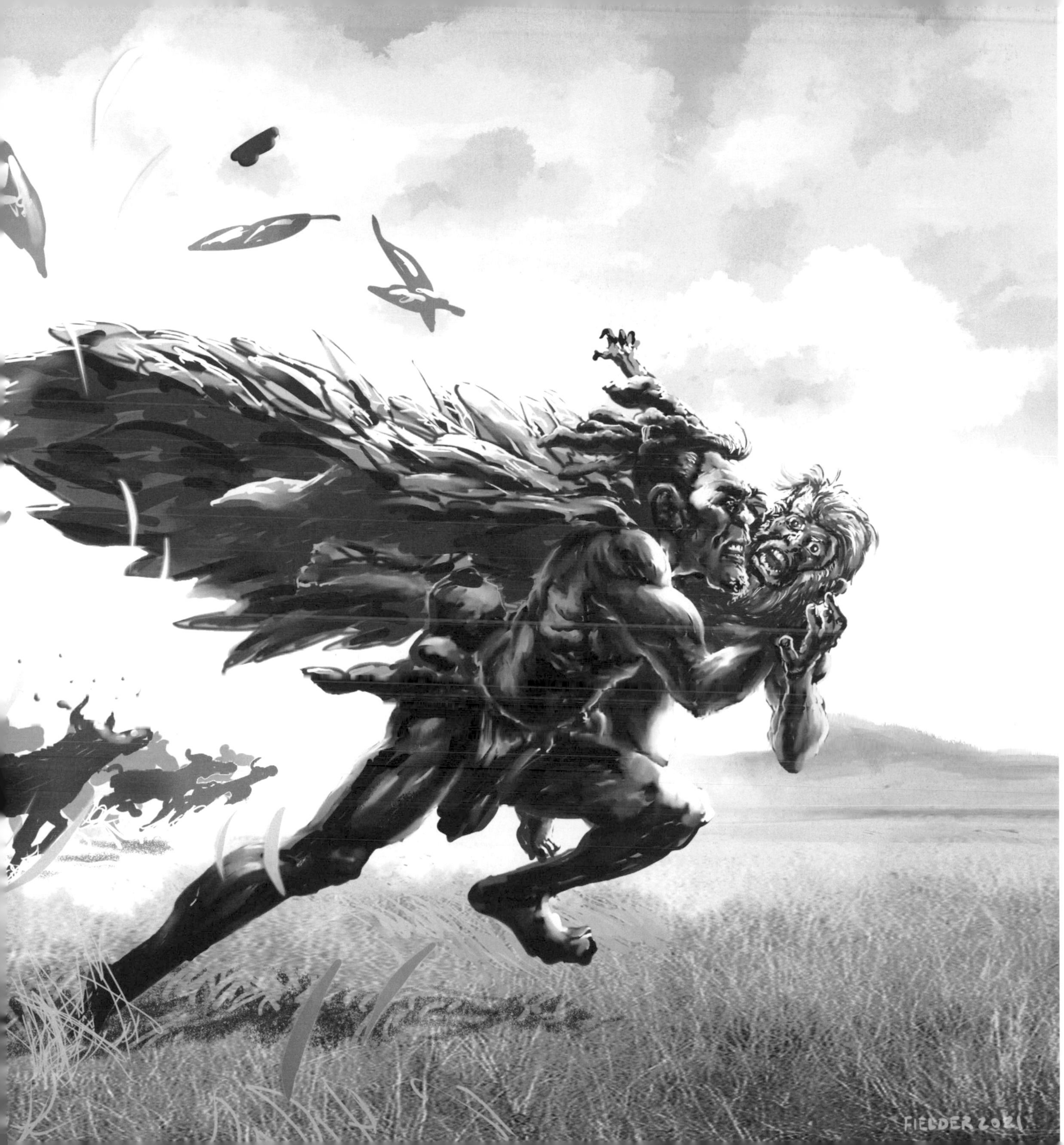
FIELDER 2021

Tuki rescues the Old Habiline
by Tim Fielder

"As a hybrid artist my work begins and ends in digital. I employ traditional 2d draw ing, photos, whatever I can use to make an image sell the moment. This part took much longer than I would have liked with the rendering and constant balancing of elements, but I'm very happy with the way it turned out."

—Tim Fielder

The Last Page

The last page of TUKI: Fight for Fire was created for the graphic novel mostly to gather up our meager belongings and set our misfits on the road to adventure together. And to tease Zee. To be continued!

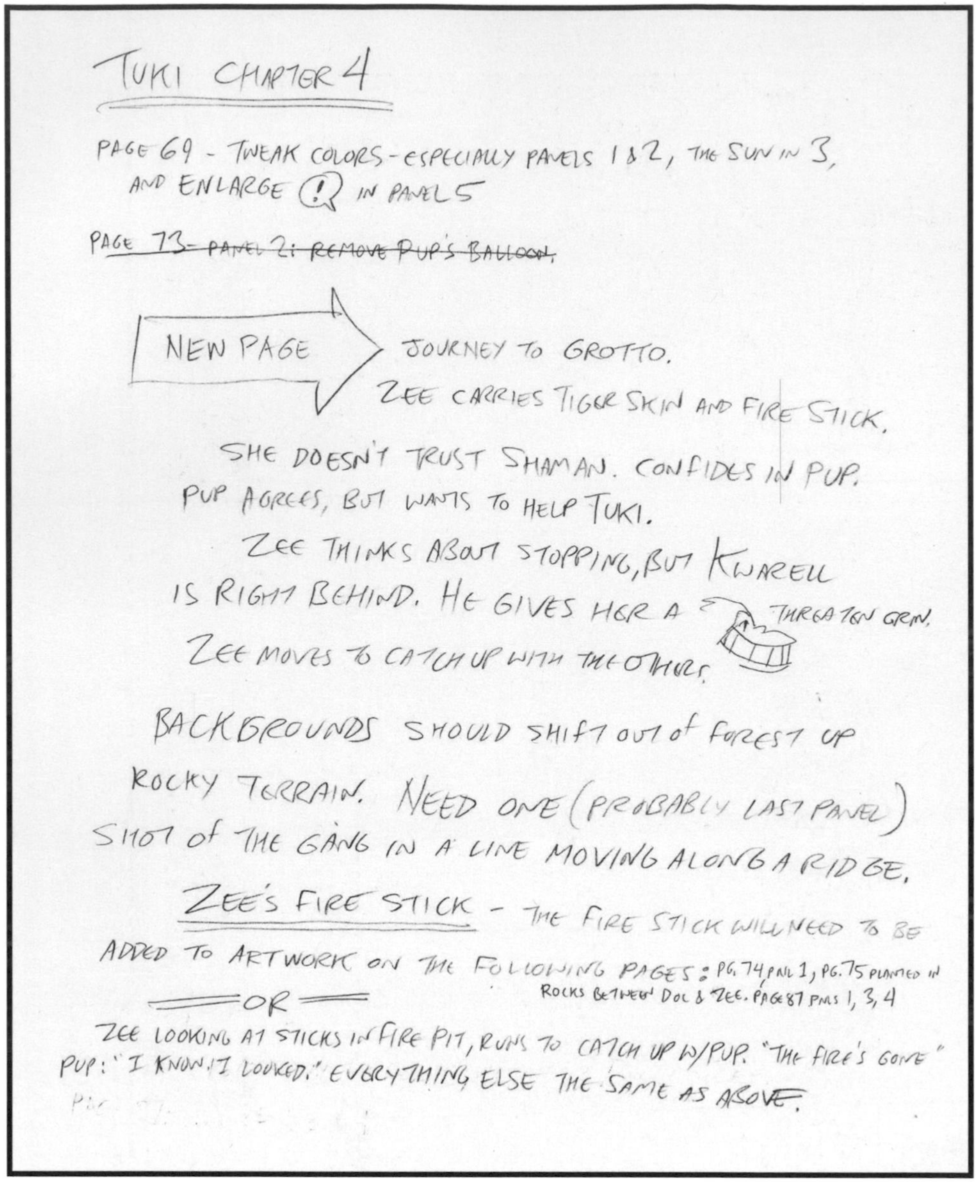
TUKI CHAPTER 4

PAGE 69 - TWEAK COLORS - ESPECIALLY PANELS 1 & 2, THE SUN IN 3, AND ENLARGE (!) IN PANEL 5

PAGE 73 - ~~PANEL 2: REMOVE PUP'S BALLOON~~

NEW PAGE → JOURNEY TO GROTTO.
ZEE CARRIES TIGER SKIN AND FIRE STICK.

SHE DOESN'T TRUST SHAMAN. CONFIDES IN PUP. PUP AGREES, BUT WANTS TO HELP TUKI.

ZEE THINKS ABOUT STOPPING, BUT KWARELL IS RIGHT BEHIND. HE GIVES HER A THREATEN GRIN.
ZEE MOVES TO CATCH UP WITH THE OTHERS.

BACKGROUNDS SHOULD SHIFT OUT OF FOREST UP ROCKY TERRAIN. NEED ONE (PROBABLY LAST PANEL) SHOT OF THE GANG IN A LINE MOVING ALONG A RIDGE.

ZEE'S FIRE STICK - THE FIRE STICK WILL NEED TO BE ADDED TO ARTWORK ON THE FOLLOWING PAGES: PG. 74 PNL 1, PG. 75 PLANTED IN ROCKS BETWEEN DOC & ZEE. PAGE 87 PNLS 1, 3, 4

OR

ZEE LOOKING AT STICKS IN FIRE PIT, RUNS TO CATCH UP W/PUP. "THE FIRE'S GONE" PUP: "I KNOW. I LOOKED." EVERYTHING ELSE THE SAME AS ABOVE.

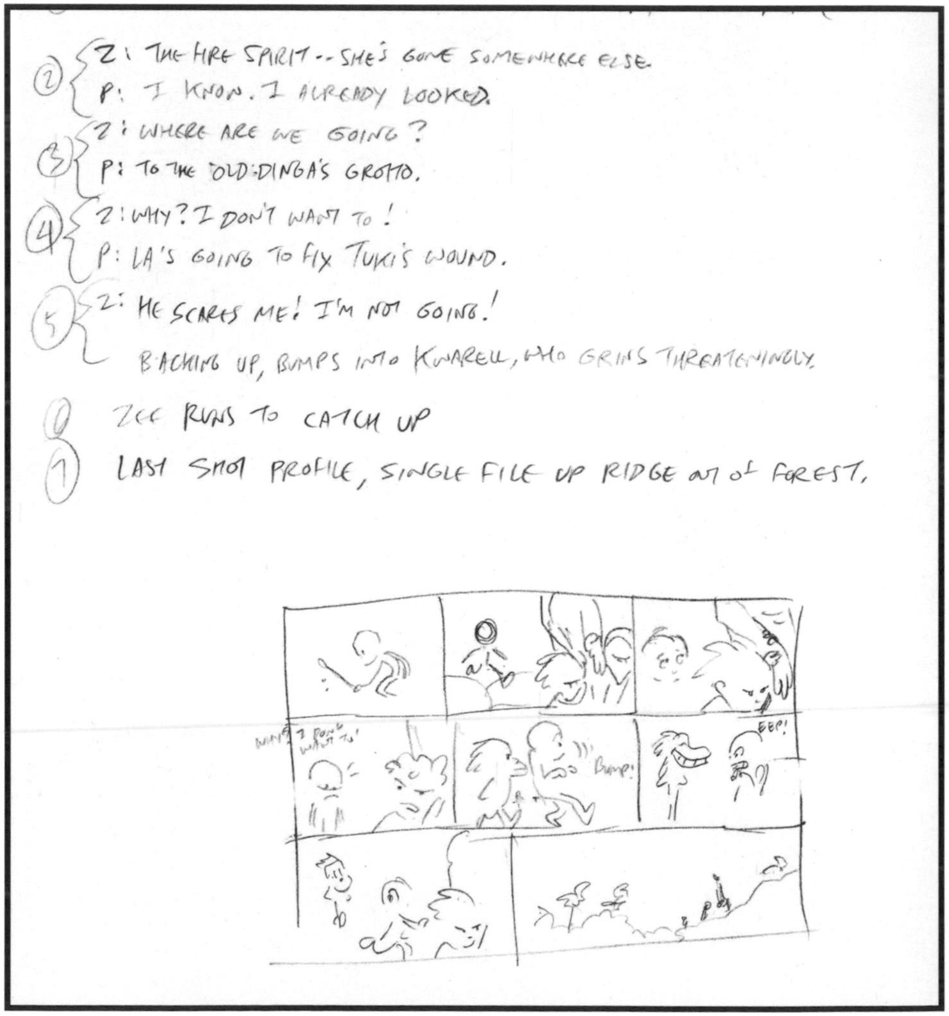
(2) Z: THE FIRE SPIRIT -- SHE'S GONE SOMEWHERE ELSE.
P: I KNOW. I ALREADY LOOKED.
(3) Z: WHERE ARE WE GOING?
P: TO THE OLD DINGA'S GROTTO.
(4) Z: WHY? I DON'T WANT TO!
P: LA'S GOING TO FIX TUKI'S WOUND.
(5) Z: HE SCARES ME! I'M NOT GOING!
BACKING UP, BUMPS INTO KWARELL, WHO GRINS THREATENINGLY.
(6) ZEE RUNS TO CATCH UP
(7) LAST SHOT PROFILE, SINGLE FILE UP RIDGE OUT OF FOREST.

Bump!
EEP!

Above left: The synopsis for the last page.
Above right: The script for the last page.

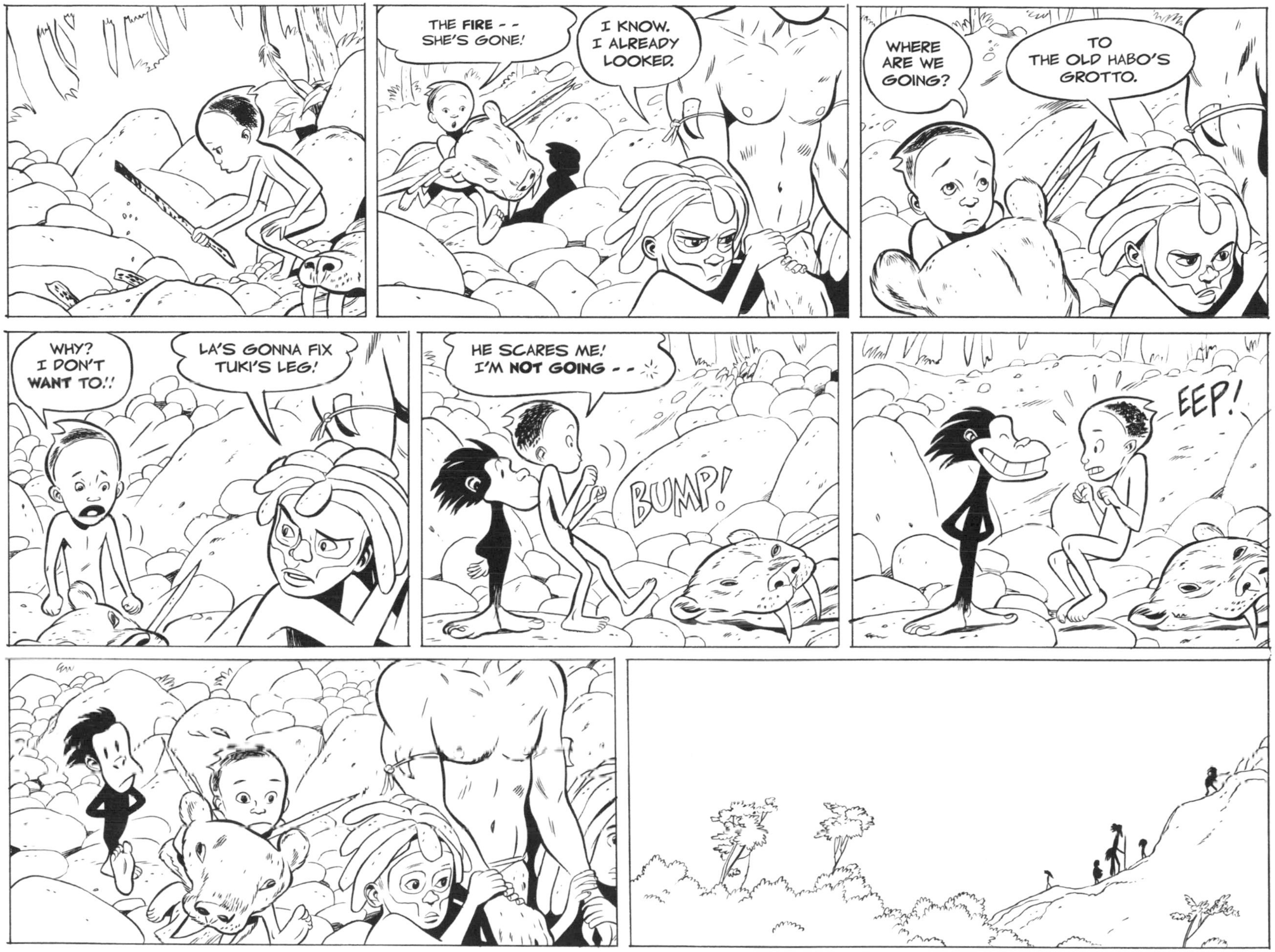
THE FIRE - - SHE'S GONE!
I KNOW. I ALREADY LOOKED.
WHERE ARE WE GOING?
TO THE OLD HABO'S GROTTO.
WHY? I DON'T WANT TO!!
LA'S GONNA FIX TUKI'S LEG!
HE SCARES ME! I'M NOT GOING - -
BUMP!
EEP!

To be continued!

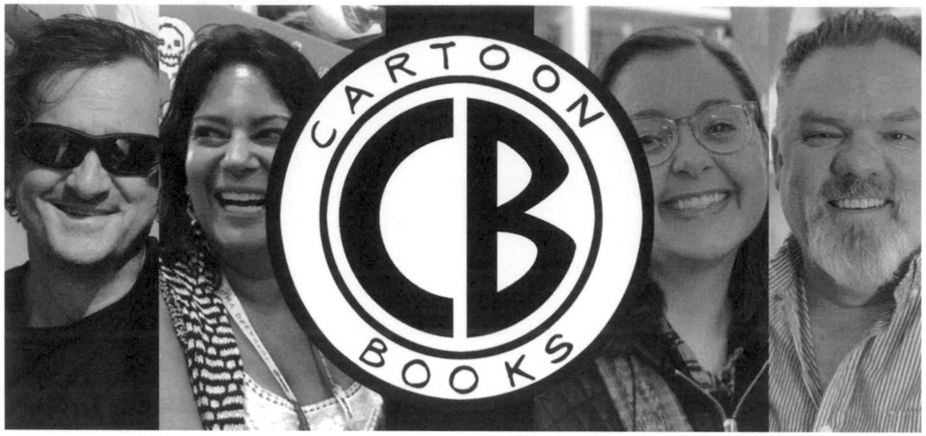
CARTOON
CB
BOOKS

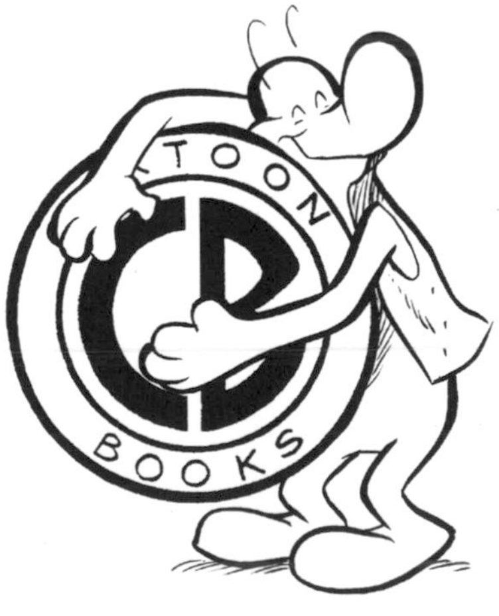
BOOKS

30 YEARS!